THE PROPELLER UNDER THE BED

Eileen A. Bjorkman

THE PROPELLER UNDER THE BED

A Personal History of Homebuilt Aircraft

UNIVERSITY OF WASHINGTON PRESS

Seattle and London

University of Washington Press
www.washington.edu/uwpress

Library of Congress Cataloging-in-Publication Data
Names: Bjorkman, Eileen A., author.
Title: The propeller under the bed : a personal history of homebuilt aircraft /
   Eileen A. Bjorkman.
Description: 1st edition. | Seattle : University of Washington Press, [2017] |
   Includes bibliographical references and index.
Identifiers: LCCN 2016049323 | ISBN 9780295741444 (hardcover : alk. paper)
Subjects: LCSH: Ebneter, Arnold, 1928– | Air pilots—United States—Biography. |
   Airplanes, Home-built.
Classification: LCC TL540.E335 B56 2017 | DDC 629.13092 [B] —dc23
LC record available at https://lccn.loc.gov/2016049323

To my mother

CONTENTS

ACKNOWLEDGMENTS

I THANK MY MOTHER, WHO INSPIRED BOTH THE TITLE AND IDEA for the book, and my father, for enduring dozens of interviews, digging through logbooks, finding old photos, and answering hundreds of questions. I also thank the many people who provided comments on the original manuscript. This book would not have been possible without my editor, Regan Huff, who had the vision to turn a rambling story about my father into a tale of homebuilt aircraft.

John Little at the Museum of Flight Research Center in Seattle, and Susan Lurvey at the Experimental Aircraft Association's Museum Library, gave me invaluable assistance in locating old magazines, letters, and books.

Finally, I must thank my cats, Scout and Butterball, who missed many hours of lap time.

LIST OF ILLUSTRATIONS

THE PROPELLER UNDER THE BED

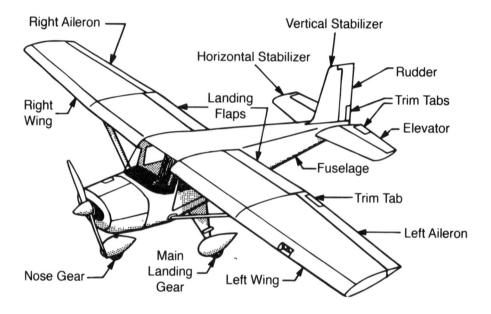

Right Aileron

Vertical Stabilizer

Horizontal Stabilizer

Rudder

Right Wing

Landing Flaps

Trim Tabs

Elevator

Fuselage

Trim Tab

Left Aileron

Nose Gear

Main Landing Gear

Left Wing

COMPONENTS OF A TYPICAL LIGHTPLANE

1

The Flight

> Every pilot knows the chances he takes at times; that's part of
> aviation. Ours is not a nation built on too much caution.
>
> Charles Lindbergh, *The Spirit of St. Louis*, 1953

JULY 25, 2010, EVERETT, WASHINGTON. SMALL AIRPLANES BUZZED overhead and trundled to and from the runways at Paine Field. On a normal weekday, jumbo jets roll off Boeing's assembly line, which is housed in the world's largest building and sits at the south end of the airport. On weekends, airplanes that could fit in a 747's baggage compartment invade the airspace. This particular Sunday was no exception.

On a ramp away from the din, a small crowd surrounded a silver airplane with a jaunty yellow nose. The airplane resembled a miniature World War II fighter resting on its tail, nose poking into the air. The cockpit was built low to the ground, so an observer—even a child—could easily peer at the instruments and controls. An aeronautical engineer present might have noticed the long wings that tapered from about four feet in width where it attached to the fuselage to about a foot at the wing-tips and deduced that this airplane, like a U-2 spy plane, was built to stay airborne for much longer than the three or four hours that most small planes stayed aloft at a time. A pilot might have spotted the three bathroom scales, one under each wheel, and realized that someone was planning something more than a routine flight.

Casual observers might have marveled at the word "EXPERIMENTAL" painted on the side of the airplane and wondered if a thin elderly man dressed in a military-green flight suit was a test pilot. That man, Arnold Ebneter, was my father; and as he wandered about the plane, he checked

3

for anything that might make his upcoming flight end sooner than the planned eighteen hours. He had conceived the airplane as a college design project and, after fifty years of persistence and procrastination, had birthed the machine in his garage and then coaxed it into its final configuration. Today, he was confident he could fly it nonstop for 2,328 miles to set a new world record for the greatest number of continuous miles flown in an airplane weighing less than 500 kilograms, or 1,102 pounds.

After satisfying himself that every nut and rivet was in place, Arnold called for a fuel truck and climbed into the cockpit. He carried only the barest of essentials for the flight—two energy bars, a quart of water, and a picture of my late mother, Colleen. When the fuel truck arrived, he asked the driver to fill the seven tanks—three in each wing and one in the cockpit. Helpers on the ground called out weights on the individual scales, which Arnold added for the total weight, all under the watch of an observer from the National Aeronautic Association, keeper of US aviation records. When the combination of airplane, supplies, fuel, and Arnold weighed a few ounces shy of 1,102 pounds, he told the fueler to stop.

Record-breaking aircraft come in all sizes and shapes—they are balloons, airplanes, helicopters, and gliders, to name just a few. Except for "absolute" records, pilots compete in aircraft type and weight classes, and nearly four hundred types of records exist for airplanes, in a dizzying array of categories, including altitude, speed, time-to-climb, duration, efficiency, payload, and distance. For record-setting purposes, balloons are Class A, airships are Class B, powered airplanes are Class C, gliders are Class D, and so on. Airplanes are further divided into C-1 for landplanes, C-2 for seaplanes, and C-3 for amphibians, and these three categories are again divided by takeoff weight, such as "a/o" for less than 300 kilograms, "a" for 300–500 kilograms, and "b" for 500–1,000 kilograms. The final classification is by powerplant, with Group 1 (or "I") being an internal combustion engine, Group 2 a turboprop, and so on.

My father's airplane fell into the C-1aI class, and his coveted prize was a "straight line" distance—the shortest route between takeoff and landing points; pilots can also set records for "closed circuits" by flying multiple times around two or more points on the ground. Seven pilots, before my father attempted it, had progressively increased the C-1aI straightline distance record, beginning in 1950 with Belgian Albert Van Cotthem in a factory-built aircraft, who flew a pedestrian 587 statute miles, a distance easily achieved by many light airplanes with a strong tailwind. The record fell three times over the next five years, all in factory-built aircraft. But in 1957, a Finnish homebuilt airplane seized the record with a 1,767-mile flight, and homebuilts have monopolized the category since. In 2010, the record of 2,214 miles for a C-1aI aircraft set in 1984 had not yet been broken, despite the fact that twenty-six years was an eternity in the world of airplane records, many of which have lives measured in months or single-digit years rather than decades.

Unlike when pilots attempted record-setting flights during the first half of the twentieth century, there were no adoring media to record my father's 2010 attempt nor any cash prizes at stake. Instead, a handful of friends and family were at the airport to see him off. His reward would be the fulfillment of his dream of proving to himself that he could design and build a record-setting airplane—although six military moves, countless deployments, the Vietnam War, kids in college, and an addiction to flying that diverted his attention and spare cash from airplane building had all conspired to thwart his record attempt until he was eighty-two years old.

My father's record attempt would have been impossible had it not been for a small band of advocates who worked with the federal government for several decades to develop mutual trust and respect and to overcome the public's fears about homebuilt aircraft and beat back overreach by state and federal governments. Homebuilding's rich history of colorful figures, visionary designers, and occasionally strange-looking airplanes provides an interesting tale, but we can also learn something from the community's success at creating the freedom to build and innovate, a freedom that might have been crushed, or at least severely limited, had the movement's leadership taken a more confrontational approach to achieving their goals.

On that July day in 2010, my father wasn't thinking about homebuilding rules and his freedoms; he was just thinking about flying. The engineer in him had designed an airplane that would hold as much fuel as possible, and the mechanic in him had built the best airplane with the best engine possible, but the pilot in him still had to cross the entire United States by himself without landing, just as Charles Lindbergh had had to cross the entire Atlantic Ocean by himself in 1927. Lindbergh's aircraft, *The Spirit of St. Louis*, was factory built but was certified in the "experimental" category, since the Ryan Company in San Diego had modified an existing design for the long crossing. When Lindbergh took off for

Paris, he wasn't even certain his flight would be eligible for the twenty-five thousand dollars offered by hotelier Raymond Orteig—the required sixty days between his application to compete for the prize and his take-off had not yet elapsed. To Lindbergh, it didn't matter—an aviation visionary even at twenty-five, he thought flying nonstop from New York to Paris would convince the world that airplanes could do anything. The day he departed, the weather was good enough, the moon was full, and the plane was ready, so he went.

The Spirit of St. Louis was crude by modern standards, but even with more than eight decades' worth of technological advances Arnold still faced challenges similar to Lindbergh's. Arnold might have to fly around bad weather, and that extra distance wouldn't count toward his record, but at least a radar image of the weather would appear on his cockpit display via satellite radio. With limited weather reporting in 1927, all Lindbergh could do was hope his meager information about weather over the North Atlantic held up for forty hours. Each pilot had to worry about fuel exhaustion or a mechanical failure of his only engine, but at least Arnold would be over land—although, since he had minimized crash protection in his cockpit to save weight, he might wind up badly injured or worse if the airplane crumpled into a ball in a farmer's field. Lindbergh had carried only minimal survival gear, to save weight, and he knew a water landing would likely be fatal even if he survived a ditching of *The Spirit of St. Louis* into the icy swells of the North Atlantic. To guard against running out of fuel, both pilots had meticulously measured fuel burn rates in their airplanes and carefully calculated multiple scenarios based on differences in the winds they might encounter. They hoped tailwinds would push them along faster, but hedged against the possibility of headwinds in some places. Arnold could check his groundspeed displayed on his GPS, but Lindbergh didn't know his progress until he made landfall on the eastern side of the Atlantic.

Lindbergh relied on youth to carry him through thirty-four hours of flying after little sleep the night before, while Arnold carried caffeine pills as a precaution. Both pilots flew on days with long hours of sunlight and a full moon to reduce the risk of getting lost and to help them see the ground below in case they had to make an emergency landing. Although Arnold had a GPS, if it failed or he lost electrical power, finding the small airport at his destination would in some ways be more challenging than Lindbergh's navigation problem, and a miscue might trigger F-16s patrolling the airspace over Washington, DC, to escort him away. "Lucky" Lindbergh figured all he had to do was keep flying east; even if he completely missed the United Kingdom, at some point he would run into the European coastline. Then all he had to do was decide whether to turn right or left and look for a road that would lead to Paris.

At 2:15 in the afternoon, Arnold and his airplane leaped into the air and headed east. He climbed to ninety-five hundred feet to cross the only major obstacle in his way, the snow-covered Cascade Mountains. During the climb, his fuel flow meter and the gauge that displayed his total amount of fuel failed. Both pieces of equipment had performed without fault during his five-year test program; but at the worst possible moment, he had no way to know exactly how much fuel remained. He still had a gauge on his cockpit tank, but during the flight he would have to calculate how much fuel he had used from the wing tanks by multiplying his estimated burn rate by the amount of time he had been airborne, much like using an odometer to estimate the fuel in a car with a failed gas gauge.

As he crossed the Cascades, the miniature radio in his cramped cockpit seemed to have failed as well, but he finally contacted an air traffic controller as he approached Spokane. Soon afterward, air traffic radars began tracking him and feeding his path over the ground to an Internet flight-following program, to the relief of family and friends watching his progress across the United States.

Approaching Montana, Arnold watched as the sun began to set behind him and a line of thunderstorms at a safe distance greeted him with a spectacular light show in the darkening sky. As the night wore on, the full moon rose and the radio fell silent. He seemed to be the lone pilot in the sky, with only his picture of Colleen, the purring of his engine, and his thoughts to keep him company.

As he passed through North Dakota, he confronted a headwind that slowed his progress and wasted precious fuel. He descended to search for better winds, flying lower and lower. When he crossed the southern Minnesota border into Iowa and descended below the three-thousand-foot-level above the ground, air traffic radars lost his signal, and the reassuring green line marking his progress on the Internet tracker vanished.

Traveling through Indiana, he watched the sunrise, and as he neared Columbus, Ohio, he computed how much gas he needed to make it to Virginia. Arnold grimaced as he stared in disbelief at the numbers on his kneeboard. He computed the numbers again, but they refused to budge, ripping his fifty-year dream to shreds as they said, "You don't have enough fuel to get to Fredericksburg. It's time to go to Wisconsin instead."

*   *   *

In my childhood houses, mounds of airplane magazines, airplane books, airplane models, and airplane parts competed for space on end tables and shelves already piled high with Dr. Seuss books and Civil War tomes. My parents, both pilots, always owned at least one airplane, but I was in my forties, and an aeronautical engineer and pilot myself, before I realized my father planned to build a record-setting airplane he had designed in college. Even then, as he showed me balsa models of his design during my trips home, I wasn't sure he would ever build the plane or, if he did, set a world record. He was often unengaged with the rest of our family as he constantly tinkered with something in the garage or at the airport while my mother uncomplainingly kept dinner warm. Even she, my father's most ardent supporter, often started sentences with: "If he ever builds that airplane . . ."

It wasn't until I passed my fiftieth birthday that I realized how few details I knew about my dad's youth. He had helped my mother achieve many of her own dreams of flight, and much of what my sisters and I knew about our father's dreams had been filtered through her lens. She portrayed him as some sort of aviation icon who always knew exactly what he wanted and where he was going. However, as my youngest sister, Kelly, and I dug into old photographs and my father's logbooks while we assembled a set of scrapbooks to commemorate his eightieth birthday, I saw that his path had been much less of a straight line than my mother had let on.

As I pieced together the story of a boy who grew up preferring science projects and slide rules to sock hops, and who would skip school to fly rather than joyride in a car, I found his life had been like that of many early pilots and aircraft designers—circuitous, unplanned, and open to both risk and opportunity. I had always viewed my father as a pilot first and engineer second, but I soon realized he wanted to design airplanes just as much as he wanted to fly them, although circumstances had thwarted that dream for years.

Many engineers, including me, also want to be pilots, and that is the easier path to take. Full-time engineers can earn a pilot's license and fly part-time, either for pleasure or professionally, piloting jump planes for skydivers, towing gliders into the air, or instructing students. It's much harder to be a full-time pilot and an engineer on the side; few businesses hire part-time engineers, although some pilots design airplanes in their spare time.

Even for a person with enough time and talent, engineering an airplane isn't a process that goes in a straight line, from the designer saying, at point A, "I'm going to give birth to an airplane," to achieving, at point B, the reality nine months later. Instead, the laws of physics and aerodynamics, resistant to all attempts at reform, make the journey much like following an errant compass that points only roughly in the right direction: on any given day it may lead you astray by dozens of miles. Designing an airplane involves hundreds of individual decisions to solve dozens of problems, some with elegant solutions, others with solutions that create unintended consequences that must also be resolved. Sometimes, it's two steps forward, one step back, and other times the designer must throw something out and start all over again. In the end, each aircraft requires such compromise that it's a wonder any of them get into the air, let alone achieve the feats they do.

Aircraft constructed outside of factories are often called "homebuilts," but the Federal Aviation Administration's formal and legal term is "experimental amateur-built," an unwieldy label meaning the aircraft are built by amateurs and issued airworthiness certificates in the experimental category. Thus, homebuilt aircraft fall into the same general category as prototypes or research vehicles, such as the X-1, which first broke the sound barrier, although the rules for certifying homebuilts are quite different from those for research vehicles.

Homebuilt aircraft make up just one part of the aviation ecosystem in the United States, but it's an important species, one that thrives on a type of individual initiative and problem solving not often seen in the manufacture of factory-built aircraft. In the twenty-first century, the United States leads the world in amateur-built aircraft—the most designs, most kits, and most airplanes. But while such aircraft were a curiosity just a few decades ago, the FAA's Aircraft Registry now lists about thirty thousand homebuilt aircraft in the United States, accounting for about 20 percent of personally owned aircraft and about 10 percent of all aircraft.

Since the 1950s, homebuilt aircraft have been a bright spot among piston-powered general aviation aircraft, often defined as any noncommercial, nonjet airplane that carries fewer than twenty passengers. While aircraft manufacturers spent decades churning out the same designs with marginal improvements, homebuilders created a zoo's worth of designs and parts: airplanes and gyrocopters not much bigger than a bicycle, racers that squeaked two hundred miles per hour out of an eighty-five-horsepower engine, sophisticated avionics at one-tenth the price of production units, and new covering systems that more than quadrupled the life of fabric-covered airplanes. Over time, some manufacturers adopted homebuilding parts and processes outright, such as fabric covering or spring-steel landing gear, and in other cases, manufacturers updated older designs to compete with homebuilt aircraft. Some aircraft originally designed as homebuilts, such as Pitts aerobatics airplanes, have even made their way onto production lines.

It's also no accident that homebuilt aircraft dominate some classes of records. In early 2016, homebuilts owned all but one of the forty-four significant distance, speed, altitude, and efficiency records for airplanes weighing less than one thousand kilograms listed by the Fédération Aéronautique Internationale, the Swiss-based keeper of aviation world records. Building an airplane without the expense and worry of certifying the design for a market filled with finicky aviation consumers, or of meeting the demands of an often unreasonable military customer, frees amateurs to design aircraft to do exactly what they want and no more, a stripping-down process that results in what engineers call elegance, described best by pilot and author Antoine de Saint-Exupéry in *Wind, Sand and Stars*: "Perfection is finally attained not when there is no longer anything to add but when there is no longer anything to take away."

A trip to the Experimental Aircraft Association's annual fly-in at Oshkosh, Wisconsin, demonstrates what elegance has brought to aviation. Ten thousand airplanes arrive every year, among them more than one thousand homebuilts, which receive privileged parking spots. Over a week's time, a half million aviation enthusiasts can see just about any kind of aircraft for sale in the United States, short of Boeing transports. Kit airplane manufacturers don't take up much real estate, but they have an outsized presence, harkening back to simpler times when people lived by their own ingenuity, designing and building for themselves all sorts of things they needed and wanted. There is perhaps some primal need in people to make things, and many of us find pride, pleasure, and satisfaction in constructing a set of shelves, sewing a new dress, painting a picture, or writing a poem. Some extend that idea to building airplanes, and in many countries, including the United States, you can do just that, and then fly your airplane, with passengers and luggage, almost anywhere. For many, it is the ultimate in freedom.

*　*　*

My family moved to Wright-Patterson Air Force Base, near Dayton, Ohio, the "Birthplace of Aviation," when I was eight. Even then, I appreciated the awesomeness of what Orville and Wilbur Wright had accomplished with the *Wright Flyer*, the first heavier-than-air, powered aircraft to succeed at carrying a human during controlled flight, so I never understood why the brothers had to share the base's name with someone who had nothing to do with building the first airplane.

Naming oddities aside, after I became an aeronautical engineer I appreciated the brothers even more, especially since they had had no formal engineering education. In an era when most inventors learned just by trying things to see what worked, the Wrights embarked on a campaign of methodically planned experiments to solve two fundamental problems: how to control an airplane in flight, and how to build a lightweight engine with enough power to get an airplane off the ground and keep it in the air.

All airplanes are subject to four fundamental forces in flight: lift, weight, thrust, and drag. Lift comes primarily from the wings, partly from the deflection of air off the bottom of the wing, which pushes the airplane up, and partly from the curved surface, which creates a region above the wing that is lower in pressure than below, causing the airplane, following the path of least resistance, to move toward the lower pressure. The weight of the airplane tends to move the airplane back toward the ground. Pulling or pushing the airplane through the air is a result of thrust, which usually comes from some sort of powerplant that accelerates a mass of air: reciprocating piston engines impart small accelerations to a large volume of air past a propeller, while jet engines impart large accelerations to a smaller volume of air passing through the engine.

Airplane designers always want more thrust, which is offset by drag, and which is, yes, a drag. Some drag, called induced drag, is a necessary consequence of producing lift, but other drag, called parasite drag, results from all the small protuberances and inefficiencies on an airplane—wires, bolts, rivets, antennae, and anywhere two surfaces come together.

When the Wrights began experimenting in the late 1800s, most would-be airplane designers had moved away from birdlike ornithopters that flapped wings to create lift and thrust, and toward the modern concept of an airplane: fuselage, tail, and fixed wing. The Wrights researched aerodynamics, built wind tunnels, and flew dozens of models and gliders to learn which wing shapes worked best and to evaluate discrepancies in data produced by previous experimenters, such as Germany's Otto Lilienthal, who lost his life in a glider crash in 1896.

From their experience with bicycles, which require constant small inputs to remain upright, the Wrights knew that control would be a key part of sustained flight. Airplanes move left, right, and forward like a car; they pitch, roll, and yaw like a boat; and unlike cars and boats, they climb and descend. The pilot needs deliberate control over these motions. In addition, the slightest gust or bump in the air, or twitch in the pilot's hand makes a wing drop slightly, or jostles the nose to the right a little, or any number of things. The airplane must be stable enough to overcome these small annoyances on its own, or the pilot must be able to quickly return the airplane to where it was.

Other experimenters had already solved the problem of pitch and yaw control using elevators and rudders, respectively, but rolling the airplane into a bank for turning remained an obstacle. The Wrights realized that to roll the airplane, the wing on one side had to generate more lift than the other; the wing with more lift would move up, the wing with less lift would move down, and the airplane would roll. How to alter the lift proved elusive until the Wrights hit on the concept of "wing warping" and used a series of wires attached to the pilot's control stick to change the shape of the wings.

By 1902, the Wrights had demonstrated their wing-warping concept with a glider, and all they needed next was a powerplant—a propeller and an engine. Steam engines were too heavy for the power they produced, and even existing gasoline-powered automobile engines couldn't produce the eight or nine horsepower the brothers demanded from an engine weighing less than 180 pounds. The Wrights outsourced the problem to one of their bicycle mechanics, Charles Taylor, who managed to build a twelve-horsepower, 179-pound engine.

Propellers at the time were designed for boats, not airplanes, so the brothers developed their own after realizing that propellers are just miniature wings that rotate. After much experimenting, the Wrights settled on two eight-and-a-half-foot-diameter spruce propellers. Bicycle chains attached to the engine completed the assembly by driving the propellers mounted at the backs of the wings.

The Wrights knew that, even with their twelve-horsepower engine, their craft would need some wind to get airborne. An airplane reacts to the wind around it, whether that wind comes from the airplane moving itself through the air or the air moving over the airplane, so every knot of headwind on the ground is one knot of airspeed the engine doesn't have to produce for taking off. To increase their odds, they returned to the windy Kill Devil Hills, North Carolina, where they had done many glider experiments.

At 10:35 A.M. on December 17, 1903, Orville Wright took to the air in the *Wright Flyer* for a twelve-second flight that covered 120 feet, a distance shorter than the 197-foot wingspan of a Boeing 787 Dreamliner. The brothers flew three more flights that day, the longest one just under one minute and measuring only about three football fields in length, but it was enough to prove that powered flight to carry humans was possible.

* * *

Underpowered and barely controllable, the *Wright Flyer* was useless for any practical application, and even after another decade of improvements, early "aeroplanes" still seemed to crash more than they flew— inexperienced pilots lost control of cantankerous airplanes, and wimpy engines often failed to push airplanes into the air. Responding to the dangers of flight, Congress enacted a law in 1913 to give flying army officers a 35 percent increase in pay, as designers around the world worked to refine both airplanes and engines.

In the early 1900s, French designer Louis Blériot had tried out some unsuccessful gliders and flapping-wing ornithopters. Despite being an engineer, Blériot followed the "just try it" approach more common for the day; fortunately, in science and engineering, what doesn't kill you makes you smarter. By late 1908, after spending $150,000 on failures, he was convinced he had found the right design.

With his indulgent wife's blessing and part of her inheritance, he pressed on with the Blériot XI, a revolutionary craft that introduced the configuration used by nearly all modern aircraft: a single wing, a front-mounted engine, a stick or yoke to move the nose of the airplane up and

Fig. 1.1. The Blériot XI, the first airplane to use a modern flight control system, May 1909.

down and to roll the airplane, and foot controls to move the airplane's nose from side to side. In addition to his modern flight control system, Blériot also added innovations such as shock absorbers for the wheels and a tail wheel instead of just a skid.

In 1908, a British newspaper, the *Daily Mail*, offered a thousand-pound prize to the first person to cross the twenty-two-mile English Channel in an airplane. After flying several flights of more than one hour, Blériot set his sights on the channel, a feat many thought foolhardy at best and fatal at worst. By late July 1909, aviator Hubert Latham had already crashed into the sea while vying for the prize, which was followed by a hair-raising rescue.

On July 25, 1909, exactly 101 years before my father set off to fly nonstop across the United States, Blériot took off at 4:30 A.M. It was light outside, but the English coast was lost in a morning haze and Blériot's state-of-the-art airplane had no compass. Wearing blue cotton coveralls over his tweed clothes to ward off the cold, and flying about 250 feet above the water, he soon spotted a destroyer below bound for England, but it proved useless for navigation—traveling at forty-two miles per hour, Blériot sped past the ship.

Ten minutes into the flight, Blériot could still see nothing and the waves below unsettled him, but he pressed on, knowing he had enough fuel to turn around and head back to France. His luck held, and he spotted the cliffs of Dover and turned toward his intended landing spot. Winds shrieking off the cliffs bounced him like a pogo stick as he crawled to the landing zone, and he considered flying back to France; but he decided he had come too far.

Above the landing field at seventy-five feet, Blériot found it impossible to make a normal landing, owing to the howling winds, so he simply turned off his engine and fell straight to the ground. The airplane crumpled as it crashed, but the aviator escaped unscathed to claim his prize.

Upon Blériot's death twenty-six years later in 1936, the Fédération Aéronautique Internationale established the Louis Blériot Medal, awarded to lightplane aviators who set certain world records, including the seven pilots who had previously set the record my father pursued.

* * *

I've heard people say that all early airplanes were technically homebuilts, since no airworthiness or manufacturing standards existed until the 1920s. However, the Wrights, Blériot, and others tried to profit from their designs and assembled airplanes in rudimentary factories, so it would be inaccurate to call them amateurs.

Whoever assembled the first true homebuilt is lost to history; but in 1910, *Popular Mechanics* began offering blueprints for what is likely the earliest homebuilt offered, the Demoiselle, a monoplane that resembled a modern hang-glider powered by a lawnmower-size engine. Amateurs eager to try their own hand at designing airplanes instead of copying someone else's didn't have to wait long for help. In 1912, Victor Loughead published a book, *Aeroplane Designing for Amateurs*; his brothers Allan and Malcolm changed the spelling of their name to Lockheed and founded what would become their eponymous aircraft company the same year. By 1915, *Popular Mechanics* ran dozens of ads for a wide assortment of aircraft parts as a small but growing population of homebuilders assembled, and in some cases designed, airplanes in their garages, barns, and boathouses.

Regardless of whether professionals or amateurs were doing the designing, airplane design still had a long way to go, and the new technologies themselves often caused even more problems, such as monoplane wings that occasionally broke off in flight. Biplanes had a "bridge-truss" structure of sturdy wires between the wings that was inherently strong and well understood by engineers at the time. Monoplane wings easily passed standard load tests that piled sandbags with a combined weight of up to six times the aircraft weight onto the wing, but wings continued to separate in flight. The vexing problem wasn't solved until after World War I, with the result that nearly all airplanes used during the war were biplanes.

In the meantime, engine technology, already behind in 1903, struggled to catch up, both in power and reliability. Designers had two ways to coax more power out of an engine: make the engine bigger, or make the existing engine more efficient. The laws of thermodynamics make the second option harder; in addition, more efficient engines produce more unwanted heat that has to be dumped overboard somehow, so most engineers just make bigger engines. But in the endless cycle of engineering trade-offs, bigger cylinders are harder to cool and they add weight. One solution is to make smaller, lighter cylinders and use more of them, but lighter parts tend to be less reliable.

Prewar engines were a maintenance nightmare, with most lasting only fifty or sixty hours before they had to be overhauled; even an airplane that flew only one or two hours each day had to have the engine removed every month or so for maintenance. By the end of the war, durability had improved to about two hundred hours, still well short of the fifteen hundred to two thousand hours seen with modern piston engines. In addition, nearly all early engines were modifications of liquid-cooled automotive designs, which led to many engine failures when the water drained out in flight after a radiator cracked or hose broke.

World War I ushered in many improvements for larger engines used in combat and then commercial aircraft after the war, but smaller engines suitable for trainers and light airplanes received much less attention. As a result, by the mid-1920s most airplanes cost at least twenty-five hundred dollars, more than a year's salary for the average worker. *Aviation* magazine thought that personal flying was the best way to reduce the cost of all flying, since, if only professionals could fly airplanes, very few would be needed, just as few people would buy cars if only professionals could drive them. When flying was so expensive that no one could afford it, how could the United States get more people interested in flying so it would be cheaper?

Then, in May 1927, Charles Lindbergh crossed the Atlantic. His landing in Paris let loose an aviation genie that will never go back in the bottle.

2

The Pilot's Rock

Aside from the loss of time, there are great advantages in building
a new plane instead of buying a standard model. Every part of it can
be designed for a single purpose, every line fashioned to the Paris
flight. I can inspect each detail before it's covered with fabric and
fairings. And by knowing intimately both the strengths and weak-
nesses of my plane, I'll be able to tax the one and relieve the other
according to conditions which arise.
—Charles Lindbergh, *The Spirit of St. Louis*, 1953

CLOUDY DAYS WERE THE BEST. FEW AIRPLANES IN 1934 NAVIGATED
by instruments, so instead of flying at high altitudes, pilots stayed
beneath the clouds to see the ground. Skimming under the cloud deck, as
low as five hundred feet above the earth, airplanes announced their
arrival with a thunderous roar that bounced off the countryside. Entire
counties ground to a standstill as the population watched the impromptu
air show.

Airplanes never got past six-year-old Arnold. As soon as he heard
rumbling in the distance, he jerked his head skyward. All work or play
stopped until he spotted the craft and then stared transfixed while it
crossed overhead and disappeared on the horizon. He yearned for a flight
in one of the magical machines.

That my father saw at least ten airplanes flying overhead every day in
the 1930s was a coincidence of geography and geology. A straight line
drawn between Chicago and Minneapolis passes close to the dairy farm
where Arnold lived with his parents, Emil and Bertha. The farm, just outside Mount Horeb, Wisconsin, was also the site of an attractive navigation

landmark for early pilots: Donald Rock, a monolith the size of a ten-story building that dominated the surrounding terrain.

Something from Charles Lindbergh's spirit must have penetrated Arnold's soul at conception, because he seemed destined to be a pilot from the day he was born in 1928, nine months after the day of Lindbergh's historic Atlantic crossing. By age six, Arnold and his cousin Carl were imitating the pilots they would both become, sporting small versions of the leather helmets and goggles popularized by the famous aviator.

*   *   *

In addition to proving what airplanes could do, Lindbergh's 1927 flight ignited a fire in millions of people in the United States and around the world. Airplane designers, manufacturers, flight schools, and new aviation magazines popped up almost overnight, and many fizzled almost as quickly. Wildly optimistic estimates of the future pilot population ran as high as ten million; after all, the United States already had forty million people driving cars. A new magazine, *Popular Aviation*, and related magazines such as *Popular Mechanics* and *Modern Mechanics and Inventions*, ran ads for flight training and lightplanes; but a commercial pilot's license cost about a thousand dollars, and airplanes still cost too much for most private fliers. Consumer loans for private autos weren't yet widely available; getting a loan for a small personal airplane was out of the question. War surplus trainers, such as the Curtiss JN-4 Jenny that entered the market in the 1920s, still cost less than a thousand dollars, if you could find one, but by the 1930s many had crashed or were no longer flyable because of age.

The Jennys might be mostly gone, but thousands of this plane's rugged OX-5 engines were still around. Engineers employed by factories churned out designs based on the OX-5, resulting in heavy, low-performing, and expensive airplanes useful only for barnstormers and for budding commercial airlines more interested in carrying lucrative airmail than in transporting passengers. Young men with dreams of flight but no funds for training or for buying their own aircraft turned to homebuilding.

August Valentine was one of those young men. Longing to build a glider to see what flying was like, he chopped down two basswood trees on the family farm and used an abandoned sawmill, which he learned to run after a few tries, to cut the logs into planks of the right size. He completed his prize in only twenty-one days and crashed on his first flight; but after some minor repairs, he made it into the air using a slingshot he had designed himself and attached to a truck.

Young men who wanted an airplane—a craft with an engine that could take off on its own—needed more than just a few local trees, and no one captured their attention more than the Heath Aircraft Corporation.

Edward Bayard Heath had had a vision: an airplane in every garage. Like the Wright Brothers, Heath had no formal education in engineering. As a young man, however, he spent many hours working with wood and metal in the family machine shop business in New York State, where the Brooklyn native had returned after spending most of his childhood in Chicago with his widowed mother and stepfather.

On October 10, 1908 or 1909 (accounts vary, but most favor 1908), Heath made his first flight in a biplane he designed and built himself, launching himself from a hill on the golf course at the Antlers Club in Amsterdam, New York. After taking off, he wobbled through the air for about forty seconds; and when he touched down about a half mile away, the landing gear broke. After repairs, he tried again on November 2, this time taking off from a horse-racing track at the Fonda Fair Grounds a few miles from the Antlers Club. After using nearly one-third of a mile to become airborne and narrowly missing a fence at the end of the track, he managed to fly for about a full minute before landing on rough ground that splintered the gear again and damaged the propeller.

By now broke, he stored the remnants of his project until the next summer, when he struck a deal to fly in a Fourth of July event. With a signed five-hundred-dollar contract, Heath persuaded his uncle to lend him two hundred dollars for repairs. But, probably because of the heat, Heath couldn't climb more than about three feet above the ground, and he hit a fence at the end of the takeoff field, this time sending the plane into the equivalent of intensive care with a smashed fuselage and broken engine mount. However, the event producers were apparently happy with their profits, so Heath received his payment, along with another two hundred dollars he made by selling photos of his dubious airplane.

Perhaps thinking he should quit while he was ahead, Heath found a factory job building motorcycles, which he soon left after getting another request to fly his airplane in an air show. After that, he moved back to Chicago to set up shop as the Heath Aerial Vehicle Company with his mother, who became his lifelong business partner. His first ad, in the

June 1911 issue of *Popular Mechanics*, stated, "Everything for Aircraft," and asked people to "send 6 stamps for catalogue." By 1914, ads for the twenty-six-year-old aviation maven's company claimed, "Five years of propeller production proves perfection."

His business sold primarily new and used airplane parts, as well as pilot supplies, such as fur-lined flying suits for fifteen dollars, Curtiss OX-5 propellers for thirty-five dollars, and spark plugs for a quarter each. With the steady income from his business, Heath continued to design and build small airplanes, selling a few, but mostly using them as personal aircraft for business ventures and vacations, such as flying into the Texas wilderness to hunt rattlesnakes. But in 1927, he and his chief designer, Clare Linstedt, hit on what would become one of the most popular home-built airplanes of the 1930s—a single-seat airplane called the Parasol, which often looked larger than it was when photographed next to Heath's five-foot-one, 105-pound frame.

Although the name "Parasol" might conjure images of British nannies held aloft by umbrellas, the fanciful name derived from the single wing above the fuselage. Unlike designers of biplanes, monoplane designers can mount the wing in multiple places on the fuselage: high, midway, or low. Although there are some performance differences among the three wing-fuselage combinations, the choice of wing position is often driven by how the airplane will be used. High-wing airplanes have better downward visibility and permit easier cargo loading, parachute jumping, and bush flying, but are generally harder for passengers to get in and out of and tend to be slower owing to the draggy external struts that usually brace the wings. Midwing planes tend to be speediest: the midwing can be mated to the fuselage by means of an optimized shape that reduces drag, but the mating process can be difficult without expensive tooling, making most midwing planes specialized craft used as racing and fighter airplanes. Low-wing aircraft with no external bracing are easy for people to get into, and they give the pilot the best upward visibility. Usually somewhat faster than high-wing aircraft because of reduced drag, low-wings also tend to be heavier, since the internal wing design must be stronger to make up for the lack of struts.

After the war, engineers had finally discovered how to analyze the complex stresses involved with monoplanes, so designers could be confident their wings would no longer depart from their airplanes in flight. But before monoplanes could really catch on, designers also needed

Fig. 2.1. The Heath Parasol, 1930s.

better airfoils. An airfoil is a streamlined shape, usually curved, that reacts with the air to create lift or some other force; systems that use or move through air or water use airfoils for all sorts of things: propellers on boats or airplanes, wind turbines, ceiling fans, and wings, to name just a few. You can see the shape of a wing's airfoil by viewing it from the side, and that shape has a significant impact on an airplane's performance.

Most modern airfoils look like a modified ellipse: round on the front end (the "leading edge"), and squashed on the other end (the "trailing edge"), like the middle and bottom airfoils in figure 2.2. Early designers thought the thin airfoils had less drag; but while they worked well in naturally strong biplane trusses, they caused problems for monoplane designs, which required beefier structures.

In the 1920s, researchers found that, in fact, fat airfoils, six inches high or more, were much more efficient than their skinny cousins. In addition to producing more lift with less drag, the thicker airfoils afforded plenty of room for a monoplane's large internal wing spar. The spar, which carries most of the aircraft load, is usually a long, solid rectangular piece of metal or wood. The spars in small airplanes aren't much more than a two-by-four like those purchased at the local lumberyard, but larger airplanes and aerobatic airplanes have spars the size of deck posts.

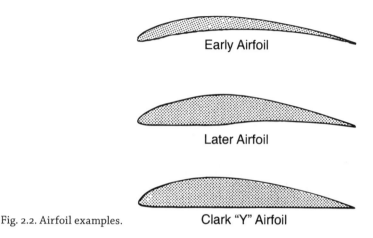

Early Airfoil

Later Airfoil

Fig. 2.2. Airfoil examples. Clark "Y" Airfoil

Most early monoplane designers opted initially for high-wing aircraft that used external struts, a configuration that was strong, light, and easy to build, and Ed Heath was no exception. Craving publicity for his new brainchild, Heath took his Parasol, powered by a twenty-three-horse-power Henderson motorcycle engine, to the National Air Races at Felts Field, in Spokane, Washington, at the end of September 1927. At the time, the races were divided into about ten different categories, about half for military planes and pilots, and the rest for civilians, with categories being further defined by engine size, aircraft weight, and payload.

Heath had been entering his designs in the National Air Races since the early 1920s, placing as high as third, good for a $150 prize, before winning an event in 1926. In 1925, he had failed to even get off the ground, but his fortunes changed when he brought a new design, the Tomboy, to Philadelphia in 1926. Heath jumped to an early lead in the Speed Race for Light Airplanes, a fifty-mile race that covered ten laps over a five-mile course. When the second-place airplane, a KRA midget monoplane, caught up to Heath, the KRA's spinner, a protective cone over the front of the propeller that reduces drag and straightens airflow, flew off with a bang. The KRA's pilot broke off from the race and circled once outside the course; finding no damage other than the lost part, he reentered the race but couldn't catch Heath. The only other contender had an engine failure and landed in a field, and Heath won with an average speed of ninety-one miles per hour.

In 1927, Heath must have been dismayed when Jack Irwin, a West

Coast competitor who offered kits and fully assembled Meteorplanes, showed up in Spokane with a special racing biplane he had finished just days earlier. Reporters soon dubbed Irwin's nameless plane, which was even smaller than the Parasol, the favorite to win; but Heath's luck from the previous year held for the two scheduled lightplane races, one consisting of five laps and the other ten laps, both around a six-mile course. The day before the races, Irwin decided to take the biplane up for some practice, and during the takeoff roll he hit a hole and tore off the right wheel. With no time to repair the damage, Heath's only competitor that year withdrew, and Heath won both races uncontested.

Heath took out a three-quarter-page ad in *Popular Aviation* touting his wins, without mentioning his lack of competition. The ads prompted readers to flood the editor with requests for information on how to build the Parasol, and Heath was happy to oblige, penning monthly articles for seven issues. The December 1930 issue of *Popular Aviation* carried the first installment, and an ad in the January 1931 magazine claimed that thousands had already completed their Parasols after "transforming dull winter evenings into hours of genuine pleasure," with one young man supposedly having built his Parasol in three weeks during the previous summer. The airplane could be built with simple hand tools, such as a screwdriver, handsaw, pliers, and a breast drill that allowed users to lean their weight into a concave fitting while drilling. Each article provided a full list of parts and supplies, such as various pieces of wood, nuts, bolts, pulleys, clevis pins, screws, washers, turnbuckles, and "aviator wire" used to help stiffen the wings and fuselage.

The Parasol had the same major components as all single-engine airplanes—wings, a fuselage, flight controls, control surfaces, and an engine. Parasol builders started on the wings, first forming ribs by bending and gluing sticks together, much like building bridge trusses.

Heath's first set of instructions described how to build the ribs. The builder could buy wood and glue, using a list of materials given in the article, or could purchase a twelve-dollar kit from Heath. A kit builder would have pulled the dozens of eight- or ten-foot lengths of $7/32$-inch-square spruce called cap strip from Heath's kit and perhaps wondered how five hundred feet of material no fatter than a no. 2 pencil could be turned into a flyable airplane. The kit also included some $1/32$-inch-thick plywood for gussets—small pieces of wood glued over joints to provide extra strength—and some larger cap strip for reinforcements and building

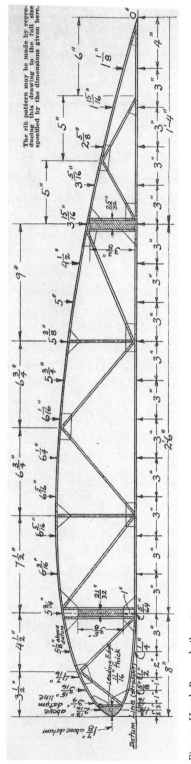

Fig. 2.3. Heath Parasol rib pattern.

some specialized pieces called compression ribs. The builder also needed one-half pound of small nails for attaching the gussets and one pound of casein glue, essentially Elmer's Glue-All.

I decided to see if an average builder could construct a rib in one evening as Heath advertised, so I first had to make a jig, a device to form the cut cap strip and clamp it in place while the glue dried. I started by enlarging the scale drawing from his article, shown in figure 2.3.

It would be a trivial operation to make the full-size pattern with a computer, but I wanted to try it with 1931 drafting tools—a pencil and ruler. A small mistake at the beginning could have rippled through and ruined the entire drawing, but in about an hour I laid out the rib on a five-foot length of US Postal Service regulation shipping paper that covered most of my dining room table. Even though my rudimentary drafting skills, gained while pursuing my engineering degree, probably gave me an advantage over most 1930s builders, I think anyone with a little persistence could have finished the drawing in an evening.

I had already ordered some ¼-inch cap strip (no 7⁄32-inch available) and plywood from Aircraft Spruce & Specialty Company, a California-based supplier of homebuilding parts; the twenty-six-dollar shipping charge had more than doubled the cost of the wood. Following Heath's directions, I assembled the jig by first taping the full-size drawing to an old wooden folding table I found in my garage. After driving one-inch nails about ¼-inch deep into points on the outline of the rib, I added nails on the inside to hold the cap strip in place, using a small piece of the cap strip to get the right spacing. I then clipped off the nail heads to make it easier to slip the wood into the jig and, somewhat in awe of what I had accomplished, called my photographer sister, Kelly, to capture the setup with a wide-angle lens.

The jig complete, it was time to "boil some water in a pail and stand about ten of the [cap] strips in the water to a depth of about twelve inches" to soften the strips for bending. While the wood was softening, I used scissors to cut small gussets, about two inches by three inches, that I would lay over the glued joints.

Then the scary part began: bending the cap strip into the curved channel outlined by the nails in the jig. I agonized as I coaxed the slender strip into the dramatic curvature of the rib's nose, knowing a misstep would splinter the wood like a broken arm. My patience paid off, and a few minutes later I sawed and filed the internal pieces to size and glued them into place.

I was starting to feel like a 1930s builder, my confidence growing with every step, as I moved on to the gussets, which sounded easy in the directions—although I first spent fifteen minutes trimming my robust plywood pieces to more appropriate sizes before gluing one on top of a joint. I selected a ⅜-inch-long nail the diameter of a sewing needle and gingerly placed it on top of the gusset to hammer it through the plywood into the cap strip. On my first tap, the nail bent at a seventy-degree angle and the gusset skidded away from the glue underneath, but after a few more tries I got the technique down.

After an hour of gluing and nailing gussets, the next step was to take the rib from the jig.

The rib wouldn't budge.

A few minutes of probing with a plastic scraper under the cap strip told me that the fifty or so nails I had driven through the gussets had also attached the rib to the tabletop, which I might have predicted had I read two paragraphs further in Heath's directions: "The nails are long enough to extend ¼ inch, allowing them to be clinched, giving added strength."

About five minutes later, the scraper had rescued my rib and an Internet search told me that "clinched" meant I should tap the nail protruding through the wood sideways to flatten it on the other side. It wasn't clear to me if I was supposed to do this before or after attaching the second set of gussets on the other side, but I went ahead and clinched the nails. At that point, I was about two and a half hours into rib construction, and since I wasn't planning to actually build a Parasol but wanted only to prove that a rib could be built in an evening, I decided to stop.

The Parasol required fourteen of these ribs, along with ten aileron ribs and two end ribs, each with separate patterns, so that when assembling one each day, a motivated builder could expect to be done in a month. The builder would then spend the next two months assembling the wing, which included the ailerons for banking the airplane, and a fuel tank made from terneplate, composed of steel coated with an alloy made from lead and tin, used at the time instead of aluminum.

The Parasol's fuselage, made from thin-walled steel tubing, was bolted together instead of welded. Although very early aircraft fuselages were made from wood, designers soon found that the aerodynamic loads imposed on the small number of long, straight pieces required by a fuselage meant they couldn't simply be glued together like a wooden wing with its dozens of spars and ribs that naturally formed a strong structure.

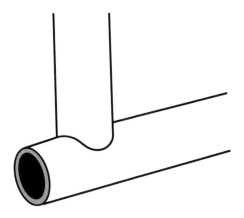

Fig. 2.4. Example of a "fish mouth" cut, which helps achieve better fit with round tubing.

At first, designers tried tying wooden fuselages together with complex metal fittings, but they soon turned to lightweight, hollow, steel tubing, with most pieces measuring about three-quarters of an inch in diameter. However, unlike gluing, which just about anyone could learn in one afternoon, welding steel tubing for aircraft can't be learned in one day. The thin walls heat up so quickly that it's easy to go from a mesmerizing puddle of melted metal to a vaporized mess in an instant, not to mention all those third-degree burns.

Even if one could master the welding process, cutting pieces of steel tubing and fitting them together was much more laborious than slicing small pieces of wood. When you cut off the end of a round tube with a hacksaw and then try to set it on another round tube for welding, there will be a gap, which makes for a poor joint when the welder melts the two pieces together with a torch and adds filler material. It's much better to make a curved cut, called a "fish mouth," on the end of the top tube so that it fits snugly. In the 1930s, a homebuilder had to manually file down the tube, a tedious and error-prone process.

Heath avoided welding by bolting the steel pieces together, although some of the directions must have made a few builders decide it would be easier to learn to weld: "Make two side struts and drill the upper ends with $^{17}/_{64}$-inch holes. Fasten the lower ends in fittings on the lower longerons at the points shown in your print and bolt the upper ends together with the top longerons to the fitting on the stern post. The ends of the longerons belong between the ends of the fitting and the ends of the struts go outside the ends of the fitting."

The Parasol's wings and fuselage were covered with fabric, usually cotton, which was sewn into "blankets" that slipped over the surfaces and tied into place with hand-sewn stitches in various places, including loops around the ribs and through the fabric. The fabric was then coated with a gluelike substance called dope that shrank the fabric as it dried, producing a taut and smooth surface.

Heath's final article gave instructions for building a windshield, a spinner for the propeller, and a metal cowling to cover the engine and cockpit. Final assembly included directions to connect the fuel system to the engine and attach the landing gear. Heath's concluding paragraph advised: "Bolt the propeller to the engine. . . . Be sure that you have six quarts of clean oil in the sump. . . . Screw the cowling in place and your HEATH PARASOL is ready to be transported to a field where, after attaching the wings, you will begin the first of hundreds of hours of joyous flights."

It's not clear how many people actually built airplanes from Heath's directions and kits, but the trophy for determination likely belongs to Stanley Rowan, who built a Parasol in his bedroom at a Chicago boardinghouse. The Pennsylvania native had come to Chicago in 1929 to learn to fly; but after the school he attended went bankrupt, he found a job paying only twenty dollars per week and decided the cheapest way to finish the two hundred hours he needed for his commercial pilot's license was to build an airplane. After visiting the Heath factory, he bought the rib kit and built the required twenty-six ribs in twenty-six days. He worried about disturbing his fellow roomers, but before long, other boarders were stopping by to see the plane-in-progress or borrow tools. Rowan's only regret was that the tools weren't always returned, adding to his expenses.

Those who completed their Heath Parasols and flew them reported that the airplane, although a bit slow, was easy to fly and nimble, even at very slow speeds, where many airplanes have sluggish responses to pilot inputs. The only real complaint was that no one seemed to achieve the eighty-five miles per hour that Heath advertised (sixty was more like it); but given the variety of engines used and the uneven quality of construction, it would be hard to say Heath exaggerated the performance of his designs.

Heath sold both land and seaplane versions of the Parasol, which he touted as having, in addition to the purported top speed, a landing speed of only twenty-eight miles per hour, about half that of most larger airplanes, meaning the planes could fly in and out of just about anywhere, landing even on deserted country roads. The small number of would-be aviators who could afford $975 for a fully assembled airplane could purchase one directly from Heath's factory, but most Parasol owners opted for the $199 kits. The kit came without an engine and propeller, which would add at least another $300, and Heath was happy to sell both to his builders. But many cost-conscious builders instead recycled engines from old motorcycles or cars.

*   *   *

Heath's pronouncement about thousands of airplane builders was premature, since he expected that those who followed the instructions in his monthly articles would not have flyable airplanes until, at the earliest, the summer of 1931. It is doubtful that thousands of Parasols ever existed, but the Aeronautical Chamber of Commerce of America listed more than 160 Heath aircraft in the section on unlicensed planes in its July 31, 1931, report *Licensed and Identified Aircraft*. Since Heath plans and kits had been around for some time by then, many of these were likely built before the *Popular Aviation* series of articles that Heath wrote, but at least some builders were succeeding.

As more Parasols flew, builders and pilots demanded more speed and better climb performance, which drove Heath to develop his first low-wing design. His marriage now in tatters, Heath moved into a room at his airplane factory, and, despite any misgivings he may have had about his ability to design the more complex low-wing airplane, the new plane was ready to fly on February 1, 1931. Normally, Heath would have taken the first flight, but he instead let two of his factory pilots try it out; each flew for a few minutes and pronounced the airplane "good."

Donning his helmet and goggles, Heath took off and climbed to about fifteen hundred feet, where he began maneuvers that put higher stresses on the airplane than the previous two pilots had. After several turns, the right wing suddenly collapsed and slammed against the tail, sending the airplane into an uncontrollable spin. Witnesses reported that Heath's helmet and goggles flew from the cockpit during the plunge, and that they saw his stoic face as he accepted his fate in the last few seconds before hitting the ground.

Heath's mother continued to run the company for several years after his death, until a combination of regulations and the dwindling private aviation market drove it to bankruptcy in 1935. Sold at auction, the company continued manufacturing airplanes, kits, and parts; but after World War II it abandoned aviation for Heathkit electronics and, eventually, computer kits that became wildly popular among hobbyists.

While August Valentine, Stanley Rowan, and others happily built airplanes and launched themselves into the air, often taking their first flying lesson while also taking their craft out for its first flight, a storm brewed. Legislatures throughout the United States had noticed the aviation Wild West in their backyards and declared war on amateur aviation.

3

Death Knell

With so many companies planning production it will not be long
before the home design of an airplane will be considered as strange
as backyard auto builders.
"That Matter of Homebuilding," *Popular Aviation*, August 1928

MY FATHER'S FIRST FLIGHT OCCURRED AT THE ANNUAL FALL FROLIC
festival in Mount Horeb. Two barnstormers arrived in airplanes with
wingspans the length of small houses, one appropriating the golf course
next to the festival, while the other used an adjoining farmer's field. The
pilots offered rides for one dollar per person, and as soon as eight-year-
old Arnold spotted the airplanes, he pleaded with Emil for a ride.

One dollar was an exorbitant amount of money during the Great Depression, especially for a farmer, but Emil didn't need much convincing—he,
too, wanted to indulge in his first flight. On spying Arnold's three-year-
old brother, Frank, the pilot proclaimed, "The little guy can go, too," so
father and sons piled together into the emerald-and-orange airplane.
Arnold sat up front, while Emil, holding Frank, crammed himself into the
back seat along with a fourth passenger.

Arnold could hardly believe his good fortune as he watched the pilot
push and pull an assortment of mysterious levers and knobs to make the
airplane move. At the end of the field, the radial engine roared to life and
the plane accelerated along the sod, bouncing as it picked up speed, until
suddenly they weren't bouncing and Arnold realized they were in the air.
He watched in awe as the ground receded, marveling at the houses that,
from one thousand feet, looked like they could fit in his hand. The dials
and equipment looked terribly complicated, and the airplane was noisy

and reeked of oil and gasoline, but Arnold soaked it all up—the smells, the vibrations that pulsed through his body, and the pilot's cool confidence.

The flight lasted only fifteen minutes, but it hooked Arnold forever—the experience made him like a stranded shipwreck survivor gulping a cup of ocean water: it only made him thirst for the thing he could not have. And he didn't want to be just a passenger—he wanted to be a pilot, to fly the airplane himself, free to go anywhere and do anything.

Too young to fly real airplanes, Arnold built models instead. Modelers' kits in the 1930s didn't have preformed plastic parts. Instead children cut out and assembled individual pieces, just as a builder would with a real airplane kit, turning modeling into an education in aircraft design and construction. Early models were built in exactly the same way as real airplanes, although with parts measured in inches instead of feet; and razors, Balsa wood, and tissue replaced saws, plywood, and cotton.

Arnold's kits cost a dime or a quarter, and although some projects became jumbled balls of balsa wood, glue, and dope that went into the trash, others became flyable airplanes that taught him the principles of flight, such as the importance of the "center of gravity," a detail pilots use to keep airplanes level and safe. His first flying model included a paper clip used as a small weight to balance the airplane like a teeter-totter. Arnold found that if he attached the paper clip too far back on the airplane, the tail was too heavy and the airplane pitched up violently and crashed to the ground. If he attached the paper clip too far forward, the nose was too heavy and the airplane dove to the ground as he launched it. Only if he put the paper clip in just the right place would the airplane balance out and fly smoothly.

But the models did more than teach the basics of flying. Arnold soon realized that each part of an airplane, no matter how small, had a purpose, and that moving those parts around and making them different shapes and sizes had a profound impact on how an airplane would perform. He decided he wanted to be a part of making real airplanes as well as flying them, although the term *aeronautical engineer* wasn't yet in his vocabulary.

* * *

The US government had not foreseen the explosion in aircraft built at home during the 1930s. Before World War I proved the utility of the airplane, not many gave much thought to regulating the new invention.

After the war, Congress chartered multiple studies to determine the best way to ensure that the military had aviation assets to defend the country. With commercial aviation and an "air-minded" country viewed as providing the backbone for a strong aviation industry and a reservoir of pilots in case of emergency, two commissions concluded in 1925 that a government organization should oversee, regulate, and promote safety and the development of airplanes, pilots, and mechanics.

Some pilots and manufacturers thought federally mandated inspections and aircraft certifications were the solution to aircraft safety, but others weren't so sure. *Aviation* magazine conceded that some sort of aircraft inspection program was needed, while cautioning that inspection programs in Britain had nearly doubled operating costs. Others worried that too much regulation would stifle innovation by adding costs for extra testing or labor to show that a new part or airplane complied with the proposed rules. Once designers already had something that worked, why would they want to improve it if they had to go through an expensive recertification process? Still others thought it best to let insurance companies sort things out, since insurers could promise lower rates for aircraft with good safety features.

New rules regarding pilots' licensing proved less controversial in an era when many pilots taught themselves to fly and commercial programs produced fully trained pilots in as few as seven hours. With plane crashes owing to pilot error making almost daily headlines, it was hard to argue against higher standards.

In 1926, about a year before Lindbergh's flight, Congress passed the Air Commerce Act, which created an Aeronautics Branch within the Department of Commerce to regulate the licensing of pilots, mechanics, and aircraft. Pilot's licenses were divided into those for private pilots, who could carry passengers but not charge them, and those for commercial pilots, who could earn money. The standards that qualified one for a private pilot license were minimal: the pilot had to be at least sixteen years old and have at least ten hours of solo time, flying an airplane as the only occupant. A commercial license of the highest level, called a transport pilot license, required two hundred hours of solo flying. That number pales compared to the fifteen hundred hours needed for a modern airline transport pilot license; but with few affordable airplanes in the 1920s, Ed Heath could tout his Parasol as a relatively easy path to becoming a transport pilot.

The Air Commerce Act also called for licensing airplanes used in interstate commerce or for commercial operations, such as hauling passengers or cargo. This licensing involved a rigorous stress analysis to ensure aircraft were safe before exposing them to the flying public. Before the act was passed, most manufacturers tested the strength of their airplanes by suspending an upside-down wing from the ceiling and loading it up with sandbags. If a wing was supposed to carry a two-thousand-pound airplane and had a safety factor of three times that limit, workers would distribute six thousand pounds of sandbags evenly across the wing. If the wing didn't break or deform, it was good to go. Many builders also dropped fully assembled and loaded airplanes from a height of five feet or so, to show that they could survive landing stresses. But experiences with early monoplanes, such as the Blériot XI, made engineers realize that physical tests weren't always enough: Blériot's wings passed all their tests but sometimes fell off in flight regardless. Only a stress analysis that considered different flight conditions, including rough air, along with the stiffness of a structure and other design parameters, could prove an airplane truly safe.

On January 1, 1927, when the act went into effect, every aircraft in the United States became unlicensed. Manufacturers could afford the estimated one thousand dollars required for the engineering expertise to do a stress analysis to obtain a license, but most individual builders could not, and few had the engineering acumen to do the job on their own. The act allowed unlicensed aircraft not used for commercial purposes to obtain a registration number, so most homebuilders simply registered their airplanes and continued to fly.

The vast majority of homebuilt and other unlicensed aircraft were at least as strong and airworthy as their licensed cousins, and only a small percentage of all aircraft accidents were due to structural failures. But the public began to equate the term *unlicensed*, including unlicensed homebuilts, with *unsafe*, their fears in part fueled by newspaper stories such as one on July 1, 1929, that described two passengers burning to death in an unlicensed plane flown by an unlicensed pilot. The term *unlicensed* devoid of context and details apparently caused readers to overlook the three crashes involving licensed airplanes that killed five people that day.

Even though most unlicensed aircraft were already safe, the nascent homebuilding community realized the value of a consistent set of standards for both pilots and airplanes, and *Popular Aviation* often railed against pilots who flew "crates fit only for the junkyard." Some even questioned the need for homebuilt aircraft at all and assumed the fad would soon go the way of homebuilt automobiles. Few in the aviation industry called for an outright ban, although some conspiracy-minded aviators thought airplane manufacturers might be in cahoots with the government to quash homebuilding and force the would-be amateur builders to buy factory-built aircraft.

Facts about safety aside, many state legislatures decided to ground unlicensed airplanes, which meant grounding virtually all homebuilt aircraft. The Air Commerce Regulations derived from the 1926 Air Commerce Act were silent on the topic of amateur-built aircraft—they weren't explicitly banned, but they weren't explicitly allowed either. The initial set of regulations allowed licensing of "special classes of airplanes," which included "racing and experimental airplanes and airplanes of unusual design," without a full-blown stress analysis; instead, the airplanes were to be "operated only in accordance with the conditions specified in such licenses." Thus, the "experimental" and "unusual design" clauses seemed to allow licensing of homebuilts, but individual states took advantage of the ambiguous language to tighten the screws on amateur builders: they simply applied the act's burdensome stress analysis rules to every airplane whose owner sought a license.

While homebuilders struggled to adapt to the new laws, a voice cried out from what must have seemed an unlikely place—a small town in Oregon. In spite of its remote location in a corner of the country, the Pacific Northwest had long been a hotbed of aviation activity. Along with a seemingly infinite supply of aircraft-grade Sitka spruce and Douglas fir, preferred by builders because of its high strength-to-weight ratio, the region had both mild winters and summers that permitted year-round flying and a long coastline that the military wanted to defend partly by using the recent invention.

Born in Cornelius, Oregon, in 1889, one year after Ed Heath, an adult Leslie Long and his family still lived on his parents' two-hundred-acre farm with his three brothers and their families. In addition to being a prolific writer of romance novels, poems, and technical articles, Long built radios, ground telescope lenses, designed electric fences, and in his spare time, sold airplane blueprints, engines, and propellers. Although his propellers were certified for aircraft use, his customers mostly used them for drying fruit. However, his small Harley-Davidson-based two-cylinder engine, the Long Harlequin, proved popular with amateur airplane builders.

Health issues stemming from a bout with the flu in the 1918 pandemic, and his reluctance to leave his house for extended periods, prevented Long from being a pilot, but he nonetheless became inspired to design and build airplanes by an aviator who landed next to the Long house in 1927. By 1928, Long, along with his brother George and a friend, Jesse Watson, had built the first airplane to fly in Washington County, Oregon. The airplane didn't have a name, but the Longs claimed it could fly at ninety miles per hour, got thirty miles per gallon, and could be sold for about twelve hundred dollars.

Long's experience building and selling radios through his company, Long Radio, convinced him that the best innovation came from amateur individuals tinkering endlessly with their radios, not from the design departments of large corporations. He believed that airplanes, too, would only get better by amateur tinkering, and nearly every month in *Popular Aviation* he moaned at the regulations that more and more states threw in the path of homebuilders. Long also noted the hypocrisy in regulations designed supposedly to protect the lives of the flying public, especially young men, while car and motorcycle accidents killed hundreds each year.

Long pleaded for other states to adopt the so-called Oregon System that accommodated homebuilt aircraft. The system was simple: "All commercial flying must meet Federal regulations. Private flying is under control of the State Board of Aeronautics. If an individual builds an airplane he simply notifies the state."

By late 1932, *Popular Aviation* had instituted the "Howl Department for Amateurs," where homebuilders could file their grievances. And as laws against unlicensed aircraft mounted, pilots and builders found creative ways to circumvent the rules. One pilot flew his airplane only around his large western ranch, and another built an airplane with no wings that he used for "hedge-hopping." Others built wingless airplanes on skis for zooming across frozen lakes. Some decided to give up on homebuilding and form flying clubs instead, buying a licensed airplane and splitting the costs among ten or twelve people.

In late 1933, Ross Peters, a twenty-eight-year-old automobile mechanic in Washington State, suffered the first documented arrest for flying an unlicensed airplane. Unable to pay the twenty-five-dollar fine, he served his time in jail instead. Laws banning unlicensed airplanes had been on the books in Washington since 1929 but hadn't been enforced; after Peters's arrest, overzealous authorities grounded at least twenty more pilots and airplanes. During the next three years, Minnesota and Iowa arrested still more pilots, and then Massachusetts upped the rule to a ridiculous level by banning gas-powered model airplanes in late 1937. At least by then, the craze to arrest pilots seemed to have died down.

The Department of Commerce added to the confusion regarding homebuilt aircraft with a 1934 update to the Air Commerce Regulations, which now stated that "aircraft flown for racing purposes or for special industrial operations, such as crop dusting, aerial photography, etc." were eligible for licenses, in addition to "aircraft flown solely for experimental purposes" and "other aircraft . . . [at] the discretion of the Secretary of Commerce." The regulations failed to define *experimental*, but in theory the update still allowed homebuilt aircraft licensed under the "other aircraft" clause, if someone at either the state or federal level were to invoke the required "discretion."

At the height of both federal and state efforts to clamp down on homebuilding, a curious thing happened: amateur building became even more widespread. *Popular Aviation*, which had been reluctant to publish more articles on homebuilt aircraft after the Heath Parasol series out of fear that no one would be able to fly anything they built, ran a set of articles for another homebuilt, the Corben Junior Ace. Articles on aircraft design and construction techniques, such as welding, abounded. Pictures of aircraft from builders, most of them accompanied by the builders' full names and addresses, poured into the magazine for use in a monthly feature titled "What Our Readers Are Building"—although it was rumored that the magazine deliberately mismatched published names and airplanes to throw off state and federal regulators.

Although a lack of regulatory response seemed to give amateur builders tacit approval, Les Long launched the Amateur Aircraft League in early 1934 with the explicit goal of opposing restrictive aircraft legislation. The organization came to the rescue in 1935, when Oregon flirted with changing its liberal aviation laws. Long put together a pamphlet that pleaded the case of the amateur and sent it, along with a personal letter, to every legislator in the state. At least seventy-five pilots and builders, including Tex Rankin, a noted Pacific Northwest aerobatic pilot and aviation executive, testified against the proposed legislation at a public hearing.

Despite the ability of renegade Oregon to keep homebuilding alive, by 1935 other states had outlawed unlicensed aircraft, and a new federal Civil Aeronautics Act that was passed in 1938 effectively precluded the possibility that any homebuilt aircraft could be licensed. Some amateur builders were still able to persuade inspectors of the newly created federal Civil Aeronautics Authority to award them a license in the experimental aircraft category, but the 1938 regulations defined *experimental* as aircraft "certified for experimentation in flight with a view to determining or improving its characteristics or those of its components or equipment." Leslie Long and other airplane designers might be able to meet the new criteria, but individuals who simply wanted to build an airplane for their own education and pleasure could not.

In March 1938, *Popular Aviation*, dominated by articles on military aviation as the United States entered the pre–World War II arms race with Germany and Japan, published "Swan Song," an article showcasing photos of small airplanes and the men it believed to be the last of the homebuilders.

But the homebuilders' cries for smaller and more affordable planes had not been unheard. In the early 1930s, some manufacturers had realized that not everyone wanted an airplane with three or more seats designed for barnstormers and the surprisingly profitable airlines, an industry that thrived during the Great Depression.

At the 1930 All-American Aircraft Show in Detroit, Aeronca Aircraft introduced the C-2, a single-seat, closed-cabin airplane with a thirty-horsepower engine that sold for $1,495, still too expensive for some, but illustrating that it was possible to produce smaller, more economical aircraft. The Department of Commerce itself launched a program in the mid-1930s to find a safe factory-built aircraft that would sell for $700 or less, but the Hammond-Standard Y-S, which it selected, never met the target cost or went into full production.

In 1931, Taylor Aircraft introduced the Taylor E-2 Cub, powered by a forty-horsepower engine designed exclusively for lightplanes. Continental Motors' four-cylinder A-40 engine solved a host of problems and defined the configuration of most modern airplane piston engines. The cylinders were mounted horizontally, two on either side of the engine, making for a flat engine that improved forward visibility from the cockpit. In addition, the cylinders had fins that pulled heat away from the engine and allowed for air cooling, eliminating the unreliable radiator.

On early A-40s, head gaskets blew, magnetos used for ignition failed, and crankshafts broke, but engineers fixed those problems and added an extra magneto and a second spark plug to each cylinder for backup ignition. Continental and other manufacturers soon cranked out reliable engines for lightplanes.

In 1938, William Piper and his Piper Aircraft Corporation, which had taken over Taylor Aircraft, finally hit an aviation home run when the first J-3 Cub rolled off the assembly line. At only $1,295.00, the two-seat airplane could be profitable for operators charging customers only $6.50 per hour, and flight schools throughout the United States, and even the military, began snapping up the yellow airplanes faster than Piper could make them. When the company ended the airplane's production ten years later, in 1947, nearly twenty thousand had been built. In comparison, Cessna Aircraft Company has sold about forty thousand of the most popular airplane ever built, the four-seat Cessna 172, but required a half century to produce those numbers.

The Cub would be to aviation what the Model T was to automobiles, economical and easy to operate; and an entire generation of pilots, and then their heirs, fell in love with the airplane, a love story that continues to this day—more than four thousand Cubs still exist in the United States.

Arnold Ebneter became one of the lovers.

4

Sprouting Wings

The only really air-minded men in this country are the ones who
have built, or are building, or hope to build, airplanes of their own.

Leslie Long, *Popular Aviation*, June 1932

IN THE SUMMER OF 1939, MY FATHER'S FAMILY MOVED TO PORTAGE,
Wisconsin, where my grandfather had found work as a butcher after
giving up farming. For Arnold, a treasure emerged from the move—
across the street from the new Ebneter residence lived an aspiring pilot
with a huge collection of aviation magazines. Arnold borrowed the pile and
pored over each issue, mesmerized by articles about pilots known for
their derring-do, such as Freddie Lund, who, when tossed from his airplane during an aerobatic maneuver, landed on the wing and clawed his
way back into the cockpit, or about a pilot who landed a plane on the roof
of a building. Other articles offered plans and instructions for building
models of real aircraft, including a zeppelin, complete with directions for
constructing a hydrogen generator using two wide-mouthed jars, hydro-
chloric acid, and scraps of zinc or iron. Intoxicating advertisements
hawked flight schools for "those good pay jobs in aviation" that yielded
up to $700 per month. But at $2,675, the cost of a transport course might
as well have been a million dollars for a Depression-era boy. Other ads
peddled model airplane kits and books on aircraft navigation, meteorol-
ogy, radios, and aerodynamics, and some offered licensed airplanes, such
as the Alexander Flyabout for $1,465. Articles about building the Heath
Parasol and Corben Junior Ace piqued Arnold's interest, but he also
noticed features about the homebuilding movement's demise and wondered if he would be able to fly such an airplane if he built one.

The magazines provided hours of entertainment, but nothing could top Portage's crown jewel, at least as far as Arnold was concerned: despite having only five thousand people, the town had an airport. It wasn't much, just a little field about one-half-mile square, with a garage-size pilot's lounge, established in 1933 by two brothers, Chet and Bob Mael, and home to a half dozen airplanes owned by local pilots. The brothers mowed two runways into the grass, one running north-south and the other north-east-southwest, crossing each other at mid-runway, so that from the air the airport looked like a farmer's field with a giant X in the middle.

A Portage native, Chet was a gifted mechanic who operated an auto body repair shop and used car dealership on the outskirts of the airfield. After graduating from high school in the late 1920s, he used extra money from repairing cars to learn to fly in a war-surplus Hisso Standard, an airplane similar to the popular Jennys. After getting his pilot's license, he earned his aircraft mechanic's license and built an airplane similar to Heath's Parasol, a Pietenpol Air Camper.

The Mael brothers owned an airplane that Chet used for flight instruction, but the majority of flying activity came from the local pilots. A windstorm had blown down the airport's main hangar, so the planes sat on the grass, exposing them to the elements and curious passersby, including Arnold and Emil. During several visits to the airfield, Arnold peppered the brothers with questions about becoming a pilot, and they encouraged him to save his money and begin lessons when he turned fifteen.

By the time he was fourteen, Arnold was spending many Saturdays at the airport, watching pilots take off and land and tagging after Chet as he prepared for a flight or refueled and repaired airplanes. With World War II raging, most pilots were flying overseas, but Chet's wife and four children exempted him from military service. To Arnold, he was like a god—he seemed capable of making an airplane do anything and could explain the mysteries of flight to novices. Arnold especially marveled that Chet had actually built an airplane. Pilot, flight instructor, mechanic, airplane builder—Arnold thought if he could be like Chet, he would have the aviation world by the tail, although he had no notion about the wild ride his life would take once he had grabbed that tail.

Arnold spent the summer of 1943 in the "little Switzerland" town of New Glarus, Wisconsin, waiting tables and busing dishes at a restaurant owned by one of Emil's sisters. He earned only forty dollars that summer, but the meager amount was enough for a few flying lessons, even after indulging in a two-dollar slide rule, a gizmo Arnold knew scientists and engineers used for making calculations. He had no idea how to use the baffling-looking device with dozens of numbers on both sides, but it came with an instruction manual, and he figured, correctly, that he would need it someday.

Back in Portage, his neighbor Floyd had finished earning his pilot's license and bought an airplane, and he offered Arnold a flight in the red-and-maroon Piper J-4. Since Floyd wasn't an instructor, Arnold couldn't touch the controls, but he was still thrilled as they followed the twists and turns of the Wisconsin River and explored every inch of Portage from the air, which included an inspection of Arnold's house. After they landed, Arnold walked into Chet's office and scheduled his first flight lesson for September 13, 1943.

On the big day, his mother drove him to the airport and waited in the car while he flew. The dreariness of the day, with gray clouds about fifteen hundred feet above the ground, didn't dampen his enthusiasm for the lesson in the Maels' Piper J-3 Cub. The trainer's two seats were aligned one in front of the other, and like other airplanes in the 1940s the Cub sat on its tail. To control the airplane's movement in the air and on the ground, each seat had a stick that poked up between the occupant's legs and a set of rudder pedals. The Cub lacked brakes but didn't really need them. The only runway available was the grass field, and the friction caused by the grass on the wheels after landing slowed the Cub more than enough to keep it from spilling off the end into a ditch or onto a road.

Arnold climbed through the door on the right of the airplane, sat in the rear seat, and buckled his seatbelt. Because they would have to shout at each other above the engine racket once they were in the air, Chet first stood outside the plane and explained how to move the controls, even though Arnold already had an idea how things worked from his models and magazines.

"Push the stick to the left," said Chet.

The stick was about an inch in diameter and had a black knob on top of it a little smaller than a golf ball. Arnold clutched the knob with his right hand and moved the stick to the left.

"Now look at the ailerons."

Arnold looked out the window to the left, and he could see the left aileron, a part attached to the rear of the wing that looked like a miniature

Fig. 4.1. The Piper Cub in which Arnold Ebneter soloed in 1944.

wing itself, sticking up. He looked to the right, and saw the right aileron sticking down.

"Wow, just like it says in the magazines," he thought. He was impatient to try it in the air, but Chet continued the ground lesson.

"If the wings are level, the stick and rudder pedals should both be in their middle positions. If the left wing is low, bring it up by moving the stick to the right and pushing the right rudder pedal at the same time. Now try it."

Arnold moved the stick a little to the right and stepped on the right rudder pedal.

Chet said, "It's like the aileron and the rudder are hooked together by a cable, and you're the cable. Got it?"

"Got it."

To start the engine, Chet put his foot in front of the right tire, grabbed the propeller, and swung it toward the ground, as if he were rotating a car's engine by popping the clutch.

Chet climbed into the Cub's front seat and then taxied about thirty yards to the runway, using the rudder pedals to turn the airplane left and right, producing a snakelike path, so he could see where he was going. The windsock drooped straight down, indicating no wind—a perfect day for a first flight.

Arnold's chest swelled with excitement as Chet swung the Cub onto the runway and said, "Now, follow me on the controls while I do the takeoff."

Arnold put his right hand on the stick and his feet on the rudder pedals, and Chet grabbed the throttle, a circular knob on the left wall of the fuselage, and pushed it all the way forward. The engine roared, and they started moving along the grass.

Chet kept the nose of the Cub straight by using the rudder pedals, and then the tail lifted off the ground. Arnold could now see the grass in front of him as they raced over the field. At about fifty miles per hour, the airplane started to climb.

"We're flying!" Arnold thought, but he had to wait two more minutes while they climbed to five hundred feet before Chet finally took his hands off the controls and said, "Okay, you got it."

Arnold took the stick and, using all his concentration, managed to keep the wings level and kept the altitude at five hundred feet for about ten minutes. Then Chet upped the ante a bit. "Okay, now bank the wing about twenty degrees and hold it there."

Arnold pushed the stick and rudder pedal to the left, and the airplane began to turn. After he made a U-turn, Chet said, "Okay, level the wings again," and the airplane headed back to Portage.

Arnold practiced flying back to the airport, and then Chet took the airplane again for the landing, which involved all sorts of pushing and pulling of knobs, buttons, and controls, with Chet talking continuously about what he was doing.

"How does he do all that and talk at the same time?" Arnold thought, wondering if he would ever remember it all.

Chet recorded the flight in Arnold's just-purchased logbook and noted they had flown "straight-level." After watching airplanes from afar for a decade, Arnold was finally on his way.

Bertha drove him home, and he spent the rest of the evening regaling her and Emil again and again with every detail from the flight.

Over the next several months, Arnold translated his magazine and model lessons into real experiences in airplanes. For example, instead of using a paperclip to balance a model plane, Arnold and other people now moved around in the Cub to make it balance properly. If two people sat in the Cub, everything was fine; but if only one person flew the Cub, he had to sit in the backseat. If someone tried to fly alone while sitting up front, the nose would be too heavy and, just like the nose of one of Arnold's models with the paper clip too far forward, the Cub's nose wouldn't lift off the ground.

Most of Arnold's earliest flying lessons focused on takeoffs and landings, which involved maneuvering the Cub in the airport's traffic pattern, a predictable rectangular path about the runway. On takeoff, the pilot flies straight ahead until reaching a certain altitude, usually about five hundred to seven hundred feet above the ground. Then, still climbing, the pilot turns the plane ninety degrees, usually to the left, onto a *crosswind* leg, followed shortly afterward by another ninety-degree turn onto the *downwind* leg. The pilot, now parallel to, and about a half mile away from, the runway, stops climbing at the *pattern altitude*, usually about six hundred to one thousand feet above the ground, and continues to fly parallel to the runway. Abeam the end of the runway, the pilot slows down and descends and then, about a half mile farther, turns ninety degrees onto the *base* leg. Shortly thereafter, a last turn aligns the airplane with the runway for the *final approach*.

After dozens of trips around the traffic pattern, Arnold was ready for his first solo, or the first time he flew the airplane all by himself, with no onboard instructor. As I would discover four decades later after my own solo, every pilot's first solo is imprinted in his or her memory with indelible ink.

For solo flight, a pilot has to be sixteen and must complete a certain amount of instruction, which in the early 1940s was a minimum of eight hours. My father was ready the day after Christmas in 1943, but he was still only fifteen. The two-month wait to turn sixteen was pure torture, and further delays caused by a hitchhiking trip to Milwaukee for his permit, and then by weather, kept him from soloing until April 2.

The long-anticipated flight began with Chet in the Cub, watching as Arnold made three takeoffs and landings. After the third landing, as they taxied back to the ramp, Chet said the magic words every student pilot longs to hear: "Okay, take it around three times by yourself."

Arnold taxied back to the runway by himself, heart pounding as he pushed the throttle forward. Without Chet's weight in the plane, the Cub jumped off the runway and climbed much faster than it usually did; and every time Arnold moved his control stick, he was distracted by the simultaneous movement of the front stick, which was connected to his. He had never noticed the front stick before, since Chet had always blocked the view.

"Focus on flying," Arnold thought.

He circled the airport three times, making "touch-and-go" landings, touching down and then immediately adding full power to take off again for another circuit. After the last landing, he taxied to the ramp, shut down the engine, and strolled into the airport office with a telling "student solo" grin on his face. Chet congratulated him and signed his logbook so he could fly by himself and build the time he needed for his pilot's license.

That evening, Arnold's parents once again endured hearing every detail of his flight, again and again.

*   *   *

To earn more money for his lessons, Arnold at first toiled in a radio repair shop for twenty-five cents an hour; but, thanks to Chet, he soon found a goldmine in the poor-quality fabrics that still covered most small airplanes in the 1940s. Even covered with dope, cotton had to be replaced every five years or so, and Chet taught Arnold how to cover airplanes; trading labor for flying, he accelerated his lessons. In addition, he gained skills that would help him become an aircraft mechanic, his second aviation goal. Before long, he would surely be like Chet.

As the US Army stormed ashore in France in June 1944, Arnold began flying solo cross-country flights, where he navigated to an airport other than Portage and landed. He soon had the forty hours of flying time needed for his private pilot certificate, but he was too young to take the required flight test, called a check ride. Then in 1945, just as Arnold turned seventeen and was old enough for the license, Chet sold his Cubs and began a series of mercurial airplane swaps involving surplus military trainers and civilian airplanes. With every swap, Arnold had to relearn to fly the maneuvers for his check ride, since each model of airplane required different speeds and handled differently. He didn't mind the extra flying, but the summer of 1945 passed with no license.

In mid-November, Chet asked Arnold to ditch school for two days and fly to Missouri with him in a Taylorcraft, an airplane similar to the Cub, to pick up a damaged Cessna airplane. The Cessna had two engines and retractable landing gear—the epitome of technology in 1945—but it needed a new rudder. Chet planned to carry a replacement part in the Taylorcraft and then fix the Cessna and ferry it back to Portage; he needed Arnold to bring back the Taylorcraft.

When Arnold arrived at the airport for the trip, he wondered if playing hooky was such a wise choice. The rudder was too bulky to fit in the Taylorcraft's briefcase-size baggage compartment, and Chet had lashed it to one of the wing struts, the equivalent of tying a surfboard to the wing of a Boeing 737.

Staring in dismay at the awkward "baling wire and bubblegum" solution, Arnold asked, "Are you sure that thing is safe to fly?"

"Well, let me take it around once by myself, just to be sure."

Chet flew the airplane around the traffic pattern without crashing, so Arnold jumped in and they took off for Missouri.

Shortly after the Cessna rescue trip, Chet inexplicably sold the Taylorcraft, once again dashing Arnold's hopes for finishing his license requirements. Chet had the only flying game in Portage; and with no car to drive to another town, Arnold stuck it out, although he demoted Chet from god to mere knight in shining armor.

The end of the war was forcing Arnold to reconsider his future in aviation, anyway. By 1945, the military had trained more than three hundred thousand pilots, and for every pilot, ten more crewmembers existed, such as navigators and tail gunners. Many of these men, too, might be interested in postwar civilian flying. Aviation futurists projected a plethora of jobs: the airlines, flight instruction, crop dusting, pipeline patrols, and aerial advertising, to name just a few, and nonpilots would be needed for support jobs such as airline maintenance and scheduling. Although no one renewed the 1930s fantasy of a United States stocked with millions of aircraft, five hundred thousand seemed within reach. The tens of thousands of military surplus aircraft expected to flow to the market after the war would hardly put a dent in demand, and lightplane manufacturers began to salivate.

With ex-military pilots now saturating the labor market, Arnold realized that being an airline pilot was probably unachievable, at least in the near-term. He reset his sights on becoming an instructor pilot like Chet; that way, he could build his flight time, just in case an airline job came calling.

Technological advances from the war had also made newer airplanes faster, safer, and easier to fly, and manufacturers were starting to apply those improvements to civilian designs. Fuel-injection systems replaced icing-prone carburetors to make flight in clouds safer; retractable landing gear streamlined fuselages and led to higher cruising speeds; and tricycle gear replaced the old tail draggers, which improved stability during take-off and landing, allowing airplanes to operate off concrete runways in stronger crosswinds. With the addition of navigation aids that guided an airplane through the air via invisible radio beams, a truly all-weather airplane could be flown by an ordinary, albeit well-trained, pilot.

Arnold realized that all those manufacturers advertising new civilian airplanes would need engineers to come up with even more new designs, and that cemented his idea to get an aeronautical engineering degree. With the degree, he hoped, he could work for a company that designed and built small airplanes, like the Piper Cub he had first learned to fly. He thought this was actually better than his original plan to work for an airline: with an engineering degree, he could design airplanes; with a mechanic's license, he could build the airplanes he designed; and with a pilot's license, he could fly the airplanes he had designed and built. What could be better? He applied to Rensselaer Polytechnic Institute, a private engineering and architecture school in Troy, New York, and they accepted him for the winter semester of 1947.

The spring of Arnold's senior year, Chet forgot to put the gear down during a landing in the twin-engine Cessna he and Arnold had rescued from Missouri. The accident heavily damaged the airplane and further tarnished Chet's image in Arnold's mind.

Unsure whether to keep flying with Chet, Arnold focused his attention on high school and pole vaulting for the Portage track team, which he had joined as the only boy who could manage the planting and twisting maneuvers required by the vault. Even more surprising, especially to himself, he won ribbons at many local and regional meets. Off the track, however, Arnold knew that his five-foot, ten-inch, 138-pound frame, while perfect for cramped cockpits, didn't lend itself to prowess as a jock. Although a member of the Latin, German, and science clubs, Arnold found that his interests didn't include members of the opposite sex, since he could never think of anything to talk about besides airplanes. The quote next to his senior yearbook picture says, "Girls can all stay on the ground. In my plane I'll fly around—alone."

With the end of the war, Arnold's chances of being drafted by the army plummeted, and he made plans to attend Rensselaer after graduating in 1946. However, he first needed to finish earning that elusive private pilot's license, and he decided it wouldn't be with Chet.

His aviation salvation came in the unexpected form of two former Army Air Corps pilots, Forrest Sommers and Joe Theena, who had pieced together a flight school in nearby Poynette using war-surplus PT-23 training aircraft and funding from Paul Gerstenkorn, the local beer distributor. Desperately needing another mechanic, the aspiring aviation entrepreneurs wooed Arnold away from Portage and Chet. Each day that summer, Arnold rode to Poynette with Forrest in his dilapidated Model A pickup truck. Before departing Portage, they filled the radiator with water, which lasted just long enough to make the twelve-mile drive to Poynette.

Arnold quickly mastered Forrest's PT-23, and within a month of pledging his allegiance to the Poynette crowd, he passed his private-pilot check ride on July 24, 1946. However, that long-awaited piece of paper allowed him only to fly his friends and family as nonpaying passengers. To earn money as a pilot, he needed his commercial license and then a flight instructor certificate; but with visions of airplane designs dancing in his head, he put those plans on hold in order to work on his engineering degree.

* * *

By the late 1930s, private aviation in the United States had slipped nearly into oblivion. The military, however, went on a shopping spree, adding thousands of sophisticated warbirds, such as Boeing B-17 bombers and Bell P-39 pursuit planes to their fleets. Young men who might have built airplanes instead joined the army or navy as the military geared up to train thousands of new pilots. Others entered college and learned to fly in university programs designed to train twenty thousand pilots each year as a pipeline for the military.

By mid-1941, the number of unlicensed aircraft in the United States had dwindled to fewer than five hundred, from about twenty-five hundred in 1931. The final death knell for the homebuilt movement occurred on December 8, 1941, when the Civil Aeronautics Board, a safety board created in 1940 along with a reorganized Civil Aeronautics Authority (and renamed the Civil Aeronautics Administration), adopted an amendment requiring all aircraft to be certified, with no exceptions, all but guaranteeing that no amateur-built aircraft would fly for at least the duration of the war. In addition, the board grounded all private pilots, requiring them to renew their licenses to establish their citizenship and loyalty before they could fly again.

Les Long had given up even before Pearl Harbor, penning an article, "The Home Builder Bows Out," for the June 1941 *Flying and Popular Aviation* magazine, in which he conceded his fifteen-year battle to state and federal authorities. He hung up his rib jigs and stored his beloved aircraft. But within two years he entered the fight again, writing letters to congressmen on the future of amateur-built aircraft and publishing a newsletter, the *Three-A-Flyer*, for a revived version of the Amateur Aircraft League that he called the Amateur Aircraft Association, or "Three-A" for short.

After sending out the April and May 1944 issues of the newsletter, Long fell ill and was bedridden by the end of July. Trying to keep the Three-A going, he asked for help from George Bogardus, a twenty-nine-year-old printer who was also a pilot. Bogardus's response was to publish a separate newsletter, the *Triple-A Flyer*, the title of which was just different enough to confuse the Three-A membership. Long never understood what Bogardus was trying to do, and the two stopped talking. Long didn't recover from his illness or clear up Three-A matters, and he died in January 1945, not knowing that one of his designs and his nemesis would play a central role in reinvigorating the homebuilt movement.

*   *   *

With the war over, George Bogardus embarked on a crusade with the federal government to ensure that a postwar homebuilding renaissance wouldn't drown in the aviation tsunami coming ashore. In October 1945, the Civil Aeronautics Administration had put out Safety Regulation Release No. 194, which made special-purpose aircraft used for air racing and exhibition eligible for experimental-aircraft certificates. Although pilots who wanted to fly homebuilts for pleasure were still out of luck, those interested in racing or air shows began dragging their unlicensed craft out of storage.

By then, Bogardus's takeover of Long's Three-A was complete, with a new name: the American Airmen's Association, or AAA. Bogardus also acquired an airplane built before the war by Oregon amateur Tom Story; named *Wimpy*, the airplane was a close relative of Long's low-wing, thirty-horsepower Longster. Bogardus rebuilt *Wimpy* for five hundred dollars, replacing the small engine with a sixty-five-horsepower Continental and rechristening it *Little Gee Bee*.

As AAA president, Bogardus continued in Long's tradition, sending a continuous stream of letters to state and federal officials regarding the amateur-builder limbo that still existed with the current rules. In the spring of 1946, John Geisse, the assistant to the administrator for personal flying development at the Civil Aeronautics Administration (CAA), invited Bogardus to come to Washington for a chat, and the AAA membership voted to use the organization's meager resources to fund his trip. Not yet having a legal airplane, Bogardus drove his 1937 Chevy across the country and met with Geisse and other CAA officials, who told him to refine his amateur-building ideas and return the next summer for further talks.

In March 1947, the CAA, at least partly in response to Bogardus's visit, published Safety Regulation Release No. 236, which allowed local CAA aviation safety agents to issue airworthiness certificates to homebuilt aircraft. The release wasn't perfect—it gave CAA agents no guidelines for deciding whether to grant a certificate; and the Civil Aeronautics Board, which held rulemaking power, still had to make the regulation permanent—but after two decades of federal inaction, it was a monumental step in the right direction. In May 1947, Bogardus received his coveted experimental-aircraft certificate and NX number, the only restriction being that he fly *Little Gee Bee* for fifty hours before taking it on a cross-country flight. On August 11, with the required hours in his logbook, he took off from Portland's Swan Island Municipal Airport and headed for Washington, DC, his NX number and the word "EXPERIMENTAL" splashed on the side of *Little Gee Bee*. After following a meandering route that included stops to promote the AAA and collect additional supporters in Long Island, New York, he arrived in Washington in late August for negotiations that resulted in rules that surely made Ed Heath, Les Long, and other late amateur builders dance a heavenly jig.

The good news was somewhat tempered by the slow pace of government: although the CAA allowed field inspectors to issue experimental-aircraft certificates to amateur builders beginning in 1947, the final Civil Aeronautics Board–approved rules on homebuilding weren't in place until

September 19, 1952, with publication of *Civil Aeronautics Manual 1*. The manual outlined the CAA's expectations for how homebuilt aircraft should be constructed, and it defined an amateur-built aircraft as an "individual or group . . . project having been undertaken for educational or recreation purposes."

However, with the Depression finally over and so many inexpensive military surplus and factory-built planes entering the market, it wasn't clear if anyone was even still interested in building his own aircraft.

5

Foundations

In a practical sense there is no justification for the expense, work
and risk involved [in building an airplane]. It would be like a man
explaining to his wife that by buying a boat and fishing tackle, he
can save on the family food bill with the resulting (?) catch of fish.
But, certainly, the satisfaction derived from designing, building and
flying your own aircraft cannot be obtained on lesser terms.

Neal Loving, *Experimenter*, June 1954

PILOTS WHO WANTED TO RACE THEIR HOMEBUILT AIRCRAFT DIDN'T
have to wait long for their reward: in early 1947, officials of the National
Air Races, held in Cleveland over Labor Day weekend, announced a
renewed category for lightplanes, with a twenty-five-thousand-dollar
purse. Now taking classes at Rensselaer Polytechnic Institute, my father
thought an air race prize might help him and his parents keep pace with
his living expenses and the recent increases in the private school's already
steep tuition. His job setting pins in a bowling alley didn't leave much for
extras, such as flying, after room and board, and he wasn't sure how much
longer his working-class parents could afford the tuition.

After a few months of classes, Arnold had only a vague idea of how to
design an airplane, so he headed to the university bookstore, where he
spotted a maroon textbook, *Analysis and Design of Aircraft Structures*, by
E. F. Bruhn, a famous professor at Purdue University. Arnold had seen the
book standing authoritatively on the shelves in his professors' offices, and
he had often thought, "This looks like a book an engineer should have."

Ignoring the impact on his dwindling cash reserves, he bought the
book and fantasized about his racer as he walked back to his room, where,

with the new book perched on his desk as inspiration, he sketched his proposed winner, *The Dreamer*. Perhaps showing off a bit, he mailed the drawing to his parents. But ambition outstripped ability, and the dream and any extra cash that might have come with it soon died, although it would reignite in another form a decade later.

Given the burden of Rensselaer's cost, and the fact that the only planes were an eight-mile bus ride away, in Albany, Arnold transferred to the University of Minnesota in the spring of 1948. In Minneapolis, he found a job as a waiter and dishwasher in a sorority house, but instead of using his earnings to finish his commercial and flight instructor licenses, he bought a car. A few months later, he pleaded with his parents for one hundred dollars, and they agreed to give it to him, but only if he handed the money over to a flight school so he couldn't spend it on other distractions.

Cash in hand, he drove straight to Hinck Flying Service at Wold-Chamberlain Airport, now the Minneapolis–Saint Paul International Airport, and in February 1949 he finished his commercial pilot certificate and then added the flight instructor certificate a few weeks later. At twenty-one, two years behind his original schedule, he had finally entered the aviation minor leagues.

*   *   *

My father found his first paid piloting job in the university's new flight program, run by Jim Magnus, the school's assistant hockey coach, who had flown C-46 cargo planes as a marine during World War II. Still a reservist, Magnus used his military connections to find five surplus army J-3 Cubs in San Marcos, Texas, and he dispatched Arnold and several other pilots to retrieve them. Arriving in San Marcos, the pilots discovered five dejected Cubs covered in ancient fabric topped with faded burnt-orange paint as cracked as a parched desert riverbed, but Arnold decided the airplanes could fly as far as Minneapolis. Once there, he helped rebuild the Cubs, and based on the new experience and his previous work with Chet and Forrest, he received his "airframe" mechanic's license. With a little more work, he expected to get his "engine" license, now called a "powerplant" license, to fulfill the "mechanic" part of his career wish list. Soon the only thing left would be the engineering degree.

While working on the Cubs, Arnold met Charlie Moore, a young meteorologist and part-time balloon pilot who worked for General Mills, which had diversified its products beyond cereal during the war. After the war, General Mills created the Aeronautical Research Laboratory, and Moore headed up the lab's US Navy program involving unmanned helium balloons that carried secret instruments to high altitudes.

Charlie recruited Arnold to chase the research balloons launched from University of Minnesota Airport. For each flight, Arnold loaded a small airplane with an observer and photographer and then followed a balloon as it drifted with the wind. Fully inflated, the balloons resembled cigars as tall as telephone poles, each with ropes, plus two instruments contained in a box the size of a milk crate dangling below. Arnold flew in circles to keep pace with his quarry, and it seemed his main job was to be sure no one in his airplane got airsick, especially in bumpy air. When a timer on board the balloon expired, a trigger cut the boxed instrument free, and the package, which was fitted with a parachute, dropped to the ground. The balloon was disposable, and it simply flew away. Arnold then radioed the location of the package to a crew in a truck so they could retrieve it.

By mid-1950, Arnold felt his life was finally in order, but all the flying and restoring of airplanes had come at a cost to his schoolwork—he was no longer making the As and Bs he had at Rensselaer. However, by the summer of 1950 his grades were the least of his worries, because the ambition of a Cold War bit-player halfway around the world was about to transform his life forever.

*   *   *

On June 25, 1950, the North Korean People's Army rolled across the thirty-eighth parallel into South Korea. The US military mobilized and, a few weeks later, Jim Magnus headed to active duty at El Toro Marine Corps Air Station in Southern California. Not long afterward, Arnold's cousin Carl, by then an air force F-80 pilot, was in Korea chasing MiG fighters.

Arnold weighed his options. He had joined the Minnesota National Guard a year earlier to keep the peacetime draft at bay, and he would have to drop out of school if his unit were activated. The draft board in his native Wisconsin might also call him. Either way, he would wind up in Korea with his aviation future on hold. Between the dual threats posed by the Guard and the draft, not to mention his declining grades and a clash with Magnus's replacement, Arnold thought it might not be worth signing up for fall classes.

Arnold realized his engineering degree and airplane designs would have to wait. He didn't mind serving his country, but he wanted to do it on his own terms.

He decided to join the air force.

In September, he rode a train to Omaha and, after passing the air force tests, waited for a pilot-training slot to open up. Even if he went to Korea, flying an airplane sounded a lot safer than dodging bullets on the ground.

As Arnold sorted out his military predicament, he added yet another element to his increasingly complicated life: a petite, brunette freshman from Saint Paul named Colleen Kroona. As a six-year-old, she had made a miraculous recovery after brain surgery to remove a blood clot in her skull; and I often wondered, facetiously, if perhaps the surgery had had the side effect of making her crazy about airplanes.

Not long before her seventeenth birthday, Colleen took her first flight in a J-3 Cub, on an April Sunday with Paul Moore, treasurer of the Minnesota Flying Farmers. She carefully recorded the details of her half-hour flight in a scrapbook to earn a Camp Fire Girls aviation merit badge, deeming the flight "thrilling" and noting that the "houses and cars looked like they belonged to a Monopoly set." Moore allowed her to take the controls for a bit, and she "managed to go up and down, turned it right and left, and also flew straight," but admitted to becoming "thoroughly lost."

Like Arnold, Colleen became addicted to flying from the first flight, and she began imagining her future aviation life, albeit one tempered by mid-twentieth-century social standards. Her idea of the perfect family was a pilot husband and an airplane that would carry her as copilot, along with their four boys.

To meet a pilot and learn to fly, she joined the University Flying Club in the fall of 1950. The club went on periodic breakfast flights; and on Columbus Day, Arnold agreed to pilot a four-seat Stinson airplane. Colleen, along with two other women, signed up to fly with him.

At nine in the morning, twenty airplanes, carrying twenty-seven passengers, flew sixty miles southwest of Minneapolis and landed at New Ulm's grass airfield in a mini-invasion that made headlines in the small town's evening paper. After arriving about ten, the group found some scrap wood and built a fire at the end of one runway to roast the hot dogs they brought. While they ate, a six-piece band from New Ulm High School descended on the field and serenaded them with German tunes, after which a city council member arrived to bring them water and more wood for the fire.

After enjoying the New Ulm hospitality for about two hours, the pilots and would-be aviators returned home. Although Colleen had sat in the backseat of Arnold's airplane on the trip out, she maneuvered into the front for the return flight. Arnold even let her fly the airplane for a bit, and she was smitten. He thought she was cute as a bug, and they began dating.

That same fall, Arnold started working full-time for Charlie Moore. Charlie had a new contract with the navy—another secret program, this one to develop manned balloons that could stay aloft for twelve hours. He needed a pilot, a mechanic, and an engineer, and he hired Arnold to be all three, despite his lack of a degree. In addition to saving money that way, Charlie found that Arnold's reticent demeanor and methodical problem-solving approach counterbalanced his own outspokenness and propensity for cobbling together scraps of materials to make balloon parts—by, for example, turning a coffee can and piece of an old tire into a valve for filling the balloons. Arnold admired Charlie's resourcefulness in manufacturing the valve, but it was an all-or-nothing affair: if it failed in flight, the helium would escape too fast for the pilot to make a safe landing. Arnold designed a real valve that released the helium more slowly during a failure, so that the pilot could land. And, at the navy's request, he converted a metal ring on the balloon to plastic to make the balloon harder to detect and track with radar. He received two patents for his efforts, and the designs would be his only engineering projects for another ten years.

Colleen landed a job at General Mills as one of several "balloon girls" who assembled the balloons used in Arnold's program. The balloon girls laid out fabric on a long table and then used a machine that simultaneously cut the fabric and applied tape to the seams. To test the completed balloons for leaks, the balloon girls injected a bubble of ammonia inside each seam and then moved the bubble along the seam using a rag soaked in a chemical solution. If the seam leaked, the escaping ammonia mushroomed into a red blotch on the white fabric and the balloon was discarded.

Despite the leak tests, photos of Colleen's handcrafted balloons do not inspire confidence that they could safely carry someone even five feet off

Fig. 5.1. Arnold Ebneter flies a balloon in New Mexico, 1951.

the ground, let alone the five thousand feet the navy wanted. Except for the use of a large single balloon, the setup resembled the "lawn chair balloon" that Californian Larry Walters infamously used in 1982 to ascend to more than fifteen thousand feet, astonishing nearby airline pilots.

The navy balloons were legal, but the US government took great pains to hide the real reason for their existence, which was never entirely clear to Arnold. Attached only by a parachute harness, the pilot dangled precariously below the balloon, which was constructed from polyethylene plastic thinner than a sandwich bag and inflated with helium. The entire rig resembled a skydiver below a parachute, except the parachute was replaced by a balloon twenty-five feet in diameter. Arnold added a plywood seat, but the unwieldy get-up still allowed for no passengers, had any been interested in a ride.

Three months after meeting Colleen, Arnold drove with the rest of the balloon team to the US Army's White Sands Proving Ground (now called White Sands Missile Range) to test their new creations. New Mexico's near perfect year-round weather allows flying almost every day, and the remote location about fifty miles northwest of El Paso, along with a restricted area almost three times the size of Rhode Island, keeps projects free of prying eyes.

Arnold took his first balloon flight a few days after arriving in New Mexico, and he subsequently flew several test flights, one of which landed early because of a leaky balloon, forcing him to hike four hours across a moonlit desert outside Roswell. On the next twelve-hour flight attempt, he took off about six in the evening; and after drifting east for about twenty-five miles, he knew the balloon would likely last through the night. In the four days since his previous flight, the moon had disappeared from the night sky. He heard a DC-3 flying into El Paso, but a few minutes later he encountered an empty and silent darkness.

With no moon, he saw nothing on the ground, and not even a howling coyote interrupted the desolate night. He had entered what Antoine de Saint-Exupéry called "another of those hours in which a pilot finds suddenly that he has slipped beyond the confines of this world." Arnold had no way of knowing if the earth was even below him anymore. In the darkness, it was possible to believe he was the only person left in the world, or that the world no longer existed, that he could float forever into space, crossing though the solar system and into the beckoning galaxies of the Milky Way above.

Arnold pressed on, trusting the wind to carry him over an earth he believed was still there, and after several hours he spotted small fires from oil operations below. Even though he hadn't minded the solitude, he still welcomed the connection to the ground. The next morning, after twelve hours and four hundred miles, he landed just before sunrise in a field about ten miles southwest of Aspermont, Texas.

Back in Minneapolis, Charlie and his navy sponsors schemed to keep Arnold in the balloon program. Together, they convinced him to resign from his now-activating Guard unit; the navy then asked the air force to remove him from the pilot training list and obtained a one-year draft deferment from Wisconsin.

With his deferment and a full-time job, Arnold thought his life was back to normal for at least another year. He moved on to the next navy project, a two-man balloon, and began teaching Colleen to fly. Within a few months, she had soloed in a Cub and started flying solo cross-country flights around Minnesota to build the time she needed for her license. For each flight, she drew a line on her aeronautical chart between University Airport and one of the dozens of small airports in the state, such as Saint Cloud, Owatonna, or Mankato. Using a protractor, she next measured the course, or the direction of the line relative to the North Pole—for example, "225" would be southwest. The last step was to adjust the measured course for instrument errors in the Cub's magnetic compass, naturally occurring magnetic variations, and the effects of crosswinds to determine what number, called the heading, she needed to maintain on the Cub's magnetic compass. Barring any major changes in the forecast winds, flying this heading would keep the airplane above the line on her map, which represented an imaginary line on the ground leading to her destination.

Three decades later, while watching as I planned one of my own cross-country flights, my mother said, "I was always amazed that I got where I was going. I'd compute the heading and how long I was supposed to fly, and then I'd fly the heading; and when it was time for the airport to appear, it was always there!"

In December 1951, Arnold and Colleen became engaged and set their wedding date for the next June, and my father became a CAA-certified balloon pilot. He hadn't needed a license while flying out of White Sands under contract for the navy, but would need a certificate to continue flying on the civilian projects in Minnesota. The CAA issued registration number N7927A to the navy's new two-seat balloon, and Arnold met the CAA examiner at University Airport on December 17, 1951. The temperature was five below zero.

Arnold showed the examiner the balloon and asked him how much he weighed. After seeing Arnold's plywood-seat contraption, the examiner had other ideas. "It doesn't matter how much I weigh," he said, "because

I'm not going up in that thing! I'm going to stand on the ground and watch you fly it. Understand?"

That was fine with Arnold. He set the balloon up and asked what to do next.

"Go up one hundred feet and come back down."

"That's all?" Arnold could hardly believe what he heard.

"Yup."

He took off, climbed to one hundred feet and stopped. Then a light breeze carried him slowly across a road and he touched down in a field next to the airport, for a total flight time of nineteen minutes. He had traveled only two hundred yards, but he was now officially a balloon pilot.

A half century later, he would use the registration number N7927A again.

*   *   *

A few months after Arnold received his balloon license, the navy decided to lie low for a while. Another contractor had crashed a balloon into some telephone wires on a Wisconsin farm, and the ensuing media hullaballoo threatened to derail the program. Arnold suddenly had nothing to do just as his draft deferment was about to expire, and despite the navy's pleas it appeared as if the Wisconsin draft board was unwilling to entertain any further deferments. Arnold decided his best bet was to go back to the air force, but if he were to enter Aviation Cadet Training, he couldn't be married. After talking things over with Colleen, they postponed their wedding, even though invitations had already been printed and mailed.

In June, while he waited to hear the final decision on his deferment, he flew balloons in Tillamook, on the Oregon coast, a trip that allowed him to avoid the moping in Minnesota over the wedding that was not to be. Colleen's father was particularly upset.

At the end of the summer, the draft board handed down its verdict: no additional deferment. Fortunately, the air force still needed pilots, and they again accepted him for pilot training, with a class date in January 1953.

As much as he had enjoyed the balloon flying and the freedom that came with it, he put his goals for finishing his engineering degree and designing airplanes on indefinite hold and, on December 28, 1952, left Minneapolis for San Antonio, Texas.

*   *   *

As Arnold drove to his air force pilot training, about three dozen home-built aircraft enthusiasts in the Milwaukee area and northern Illinois found postcards mailed from Hales Corner, Wisconsin, mixed in with their Christmas mail. Prepared by Air National Guard pilot and amateur builder Paul Poberezny and his wife, Audrey, at their kitchen table, the hand-typed cards announced a January meeting for a local homebuilders club, tentatively named the Experimental Aircraft Owners and Pilots Association.

As a boy in Milwaukee, one hundred miles east of the Ebneter farm in Mount Horeb, the young Paul Poberezny had, like the young Arnold, looked to the skies whenever airplanes flew over, courtesy of an airmail route between Minneapolis and several Wisconsin cities. On May 21, 1927, the mother of five-year-old Paul dashed from a neighbor's house into the Poberezny kitchen and shouted, "Lucky Lindy made it! He landed in Paris! What a thrill!"

At age fourteen, Paul began making daily treks to nearby Milwaukee County Airport to watch the aviation action as Midwest Airways and Westphal Airways airliners took off and landed. During one of these visits, he found a prize behind the Midwest maintenance hangar—a discarded piece of airplane fabric. He had no idea what sort of fabric it was or if it might be useful for building an airplane, but it became the first piece of what turned into a lifelong collection of airplane parts and airplanes in various stages of repair and disrepair.

When Poberezny wasn't collecting castoff parts of questionable parentage, he attended high school as a less-than-stellar student who skipped class every Monday and required an extra year to graduate. However, he found an outlet for his aviation aspirations in the high school model airplane club. The teacher who ran the club convinced the industrial arts teacher to build a real glider as part of his class; Poberezny took the class and found he enjoyed school for the first time.

The model-club instructor must have seen something in Poberezny beyond his academic shortcomings, because one day he approached the now fifteen-year-old boy and asked if he would be interested in restoring a glider damaged in a landing accident.

Although Poberezny was thrilled and flattered, his first thought was a problem common for a Depression-era youth: "But I don't have any money."

"I'll give you the glider."

"But I don't have money for parts either." Even at fifteen, Poberezny knew his menagerie of castoffs wasn't likely to return the hapless glider to flying status.

"I'll pay for everything—glue, dope, fabric, whatever you need," the teacher assured him.

For the next six months, Poberezny spent most of his spare time on the glider, consulting his 1931 *Flying and Glider Manual* whenever he couldn't figure out how to fix something on his own. Published annually for five years beginning in 1929 by the magazine *Modern Mechanics and Inventions*, the manuals included dozens of articles on flight lessons as well as on how to design and build airplanes, gliders, engines, and their associated parts.

In addition to making his wrecked glider flyable, Poberezny improved on the original design by replacing a pair of rudimentary landing skids with real landing gear he designed himself and had welded up by a local shop. In the spring of 1937, the glider was ready to fly, but Poberezny hadn't had any flying lessons; in fact, he had yet to fly in any aircraft. Like many of his predecessors, he read the directions in some books and his *Flying and Glider Manual* and gave it a try. Most modern gliders are towed into the air by a rope attached to a powered airplane, but he had no such luxury. Instead, a car with a four-hundred-foot rope tugged him along a bumpy field until he had enough speed to get airborne. After climbing about twenty feet above the ground, he released the rope and the nose of the glider pitched up violently, nearly ending his first flight in disaster. Somehow, he instinctively pushed the nose forward, and the glider settled back onto the grass field.

Over the next several months, Poberezny learned to fly the glider through trial and error and then joined the Milwaukee Flight Club with money earned from working in a gas station. He soon began taking flying lessons in the club's Porterfield, a small airplane similar to the J-3 Cub, and soloed in May 1939.

By then, Wisconsin authorities had driven the Milwaukee area's bright and creative homebuilding community underground. The county airport in Waukesha, located just outside Milwaukee, had been a homebuilders' paradise where amateurs glued together wooden ribs, welded steel-tube fuselages, and tinkered with converted motorcycle engines. In fact, the airport wouldn't have existed had not the Waukesha Aviation Club, which formed in 1931 and counted many homebuilders among its members, convinced the county in 1933 to apply for federal funds to build the airport and, at least temporarily, provide some local employment. Club volunteers oversaw much of the construction and ran the airport until the county took over for good in 1938.

On October 20, 1936, a pilot died when he crashed the homebuilt monoplane he was flying into the woods just east of the airport. Within three days, the accident had faded from the front pages of Waukesha's *Daily Freeman,* but the *Milwaukee Journal* ran a headline story on Sunday that shouted, "Airplane Crashes Follow Lax Air Rules in State." The story railed against the five unlicensed planes out of nine at Waukesha and implied that the local sheriff, who was a pilot and Waukesha Aviation Club member, wasn't enforcing Wisconsin laws that banned homebuilt aircraft.

Waukesha County Board officials must have been torn. The home-builders provided most of the activity at the airport, and the county wasn't ready yet to take over operations. Nevertheless, the county decided to appoint a temporary airport manager, and the sheriff agreed to station a deputy at the airport whenever there was flying to ensure that only licensed planes were in the air.

The lawbreaking homebuilders took their airplanes five miles north to a little grass field with rotting, tin-roofed hangars. Their flying activities partly obscured by a hilly wooded area, the pilots named their new home "Outlaw Field." Once he had soloed, Poberezny became a frequent visitor. Then, when he bought a biplane, he became an Outlaw Field occupant, not because the biplane was unlicensed—it was a licensed factory-built aircraft—but because he wanted to fly passengers and teach others to fly, illegal activities since he had yet to earn his private pilot license.

Not long before Poberezny graduated from high school, his aviation career suffered a minor setback when he flew a friend's homebuilt air-craft, the *Munson Special.* After realizing the field he had taken off from was too short for a safe landing, he instead landed at the West Bend airport. He moved the *Munson* to Waukesha a week later, where he removed the propeller in an attempt to make it look like no one was flying the banned homebuilt. After a few days, he sneaked to the airport at dawn, reattached the propeller, flew the plane to an open field near his house, and then taxied the plane through the streets to a vacant lot across from his parents' home. A few days later, a CAA inspector spotted the strange sight in the vacant lot and grounded the *Munson* by hanging a red tag on the ignition switch. Several months passed before Poberezny received a letter from the CAA saying they wanted to talk to him. The CAA inspector wanted to check on a report that Poberezny had been flying passengers in his biplane; but thinking the CAA was wise to the homebuilt, Paul confessed to the illegal flights in the *Munson* before the inspector could even ask about illegal passengers. On December 5, 1941, the Civil Aeronautics Board revoked Paul's student license; it would be a year before he could apply for reinstatement.

Three days later, the loss of a license meant little after authorities grounded all unlicensed airplanes and required pilots to renew their certificates. Like many other young pilots, Poberezny turned to the military; but the army rejected him for pilot training because of his lack of college. Instead, he entered a program in which he learned to be a glider pilot and worked his way up to powered-aircraft instruction; then he ended the war with the Air Transport Command, ferrying cargo and fighter aircraft around the United States.

After the war, Poberezny returned to Wisconsin, where he bounced around, taking various jobs as a flight instructor, welder, and mechanic. Later, during a short-lived attempt at operating his own aviation business, he learned that few people paid their hangar rent and aviation bills on time, since other household expenses took priority. By 1948, now married to Audrey and with a young son, Tommy, Poberezny accepted a full-time job with the Wisconsin Air National Guard.

His finances finally secure, he turned his attention back to homebuilding, courtesy of the relaxed CAA rules made possible by George Bogardus. Although the CAA had yet to codify those rules into regulations and manuals, local inspectors were at least once again issuing airworthiness certificates for experimental craft to amateur builders. In the spring of 1948, Poberezny hauled the remnants of a Taylorcraft into his Hales Corner garage to resurrect it as a "clip-wing," which was just what it sounds like—the new wing was shorter than the original. With a clipped wing, an airplane can roll faster and handle the higher loads required by aerobatic maneuvers such as loops and rolls; many air show pilots also add larger engines to create higher climb rates and crowd-pleasing noise.

Clipping a wing requires a lot more than just sawing a few feet off each end. For one thing, the ailerons that roll the airplane from side to side usually run from about midwing to nearly the wingtip on most airplanes, and you can't just lop off part of an aileron and still fly safely. Shortening the wing also changes the overall aircraft structure, so the wing and its supporting members are usually almost entirely rebuilt.

With a cigar often clamped in his mouth as he turned wrenches, Poberezny worked for three years to rebuild the Taylorcraft, dubbing it *Little Poop Deck*, after the "Poop Deck" nickname he had gained in high school and used during his military career. When he tried to certify the airplane, he ran afoul of the new rules published by the CAA, which took a dim view of amateur builders who modified standard factory-built aircraft instead of constructing airplanes from scratch, even though his project was for "recreational purposes." The CAA would certify *Little Poop Deck* only in the "experimental exhibition" category—he would only be able to race the airplane, fly it in air shows, or use it to practice for those activities. The restriction annoyed Paul at the time, but years later he would change his mind after the distinction between modified standard and scratch-built airplanes caused much controversy in the homebuilding community.

As *Little Poop Deck* grew in Poberezny's garage-turned-airplane-factory, he organized a small but highly successful air show for the 1950 Labor Day weekend at the Hales Corner Airport, a two-thousand-foot-long grass strip at the small town's southeast edge. His ease in recruiting everyone from aircraft mechanics to the owner of the Miller Brewing Company as air show volunteers, and the many local builders who visited his garage to see *Little Poop Deck*, convinced Poberezny he should start a club dedicated to homebuilding and flying for fun.

Before he could hold more than a handful of meetings of his as-yet unnamed eight-person club, Poberezny's Air National Guard unit sent him to Korea to fly C-47 cargo airplanes. Returning from Korea in late 1952, he found his ragtag homebuilder band in disarray—the person left in charge apparently lacked Poberezny's vision and organizational skills.

Undaunted, Poberezny knew there was a pent-up need for some sort of club to help homebuilders and sport aviation enthusiasts. After all, the decade had started with a homebuilding bang when the August 1950 *Air Trails Pictorial* magazine had printed an article titled "The Home-Bilts [sic] Are Back." The old *Popular Aviation* magazine, now renamed *Flying*, followed up two years later with an article advocating kit-built aircraft as a way to get more youth involved in aviation, which prompted a flood of letters from readers who wanted to buy kits or otherwise build their own airplanes. Poberezny was one of the letter writers, telling the *Flying* editor that he was "reorganizing" a group he now called the "Experimental Aircraft Owners and Pilots Association" and asking that anyone interested in joining contact him at his home address. He claimed that thirteen homebuilt aircraft existed in the Milwaukee area, and he boasted, "From some of the performance we get in home-built aircraft, manufacturers could take note." The term *experimental* in his fledgling group's title derived both from the CAA airworthiness category for homebuilt aircraft and the word "EXPERIMENTAL" that had to be printed in capital letters at least two inches high (but no more than six inches high) next to the cockpit or cabin entrance of amateur-built aircraft.

The letter wouldn't be printed until April 1953, so in the meantime he and Audrey sent invitations for the January meeting, to be held at Curtiss-Wright Airport, located in the northwest part of Milwaukee. Bill Lotzer, owner of Gran-Aire, the airport's fixed-base operator that provided tie downs, hangars, fuel, and flight training, offered a free classroom for the meeting.

On January 26, 1953, thirty-six people arrived at Gran-Aire; several, including Duane Cole, a pilot who flew his clipped-wing Cub in air shows, braved two hundred miles of wintry roads from Illinois to attend. Poberezny had also invited Tony Maugeri, a maintenance inspector for the CAA. After Maugeri's short talk on CAA certification procedures for amateur-built aircraft, the group elected officers: Poberezny as president, Carl Schultz as vice president, and Bob Nolinske as secretary and treasurer. The meeting adjourned at 10 P.M., but many people stayed around to talk until midnight.

Audrey typed up her husband's scribbled notes from the meeting, and Paul added a few short descriptions on current member projects for the first edition of the organization's newsletter, two legal-size pages with "THE EXPERIMENTER" hand-printed in one-inch block letters at the top of the first page and "BUILD AND FLY SAFELY" embedded in a cartoon cloud at the bottom of the second page.

In February, at the second meeting, the membership voted to shorten the organization's name to the "Experimental Aircraft Association." Their attention then turned to additional people they might encourage to become members. Duane Cole advocated contacting Neal Loving, a racing pilot and homebuilder who ran a flight school in Detroit, despite losing both legs below the knees in a glider accident years earlier.

"I heard that Loving is black," someone said. "Is that true?"

"Yes," Cole confirmed, his temper rising at the thought that Loving's race might be an issue.

Before he exploded, Cole realized the questioner's tone was curious, not negative. The short discussion that followed led to an egalitarian membership policy for the 1950s: anyone could join the EAA, regardless of sex, race, creed, religion, or any other affiliation.

Over the next few months, various members gave talks at monthly meetings and planned a fly-in, an event they hoped to repeat every year. Poberezny's biggest catch was Steve Wittman, who, despite being nearly blind in one eye, had a long history of racing both production and home-built airplanes. In 1931, he had named his first homebuilt racer *Chief Oshkosh*, after the Wisconsin town where he lived on Lake Winnebago, and in 1938 he was awarded the Louis Blériot Medal for a speed record of 238 mph set the year before. Wittman didn't just build racers; in 1937, he designed a factory-built lightplane called the Buttercup that had side-by-side seating—two seats next to each other as in a car. World War II intervened before Buttercup production could begin, but Wittman patented the spring-steel landing gear, which was his own design. He later sold the manufacturing rights to multiple designers, most notably Cessna, who put the gear on tens of thousands of production airplanes.

Wittman traveled from Oshkosh to Milwaukee and gave a talk emphasizing safety while pointing out that, although some CAA homebuilt restrictions still existed, such as the ban on carrying passengers, the new rules were quite liberal. Reminding the crowd that freedom comes with responsibility, he admonished members not to do something stupid that would ruin things for everyone—and, when someone of Wittman's stature spoke, everyone listened.

CAA inspector Tony Maugeri was another popular speaker, and he suggested that if builders exceeded the certification requirements and flew safely, their lobbying efforts to relax restrictions on homebuilts would carry more weight with the federal government.

Poberezny soon started planning the EAA's first fly-in for September 12–13 at Curtiss-Wright Airport, while simultaneously building an airplane he hoped to race at the event. He created *Little Audrey* from the burned-out shell of a racing airplane damaged in a hangar fire, along with a pair of wings from a Luscombe that he attached to the middle of the fuselage. The name was chosen perhaps at least in part to appease his wife: with airplanes, engines, and parts clogging every square inch of the garage, Audrey parked the family car outside all winter.

By the time of the fly-in, the EAA had about seventy members, but only twenty-one airplanes arrived, one flying all the way from Florida. The small number turned out to be a blessing, since Poberezny had apparently spent more time building *Little Audrey* than thinking about the logistics of running a fly-in. As arriving airplanes taxied in after landing, he scrambled about the airport playing ground traffic cop, chief greeter, ambassador, information desk attendant for finding hotels, and maintenance specialist. He also hadn't thought about toilets and trash, and after everyone left on Monday morning, the airport looked like a garbage dump that had exploded. While cleaning up napkins and chicken bones by himself, he vowed that cleanliness would be a high priority at all future fly-ins.

Despite the mess, Poberezny and the rest of the EAA leadership deemed the first annual fly-in a roaring success. The airplanes that showed up were a happy hodgepodge of the eclectic craft prized by the homebuilding crowd: a Curtiss Jenny; an eye-watering 450-horsepower Stearman owned by Duane Cole's brother, the International Aerobatic Club champion Marion Cole; and a Heath Parasol. Steve Wittman, in his racer, *Buster*, topped out at 235 mph to beat four other pilots, including last place Poberezny in *Little Audrey*, in a two-lap, sixteen-mile race. Fred Miller treated 140 fly-in attendees to an evening party that started with a tour of his Miller Brewery and ended with dinner and drinks at the Miller Inn.

Although people drove to the fly-in from as far away as Washington State, one prominent homebuilder was conspicuously absent. George Bogardus reportedly considered the upstart organization a competitor of his American Airmen's Association, and he never joined the EAA. He also apparently lost interest in aviation by the mid-1950s. However, in a curious and unexpected tribute to his rivals, he left his entire estate to the EAA's Chapter 105, in Portland, Oregon, when he passed away in 1997. Amid decades' worth of detritus, which included old radios, rifles, and stacks of magazines, chapter members found the remains of *Little Gee Bee*, the barely legal homebuilt aircraft Bogardus flew to Washington in 1947. Restored by chapter members to its original condition, *Little Gee Bee* now resides at the Steven F. Udvar-Hazy Center of the Smithsonian's National Air and Space Museum.

* * *

On the West Coast, Michigan transplant and homebuilder Ray Stits thought Milwaukee a bit far to travel for a monthly meeting, so he dashed off a letter to the EAA asking for permission to form a local chapter, not allowed by the original constitution. When he wasn't working night shifts for two aircraft manufacturers, Stits designed and built several airplanes at Riverside Airport, just west of the San Bernardino Mountains. His airplanes covered a multitude of designs, including a low-wing monoplane he called the Playboy, which he offered for sale as a kit, and the Stits Junior and Sky Baby, billed as the world's smallest aircraft and smallest biplane, respectively. Five Sky Babies, each with a wingspan of only seven feet, could fit into the same hangar space as a single J-3 Cub. In later years, Stits also developed a cloth covering system, Poly-Fiber, used on both amateur-built and production aircraft. Wildly popular among homebuilders, Stits's system played an unwitting role in an accident that claimed the life of Steve Wittman in 1995.

In the 1950s, Stits wanted a chance for the Riverside Airport's already diverse sport aviation population to be a part of the EAA without having to fly across half the country. In 1943, two local aviation enthusiasts, Flavio Madariaga and Bob Bogen, bought the airport, which had been founded in 1925, and turned it into an aviation mecca for all manner of homebuilders: aerobatic pilots, air show performers, racers, and those who just wanted to fly for fun. In the mid-1950s, to avoid confusion with a newer and larger municipal airport built a few miles away, the owners mashed up their first names and rechristened the airfield with a fanciful moniker, Flabob.

Paul Poberezny read Stits's letter aloud at the October 1953 EAA meeting at Curtiss-Wright Airport; and at the November meeting, the members present passed an amendment to allow chapter formation. Two months later, twenty-six members of the EAA's Chapter 1 in Riverside elected Ray Stits as their president. By the end of 1954, the EAA had seven chapters and more were being formed.

* * *

While the EAA was experiencing a grassroots expansion into chapters, the March 1954 *Mechanix Illustrated* ran an article that garnered the group additional national publicity. John Scherer's "They Build 'Em and Fly 'Em" listed many reasons for building an airplane: the favorable cost of building versus buying a used airplane, the opportunity to spread costs out over several years of building, the satisfaction of building your own airplane, and being intimately familiar with every part of your airplane. Enchanted by accompanying photos of a plethora of homebuilt models—biplanes, low- and high-wing monoplanes, and racers with top speeds of up to two hundred miles per hour—readers agreed with Scherer and wrote 1,758 letters to the EAA in one month. Many of the letter writers wanted to build their own airplanes, even if they didn't have the know-how to design one on their own. The response convinced Poberezny that the traditional aviation industry hadn't done enough to meet the interests of the average private flyer, and he saw a great future for kit aircraft that, like the Heath Parasol, could be purchased as partial kits in a pay-as-you-build fashion.

With all the attention, excitement ran high in the close-knit home-building community, and even the CAA's branch chief for general aviation maintenance, Bob Burbick, crowed that, unfettered by regulations and assembly lines, homebuilders would soon be cranking out creative designs, including a flying car. Railing against older kits that produced airplanes too hot to handle or underpowered, he envisioned a just-right kit to satisfy many builders. Burbick thought the EAA could become the organization that would build a nationwide consensus on homebuilding issues, and that Poberezny would be the homebuilding high priest who would interface with the CAA.

For the 1954 fly-in, held August 6–7 at Curtiss-Wright Airport, Paul assigned chairmen and committees to tend to various duties, which included overseeing awards, hangars, lodging, aircraft welcoming, parking, and the overall program. CAA volunteers—the ever-supportive Tony Maugeri and Bob Burbick—agreed to judge participating homebuilt aircraft and make awards based on outstanding design and workmanship. Neal Loving, whose nomination had resulted in the EAA's open arms membership policy, earned the Most Outstanding Design Award with his *Loving's Love*, a two-hundred-mile-per-hour racer with a sleek, all-wood design and a wing shaped like a gull's. Poberezny won the air race in *Little Audrey*, and Duane Cole and his brothers put on an aerobatic air show. More than five hundred pilots and amateur builders wandered the airport grounds throughout the weekend, examining the thirty airplanes that showed up and exchanging ideas for new designs. Speakers from the CAA, the Wisconsin State Aeronautics Commission, and the Aeronautical

University in Chicago gave presentations on Sunday morning to a crowd of two hundred. To help create enthusiasm in a new generation of potential pilots, some members gave free airplane rides to local teenagers in what they dubbed "Teen-Hi Airlift." Membership had increased tenfold from the previous fly-in, from seventy-three to seven hundred, and the EAA had seventeen hundred dollars in the bank.

* * *

Although John Scherer's *Mechanix Illustrated* article had generated much enthusiasm among potential amateur builders, most still had no idea how to design or construct an airplane. The 1950s homebuilders were a breed unlike those of the 1930s, who tended to be impetuous young men bereft of building experience but, wanting to fly and unable to afford a factory-built aircraft, were willing to try just about anything. The newer generation was instead composed of experienced pilots whose average age was thirty-one. More mature, better funded, and many with families, they wanted to fly safely and for pleasure, and weren't interested in either flinging themselves in gliders via catapult or purchasing the training or business airplanes being produced in factories. Certified aircraft manufacturers cranked out the equivalent of Chrysler sedans, but many homebuilders longed for something more like a Chevrolet Corvette. However, at least initially, the homebuilt movement had few options to offer those not capable of designing their own airplanes.

A homebuilt could be constructed using someone else's plans, but most sets of plans didn't come with detailed instructions. The few kits that were offered included mainly raw materials, which saved the builder time otherwise spent chasing down aircraft-quality wood and aluminum. But the amateur still had to buy nuts and bolts and hundreds of other parts, as well as to decide how to build jigs, cut pieces to the correct size, and assemble everything in the right order. Many aircraft builders still joke that they wind up building two airplanes, with the first of each part for practice and the second for keeps; this is especially true of builders who, working from plans only, have to figure everything out for themselves. Experienced, talented, or patient builders could complete plans-only aircraft, but most would-be homebuilders needed help beyond how-to articles in *Experimenter* and advice from their local chapter expert, who was probably already overwhelmed with his own personal life and homebuilding project. Even so, Paul Poberezny and the rest of the EAA leadership, possibly overoptimistic regarding the mechanical abilities of most pilots and their time available for building, were slow to see true kits, with prefabricated parts, all required materials, and sets of good directions, as essential to growing the amateur-built fleet beyond perhaps a few thousand airplanes. Plans were synonymous with homebuilding, and plans it would be.

With the plans dogma in mind, Scherer approached Poberezny regarding a second article about building an airplane, similar to those that ran in *Popular Aviation* in the 1930s. Since most designers, like Ray Stits and Steve Wittman, were trying to sell their airplane plans for profit, Poberezny decided to write the article himself. He had purchased the remains of the Corben Sport Plane Company for two hundred dollars in the fall of 1953, hauling engines, drawings, jigs, fixtures, crates of wing ribs, and even a complete airplane from Madison to Hales Corner using two rented farm wagons. With the magazine article, he saw the opportunity to further EAA goals while also reviving his dormant airplane factory.

Poberezny collaborated with several experienced builders to create drawings and modify the Corben Ace design to use some certified parts, such as J-3 Cub landing gear. Originally designed in the 1930s, the Ace used the structural configuration common for those days—a welded steel-tube fuselage and a wooden wing. Ed Heath had dealt with the fuselage problem by bolting the steel tubes together, but most designers considered that a second-rate way to do the job. Poberezny chose to offer instead a prewelded fuselage for his airplane, a choice that still seemed to maintain the spirit of a true kit, even if a full-blown fuselage seemed to violate the intent of the CAA regulations.

Poberezny spent most of his spare time in the latter half of 1954 building the first redesigned Corben Ace in his garage. When it was finished, he hauled the airplane to Milwaukee's Mitchell Field, assembled it, and called Tony Maugeri to come inspect it.

The CAA inspector climbed into the cockpit, moved the controls a few times and said, "Poop Deck, what's this? You push the stick left and the left aileron comes down?"

The left aileron should have come up; Poberezny had installed the control cables backward. At least twenty-five people had sat in the cockpit and moved the controls as he built the airplane, and not one had noticed.

Fig. 5.2. Paul Poberezny's "Baby Ace" on the cover of the May 1955 issue of *Mechanix Illustrated*.

After repairing his embarrassing error, Poberezny showed Maugeri the paperwork required to get his airworthiness certificate: the "builder's log" used to document progress during construction; applications for registration and airworthiness; drawings of the airplane viewed from the side, top, and front; information about weight and balance to use for loading cargo and fuel; and an affidavit of ownership certifying the pedigree of the materials Paul used in construction. Maugeri first gave the airplane a three-day certificate to allow Poberezny to fly and do some adjusting, and then awarded him a six-month certificate for his flight testing, which required him to remain within twenty-five miles of the airport and wear a parachute, typical restrictions during the 1950s.

For his first flight, Poberezny opened the throttle at the end of the runway and the Corben took off within 125 feet. After climbing for a while, he found himself pushing forward on the stick to stay in level flight, and the ailerons were a bit stiff, both easy-to-fix problems. Thrilled to be airborne in his own creation, he didn't even notice the frigid winter air whipping past the open cockpit.

Now called the Baby Ace, the airplane graced the cover of the May 1955 *Mechanix Illustrated*, and the magazine included the first installment of directions. Like Heath, Poberezny started his builders out by making the ribs.

EAA membership continued to grow by word of mouth and additional articles about homebuilding in *Flying*, *Time*, *Air Progress*, and even a British Publication, *Flight*. Poberezny also recruited members as he flew around the country as part of his Air National Guard duties. However, despite the success of the 1954 fly-in and the growing membership, as 1955 dawned a controversy brewed that threatened to tear apart the band of builders.

6

The Dream Begins

Sometimes it's pretty wonderful to be able to dream anything
you want as long as you don't carry it too far. If you can put those
dreams into practice, that's better still.

Arnold Ebneter, in a letter to his parents
written during pilot training, 1953

MY FATHER REPORTED TO AIR FORCE PREFLIGHT TRAINING AT
Lackland Air Force Base on December 30, 1952. While friends and family
back home cheered in the New Year, he and his fellow cadets exchanged
civilian clothes for khaki uniforms and learned to salute, march, and
generally just shut up and do whatever told to by their trainers. Going
from the freewheeling, make-it-up-as-you-go-along life at General Mills
to a structured organization with rigid rules required some adjustment,
but Arnold soon fell into the rhythm of daily military life. After two
months of basic training, he transferred to Goodfellow Air Force Base,
near San Angelo, Texas, to train in the L-21A Super Cub; although similar to his beloved J-3, the high-powered, heavier, military version tended
to produce something resembling controlled crashes instead of gentle
touchdowns.

Military pilot training was fast-paced, and about 40 percent of the
cadets washed out; a cartoon in the class yearbook quipped, "I dropped my
pencil yesterday and missed the hydraulic, electrical, and induction systems lecture." With thirteen hundred hours of civilian flying experience,
Arnold quickly progressed to the 550-horsepower T-6G Texan and then
moved to Foster Air Force Base, near Victoria, Texas, located about thirty
miles northwest of the Gulf Coast's midpoint, for more advanced training

in an 800-horsepower T-28A. Going from a Cub to the three-hundred-mile-per-hour T-28A was like going from a Model T to a Studebaker, but moving to the jet-powered T-33 was like jumping into an Indy racecar. He found the jet's acceleration during takeoff and climb breathtaking; and, after five years in the minors, the six-hundred-mile-per-hour T-33 hurtled him into aviation's major league the day before Thanksgiving.

Despite my father's new experiences, he was not yet certain he wanted to make the military a career. He wrote to his parents: "The military stifles originality too much; one of the reasons I liked working at General Mills was that I was given a free hand to develop my ideas."

The air force commissioned Arnold as a second lieutenant and awarded him his silver pilot's wings on March 15, 1954, and he was on his way to becoming a fighter pilot at Nellis Air Force Base, just north of Las Vegas. But first, he had some unfinished business in Minnesota to take care of. With no time to spare, he made a mad dash to Saint Paul and married Colleen on March 18, ending her patient two-year wait as he romped around the United States.

After the wedding, his furious pace continued unabated; my parents drove west to Las Vegas, arriving in time for a brief vacation. Like many military couples, they had no real honeymoon, but at least it was free—the air force paid for the drive to Vegas.

At Nellis, Arnold flew the F-86, the air force's most advanced fighter airplane, while he absorbed a bewildering array of fighter pilot tools and techniques: guns, missiles, and bombs used for dogfighting and attacking ground targets; enemy and friendly aircraft recognition, which afforded the pilot two seconds to get the right answer; flight physiology to understand what high altitudes do to a body; and land and water survival skills in case he had to eject. He also immersed himself in fighter pilot culture, which customarily involved self-confidence bordering on cockiness, a penchant for hard partying, and an obsession with using nothing but black ink to carefully record each flight in one's logbook. Neither of my parents had a taste for alcohol, but it wasn't long before Arnold started fussing over the appearance of his flight suit and Colleen could no longer find blue ink cartridges in the apartment to fill her fountain pen, Arnold having tossed them all to keep their dreaded color from entering his logs.

After F-86 training, Arnold and Colleen returned to Foster. Coming from Saint Paul, my mother must have viewed the base as the end of the world. Victoria, the nearest town, five miles southwest, had a population of about twenty thousand. San Antonio and Houston each lay two hours away.

Although Foster had been a training base when Arnold left, when he returned it was an operational fighter base assigned to the Tactical Air Command, a far-flung organization led by a four-star general responsible for most of the fighter aircraft in the air force. The base had a main runway nearly two miles long and a ramp area large enough to park twelve dozen F-86s. Maintenance hangars the size of high school football stadiums dotted the flight line, along with white, wooden, World-War-II surplus barracks that housed the pilots and other airmen as they planned and scheduled flights, did ground training, and maintained their parachutes, helmets, and survival gear. Colleen was amazed at the effort required to keep fewer than two hundred pilots in the air: three thousand support officers, enlisted personnel, and government civilians fixed and refueled airplanes, maintained buildings and runways, and cared for the military people and their families—food, clothing, pay, doctors, lawyers, even entertainment.

Training at Foster involved endless exercises in gunnery, air combat maneuvering, and instrument approaches; but not long after arriving, Arnold and several other pilots flew their F-86s to Miami for the weekend, ostensibly to practice their cross-country flying skills. Colleen waited in their apartment, adjusting to the lonely life of military spouses. She told her mother-in-law in a letter: "I've spent three nights alone now and I'm sort of getting used to it. Now that we have the phone, I don't mind it so much. About all that's left is for me to learn how to drive." She was already thinking about making frequent moves, buying end tables with legs that unscrewed for easy shipping.

Colleen also soon learned to keep a ready supply of large books and bug spray to annihilate roaches seemingly as large as armadillos that sought refuge in the apartment whenever a storm blew through. The joke around Victoria was that you could never get rid of the bugs, but just put up a good fight. Thunderstorms and tornadoes pounded the area on a regular basis; and after a storm, kids swam in three feet of water standing in open ditches by the roadways.

Although many of the local businesses stated, "No Army wife," in their help wanted ads, Colleen found a typing job in the base finance office that brought in extra money for shopping trips to San Antonio. Married life soon settled into a routine of working during the week, with an occasional evening instructional flight for Colleen in a Cub at nearby Ball Airport—she had finished training for her license before Arnold joined the air force, but she had not yet taken her check ride. On weekends, they drove to an airport in Beeville to work on yet another civilian airplane Arnold had bought. Colleen enjoyed helping with the airplane, but she occasionally bemoaned the loss of shopping opportunities during the weekend restoration trips.

On New Year's Day 1955, Arnold and Colleen attended a traditional military reception at the Officer's Club, where hungover officers in mess dress, the military equivalent of a tuxedo, and their suit-wearing wives passed through a receiving line made up of seven colonels and their wives, followed by free punch and liquor. The first six colonels in line mangled the Ebneter name, but Colleen was thrilled to hear Arnold's new group commander say, "Hello, Mrs. Eb-netter," in a perfect pronunciation. She wasn't so thrilled six months later when the same colonel, apparently disappointed at the turnout for one of his parties, announced at a meeting that he expected the entire group to be at the next party. After a year of marriage, Colleen wasn't sure she was rah-rah enough for Arnold to stay in the military.

A few weeks after the New Year's reception, one of Arnold's pilot training classmates, First Lieutenant Elton J. Bocage, ejected after his F-86 suffered a mechanical failure and went out of control during a bombing run, but he was too low for the parachute to save him.

Word of fatalities was not supposed to be public knowledge until a pilot's surviving family had been notified, but information often leaked, strict military regulations being no match for the emotions and grief that poured from the surviving pilots, even those hardened by combat and other peacetime accidents. Someone always knew who had died, and keeping that information inside was more than some could bear. The real miracle was that the air force ever kept a death under wraps long enough to let the official team do their job.

Once word of an accident or fatality made it to the close-knit group of officer wives, the waiting began. Someone, somewhere, would see a dark blue air force staff car pull into her driveway. A senior officer from the pilot's unit would get out, along with the chaplain and, perhaps, another member of the pilot's unit. The officers, all dressed in their finest blue service uniforms, walked to the front door and knocked. Some wives refused to answer.

The pilots and their families knew the dangers of the job, but each pilot believed he would never make a fatal mistake, a bit of self-deception required to climb into a combat aircraft. If the leader of a mission told twenty pilots that only one of them would return safe and sound, each pilot would look at the other nineteen and think, "I sure am going to miss all you guys." Still, an accident like Bocage's was hard to reconcile with the can't-happen-to-me attitude—he had done nothing wrong and yet he was still dead.

Even with the risks, few pilots could voluntarily give up the challenge, thrill, and prestige of flying the hottest airplanes on the planet, and in 1955 the Foster pilots got a jet even hotter than the F-86: the F-100 Super Sabre. Compared to the chubby and docile F-86, the F-100 was much sleeker and faster, but it already had a reputation as a killer. George Welch, a civilian test pilot for the manufacturer, North American Aviation, had died a year earlier at Edwards Air Force Base when he lost control during a high-speed dive; the vertical tail wasn't big enough to re-center the airplane when it began slipping sideways, and the excessive side force ripped the structure apart. The F-100s were grounded until the tail could be replaced with a bigger one.

Once airborne, the F-100 flew much like the F-86; but on the ground, the newer jet could be as unpredictable as a bucking bronco. Engineers had sacrificed slower takeoff and landing speeds in order to reach the supersonic speed worshipped by the air force. At higher speeds, increased aerodynamic forces twist an airplane's wingtips, distorting airflow and reducing the effectiveness of outboard ailerons. To solve the problem, designers moved the F-100 ailerons inboard, near the fuselage. But the clever solution left no room for the flaps that a pilot could have lowered to add the extra lift and drag needed to slow down for landing. Even with a drag parachute that popped from the F-100's tail on landing, the 170-mph touchdown led to many blown tires, locked brakes, collapsed gear, and runway departures.

Other than the messy landings, the F-100 was a joy. Most airplanes, you climbed into them and made them fly; but Arnold felt as though he strapped the F-100 on like a backpack and, together, they flew as one, climbing, diving, and soaring with the seamless motions of an eagle. The F-100's light controls and stability made it easy to do almost everything better than in the F-86; with the newer airplane's pitch and yaw dampers holding the nose on a target, Arnold's scores at strafing ground targets doubled. It wasn't long before the F-100 replaced the Cub as his favorite airplane.

* * *

By 1955, many air force and civilian leaders became concerned that the United States had become overreliant on atomic weapons, which would deter only a large-scale war. What could the air force do against brush fires that might pop up around the globe? In response, air force planners started flinging fighter squadrons around the United States and North Africa, Europe, and eventually Japan to practice moving dozens of airplanes, maintenance equipment, and people thousands of miles on short notice.

F-100 aerial refueling began in the summer of 1956. Intended to extend the F-100's legs—the distances it could fly without landing—during deployments, the refueling system created a host of problems. The F-100 had a probe, a tube about six feet long and six inches in diameter, mounted underneath the right wing. The probe slid into a receptacle called a drogue, which resembled a laundry basket on its side as it flew in the slipstream behind a KB-50 tanker, attached via a long fuel hose. All the pilot had to do was fly his airplane up to the drogue and plug in the probe. However, while sitting in the cockpit, the F-100 pilots couldn't see the probe, turning what should have been a relatively easy task into a nightmare.

Instead of smoothly sliding the probe into the basket, pilots often crashed the noses of their jets into the heavy fueling nozzle inside the basket, resulting in unhappy F-100 maintenance crews who had to repair the cracked canopies and gouged fuselages. When pilots did manage to hook up, some ripped the basket and hose off the tanker and flew home with them still attached. And at least one hapless pilot showed up behind a tanker only to realize he hadn't noticed during his preflight walk around the airplane that maintenance personnel hadn't attached a probe to his airplane. After several years of aerial refueling mishaps, engineers finally came up with a probe that bent upward so pilots could see it.

Once they had mastered the basics of refueling, Arnold and five other pilots in his squadron planned a simulated attack on the Panama Canal as part of an exercise in the fall of 1956. With a scheduled takeoff time of 4:30 A.M. and wakeup call at 1:30 A.M. to prepare, someone decided the pilots should spend the night at the base hospital. Although the pilots went to bed as ordered at 5:30 P.M., it was apparent from the bellyaching at breakfast that no one had slept.

In spite of the grumpiness, everyone was excited and ready to go, but things did not get off to a good start. Of the six airplanes, two spares broke before even taking off, and as the remaining four airplanes passed through twenty-five thousand feet on their climb to cruise altitude, one pilot noticed his canopy was coming open. He tried several times to reclose the miscreant canopy, but it continued to inch upward and the resulting swirl of air vacuumed out everything not firmly tied down. Charts, checklists, and pencils spewed into the night and plunged into the dark waters of the Gulf of Mexico. By now, the command post monitoring the mission had heard enough and ordered the pilot back to Foster.

The remaining three aircraft, including Arnold's, continued toward Panama. Refueling tankers met them over Yucatán, but there was no time for sightseeing. After a fortunately uneventful refueling, the pilots proceeded to Panama for the simulated bombing and then turned back north for another rendezvous with the tankers.

During the last part of the long journey, Arnold gained an appreciation for how taxing long-distance flying could be, when it involved more than just drifting across the country in a peaceful helium balloon. He had been awake for more than thirty hours and had never felt more exhausted. He still had three hours of formation flying ahead, yet he craved sleep. He remembered from Charles Lindbergh's autobiography how the famed aviator fought to stay awake during his demanding Atlantic crossing, having had no sleep the night before. Although Arnold would never compare himself to Lindbergh, at that moment he felt empathy for the man to a degree that few others could ever have felt.

However, Arnold had something Lindbergh didn't—a flight-surgeon-approved "go pill" that he finally downed. The pill overcame his drowsiness, and he landed at 1:30 P.M. after eight hours of nonstop flying.

*　*　*

On July 31, 1955, Colleen passed her check ride and became the second pilot in the young family. Women pilots were still rare at the time, even among the wives of aviators, but Colleen, not knowing yet that she was six weeks pregnant, expected to start working on her commercial and instructor licenses soon. Even when she learned she would be a mother, she didn't fathom the impact that parenthood and being a military wife would have on her aviation dreams.

By the time my older sister, Maureen, was born, in March 1956, my father and the other pilots were away from Foster so much that my mother and many of the other young wives jokingly referred to themselves as "widows," but always with quotation marks to distinguish themselves from women who were unfortunate enough to be real widows. My mother had quit her job for full-time motherhood, and although she still dreamed of being a flight instructor, my father's long absences left her no time for additional flight training. Even if she'd had the time, she would have needed my father to drive her to the airport, since she still hadn't learned to drive.

In the summer of 1956, Arnold neared the end of his three-year commitment to the air force for his pilot training. He looked into returning to General Mills, but after flying the F-100, the balloon research projects didn't enthrall him as they once had; plus he wanted to design and fly airplanes, not balloons. The airlines, still feasting on the glut of pilots from World War II and Korea, were a long shot. Colleen wasn't enthused about the social requirements of being an air force wife, but she told Arnold she would support him if he decided to stay in the military.

The air force soon dangled a carrot that Arnold couldn't resist—if he would stay in, he could fly the F-104, an even newer, sleeker, faster jet than the F-100. In November, Arnold and five other Foster pilots spent one month in Palmdale, California, learning about the F-104's performance and weapons from Lockheed, the jet's manufacturer. The pilots then returned to Foster to fly the F-100 while they waited for an F-104 flight-training date at Edwards.

In January, the Foster wives went on high alert when two F-100 pilots died in landing accidents as Arnold and his unit flew across the country for an exercise. Everyone else arrived safely at Wendover Air Force Base, Utah, but the carnage wasn't over yet.

One afternoon, many of the deployed pilots assembled near the end of the runway to watch a landing by one of the colonels with a reputation for scraping the tail of his airplane on the runway. As the aviators waited for the potential tail-scrape entertainment, a flight of four F-100s departed for the gunnery range.

Shortly after taking off, the pilot leading the departing flight radioed, "I've got a fire warning light."

Seeing smoke trailing from the stricken aircraft's engine and a bright red spot on the side of the fuselage, one of the wingmen called out: "Eject, eject, eject!"

The lead pilot thought he could make it back to the airfield, and he turned around. Just short of the runway, he reported, "The controls have frozen."

The F-100 slammed into the ground and the rear half of the jet exploded in a fireball. The cockpit skidded forward, stopping just short of the runway, bringing hope to those on the ground that the pilot had survived.

Back at Foster, phones began ringing.

* * *

As my mother played with my sister and contemplated what to do over the weekend with Arnold gone in Utah, someone knocked on the apartment door. Colleen wasn't surprised to see one of the squadron wives, since they often dropped in on each other uninvited.

"Can I come in for a minute? I have something to tell you."

Once inside, the other wife said, "We need to sit down."

Her curiosity piqued, Colleen led her to the dining room table.

"I wanted to tell you this so you'll be prepared. There's been an accident in Utah."

Colleen's head started spinning, but she didn't say anything.

"I heard it was one of the guys who had the F-104 ground school."

"That's six guys," said Colleen.

"But only two of them are in Utah. Arnold and John Hungerford."

Colleen showed the other woman out and tried to comprehend what might have happened. If Arnold had crashed, he must have messed up. But she didn't think he would have messed up. On the other hand, he wasn't perfect; he had almost crashed on his first takeoff in the F-100, and he had blown tires on landings. And even if he hadn't made a mistake, something could have happened to the airplane he was flying. What about Elton Bocage, who had been killed flying the F-86? He hadn't done anything wrong. But if Arnold was dead, why wasn't someone from the base here to tell her? When Bocage had died, they hadn't been able to find his wife right away—but she had been out shopping or something. Colleen had been in the apartment all day. But why hadn't he called to say he was okay?

At first, Colleen's horror grew with each passing minute, but as the minutes turned into an hour, and then two, and then three, she realized that perhaps Arnold wasn't dead or dying after all. Surely, someone would have arrived by now. She called no one. What could she say without letting on that she knew something? And if Arnold were alive, her joy meant sorrow for someone else.

About eight o'clock, the phone rang and, as she heard Arnold's voice, anger replaced relief.

"Why did you wait so long to call me?"

Arnold was speechless, having no idea she had heard about the accident.

He told Colleen he had been strapped into another F-100, waiting to taxi for takeoff, when the accident happened. After the crash, the senior officer at Wendover had cancelled all flying for the rest of the day, and Arnold had shut down his F-100 and joined the other pilots as they consoled each other.

* * *

While my mother waited to hear my father's fate, she didn't know she was two months pregnant with me. I was born in August 1957, and one week before that, my parents flew loops in a J-3 Cub, the upside-down maneuvers and g-forces perhaps instilling in their second daughter a passion for roller coasters and jumping off rooftops. Still, one of the downsides to growing up in a flying family is that you don't get to remember your first flight in a little airplane; like all my sisters, I had my first flight before I was a month old. In our family, everyone flew, except for the cat.

In the summer of 1957, the air force announced that F-104s wouldn't be coming to Foster after all; in fact, the air force was closing the base. Although disappointed about the F-104, Arnold knew that if he wanted to fly and make decent money doing it, the air force was the best option, despite the risks. But what to do next?

His most pressing unfinished business was the engineering degree. The lack of that piece of paper was starting to haunt him—his superiors had recommended on his efficiency reports that the air force select him as an experimental test pilot, but he needed a degree to qualify. With a degree, maybe he could also design new planes for the air force; so he applied to an air force college program.

While waiting to hear if he had been accepted by the program, Arnold flew to George Air Force Base in California for an exercise in crossing the Pacific Ocean to Japan. He told Colleen he should be home for dinner in two days, since he was only a spare in case one of the other airplanes broke. But chaos during the airborne refueling after takeoff from George meant that not enough of the F-100s had sufficient fuel to keep flying across the ocean. Instead of returning to George and then flying back to Foster, Arnold was ordered by his superior to fly to Hawaii.

The next day, Colleen's concern over Arnold's dinnertime no-show turned to alarm as the night dragged on. The next morning, she called the operations desk at Arnold's squadron, and the duty officer answering the phone said, "Why ma'am, your husband had to deploy." That no one had bothered to call Colleen didn't strike him as a problem—during the Cold War, wives and children were not an air force priority. In the meantime, Arnold was sitting in a briefing room in Hawaii, preparing to fly to Guam.

Colleen calmed down and waited for a postcard or letter from Hawaii, or perhaps Guam or Japan, but nothing came during the monthlong deployment. Arnold later claimed there had been no time to write a letter, and a letter would have taken too long to reach Texas, anyway. He must have realized he was in trouble, though—he returned to Foster bearing a string of pearls.

Arnold's arrival back at Foster was accompanied by good news: the air force had accepted him in the program to finish his degree. In July 1958, the growing family—a pregnant-again Colleen, a toddler, an infant, a cat, and the new family airplane, a Stinson 108—moved to College Station so Arnold could attend Texas A&M, the school chosen by the air force.

In January 1959, my mother gave birth to Kathleen, and my father took his latest addition for her first flight when she was two weeks old. That summer, he sold the Stinson and bought a Cessna 170B to carry our larger family. Now three for three with girls, and with three children under three years of age, my mother decided the family was complete. She had wanted four children, but after Kathleen's birth, she reached the limits of her household organizational skills—toys, books, and magazines mingled with airplane parts on every horizontal surface in the apartment. Adding a fourth child to the mess seemed impossible.

Arnold reveled in the mess. Eight years older than when he had made his last try at college, with no money worries and his flight appetite sated

Fig. 6.1. The Ebneter family airplane in 1961 and (*left to right*) Colleen, Kathleen, Eileen, and Maureen.

on the weekends either by the Cessna or by occasional flights in an Air Force T-33, he devoted full attention to his studies. Instead of the Ds and Fs he had earned during his last few quarters at Minnesota, he received As and Bs. Soon, the only thing left before graduation was a senior project on a topic of his choice.

*   *   *

In July 1957, as my parents anticipated my arrival, Juhani Heinonen, an engineer for the airline Finnair, took off on a hazy day and flew 1,767 statute miles nonstop from Madrid, Spain, to Turku, Finland, in his C-1aI class HK-1 Keltiäinen, a model name that translates as "yellow meadow ant." Heinonen had originally designed and built the all-wood HK-1 as an aerobatic airplane, but for his record attempt he added some fairings to streamline the somewhat boxy fuselage and two fuel tanks to maximize his distance capability. To minimize weight, the HK-1 had no brakes, radio, electrical system, or lights, so flying at night was out of the question. Taking advantage of the lengthening day to the north during summer, Heinonen chose a south-to-north route, which also gave him a prevailing tailwind. After departing Madrid in cool air at 5 A.M., the HK-1 struggled with the heavy fuel load, and the engine temperature hit worrisome highs as he climbed to six thousand feet for crossing the Pyrenees. But the temperature dropped to normal once he leveled off and throttled back to a cruise power setting. Once he was safely across the mountains, clouds forced him to fly at low altitudes for much of the remaining flight, but he landed in Turku at about 11 P.M., just before sunset, after flying for seventeen hours.

While Arnold pondered what to do for his senior project, he stumbled over Heinonen's feat in *Jane's All the World's Aircraft*, a three-inch-thick, hardbound annual publication that catalogs new aircraft, aviation achievements, and technology advancements. The record fascinated Arnold, and he wondered if he could design an airplane to go even farther. He still occasionally toyed with the idea of the midget racer he had sketched at Rensselaer more than a decade earlier, and something approximately that size might work for a record flight. With his additional three years of engineering education, he might now have the skill to make his idea into a reality that would actually fly and permit him to accomplish all his goals: design an airplane, build it, and fly it. The world record would just be gravy if it happened.

A few days later, Arnold's faculty advisor, Ben Hamner, blessed the attempt at a record-setting design and set the course of my father's life for the next fifty years.

* * *

By 1960, most aircraft designers had adopted a three-phase approach based on science, ingenuity, art, and a little luck: conceptual design, preliminary design, and detailed design. During the conceptual phase, the designer determines aircraft requirements—what the airplane is expected to do—and makes major tradeoff decisions, such as the fuselage shape, whether to mount the engine on the front or back of the airplane, and the location of the landing gear. During the preliminary phase, the designer lays out a sketch of what the airplane will look like once built, determines major measurements such as wing size, and makes a cost estimate. During the detailed phase, a designer makes decisions about which parts to buy and which parts to build, and how to construct the parts that will be built, which might be everything from small brackets to landing gear and wings. The three phases aren't always completed sequentially; often a problem that arises in a later phase, such as too much weight or too little lift, sends the designer scrambling back to an earlier phase to adjust requirements, or tail size, or onboard equipment, among other things. Many designers wait until their ideas are complete before they start building, but others begin construction as soon as they can, working out solutions to problems that arise as they build. In practice, most designers wind up doing some of the latter, since few aircraft are built or fly exactly the way the design engineer had in mind.

For his senior project, Arnold had time only for a conceptual design and part of his preliminary design. He started with his requirements.

The overall vision of what an airplane is expected to do—for example, carry a pilot, three passengers, and two hundred pounds of baggage at least five hundred miles, or pull six times its own weight (Gs) so a single pilot can perform aerobatics—immediately narrows the designer's options. Other requirements, such as desired sales price and operating costs can further reduce options: for example, retractable landing gear and bigger engines improve performance but also cost more to build and maintain, so many lightplane designers turn to fixed landing gear and smaller engines.

Arnold's requirements were simple:

1. Maximum weight = 1,102 pounds
2. Fly as far as possible before landing

Arnold next estimated the empty weight of an airplane that would meet his requirements. The empty weight includes all the aircraft structure and the engine, but not the fuel, pilot, passengers, or any baggage. Most designers estimate their empty weight by studying aircraft similar to the one they are trying to build, so Arnold examined several long-distance airplanes, such as Lindbergh's *Spirit of St. Louis* and an experimental Russian aircraft, the ANT-25. He found that, on average, their empty weight compared to total weight was 37 percent. Thus, his target empty weight was 37 percent of his maximum allowed weight of 1,102 pounds, or 410 pounds.

Arnold thought 410 pounds was ambitious, but achievable, even though the lightest production airplane at the time, the Mooney M-18 Mite, weighed 550 pounds empty. However, some recent homebuilt midget racers weighed 465 pounds, and those planes had somewhat heavy structures to survive high-g turns. Arnold was sure he could build something much lighter.

Next he figured out how much fuel he could carry. Most designers base their fuel-capacity estimates on how far they want to fly without stopping, but since Arnold was weight limited, he worked backward. Assuming about two hundred pounds for a pilot and all the things a pilot needed—clothes, water, a little food, some charts for navigation—left 492 pounds for fuel. Fuel weighs about six pounds per gallon, so that meant eighty-two gallons, which Arnold rounded off to eighty gallons. He decided to put fifteen gallons in a tank in the fuselage and the remainder in the wings.

Next came the wing. An airplane's flight controls and control surfaces, such as the rudder and ailerons, are like a human's muscles and bones, and the engine is its heart; but the wing is its soul, having more impact on an airplane's personality than any other component. Workhorse bush planes in Alaska have fat wings with gigantic flaps to make slow and steep approaches to Lilliputian landing areas on glaciers and sandbars. Fighter airplanes, the thoroughbreds of aviation, have short, skinny wings that fly at twice the speed of sound, propelled through the air by powerful jet engines. Graceful airliners have long, elegant wings that effect a compromise between fast flight and passenger comfort. Gliders have long, skinny wings that maximize lift while minimizing drag, allowing them to catch thermals in the air and ride them upward like waves, occasionally far into the stratosphere. The wing generates the majority of the lift the airplane needs to counteract the weight of the airplane. The amount of lift depends on the shape of the airfoil, the wing's angle relative to the air the aircraft is flying through, the density of the air, the surface area of the wing, and the speed of the aircraft.

Unfortunately, whenever the airplane is producing lift, it is also producing drag. Air spilling off the ends of the wings produces miniature horizontal tornadoes called vortices that flow back onto the wing and create what's called induced drag, since it's a by-product of lift. The vortices impinge on a larger percentage of a short wing than of a long wing, so a shorter wing's induced drag is greater.

If a shorter wing has more induced drag, why aren't all wings long and skinny? Aside from needing wider hangars and wider runways, long and skinny wings are best for unpowered or low-powered aircraft that fly slowly and stay airborne for a long time, like gliders and spy planes;

the long wings generate a lot of lift at slow speeds. Speedier aircraft use shorter wings because the induced drag penalty largely goes away the faster the airplane flies. Parasite drag dominates at higher speeds and can be reduced by streamlining anything that protrudes from the airplane.

In addition to the wing's length and width, the wing's shape when viewed from above, called the planform, also affects performance. Rectangular wings are easy to build—since all the ribs are the same size—but tend to have the most drag. The shape with the least drag is an ellipse, but elliptical wings are difficult to build—not only is every rib a different size but also the entire wing surface has a continuous curve. Only a handful of production airplanes, such as the World War II P-47 fighter, have had elliptical wings. A good compromise is a tapered wing; the rear of the wing is straight, and the wing's width tapers at the front, ranging from several feet at the fuselage to perhaps only a foot at the wingtip. The tapered wing gets much of the drag benefit of the elliptical wing while still being relatively easy to build.

After dozens of calculations with his slide rule, Arnold settled on a somewhat plump airfoil to make room for the fuel he needed, and a tapered planform to reduce drag, a compromise he thought wouldn't be too hard to build in a garage. To fit sixty-five gallons of fuel in the wing, he figured he needed a wing area of 56.5 square feet, but then had to decide on length and width.

Arnold turned to the aspect ratio, another number with a big impact on an airplane's performance. The aspect ratio of a rectangular wing is the wing's span (wingtip to wingtip) divided by the chord (distance front to back). The aspect ratio of a nonrectangular wing is the span squared divided by the wing area. A sailplane might have an aspect ratio of forty or more, while a typical light airplane is around eight, and a jet fighter is around two. Arnold knew he didn't want a glider, but he wanted something a little higher than a typical light airplane, so he chose an aspect ratio of ten. When he laid everything out, his wing was about twenty-four feet long and almost four feet wide at the fuselage, tapering to about sixteen inches wide at the wingtips. He also decided to attach his wings at midfuselage; not only would it reduce drag, but also gravity would transfer fuel from the wing into his fuselage tank, which would save the weight of a fuel pump.

Next Arnold picked the heart of his airplane: the engine. He calculated that he needed only a fifty-five-horsepower engine, but no certified engines that small existed, so he selected an engine from his Cub days:

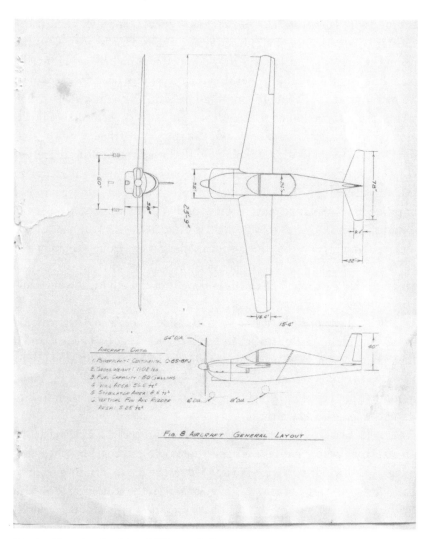

Fig. 6.2. First sketch of Arnold Ebneter's E-1.

an eighty-five-horsepower C-85 Continental. The C-85 was a bit heavy, but when combined with a metal propeller the engine would provide enough acceleration to take off in a short distance and still get good gas mileage while cruising, especially if he could minimize drag.

Since one of the biggest sources of drag on an airplane is the landing gear, he decided a retractable landing gear was a must-have; plus, it would look cool. His slide-rule calculations showed him that fixed landing gear would cost him fifty pounds of drag, which translated to almost ten gallons of fuel, and his optimism told him he could easily build a device to raise and lower the gear that weighed only ten pounds. Thus, he could save forty pounds for other things, such as some survival gear, drinking water, and a few navigation instruments. Still, he didn't expect to have enough instruments to fly through clouds. Like Heinonen and most other record setters, he would take his chances with the weather.

Every ounce had to earn its way onto Arnold's airplane, although he was willing to make a few concessions to reduce fatigue, a lesson learned from his many long F-100 flights. He would need a comfortable seat, and to deal with the long flight time, he designed a seat that reclined thirty degrees. He also widened the cockpit a bit, to about two feet, to give him more shoulder room and help with stretching.

For building materials, he needed something readily available. He chose a tube-and-fabric fuselage similar to that of the Cubs he had spent so many hours recovering, and although most homebuilders still used wood wings in 1960, Arnold decided to use aluminum. He hadn't worked much with aluminum and would have to buy some special tools, but he wanted a "wet" wing to save weight; the fuel would go directly into the wing instead of into separate tanks installed in the wing, and wood wouldn't be practical for that.

To save even more weight, he used a new type of tail called a stabilator. To move an airplane's nose up and down, most designers use a two-part horizontal tail consisting of a fixed stabilizer and moving elevator. The stabilator combines the two pieces into a single slab that is aerodynamically more efficient, so the stabilator can be smaller and lighter. But, there is a trade-off—a stabilator is harder to build than a simple elevator and horizontal stabilizer.

To save a little more weight and make extra room for fuel in the wing, Arnold used a trick from his F-100 days: he moved the ailerons inboard. With the control surfaces closer to the cockpit, he reduced the amount of hardware needed to connect the control stick to the ailerons and freed up the entire outboard portion of the wing for fuel. Like the F-100, his design had no flaps; but with the airfoil he selected, the airplane should slow down enough to make a safe landing. As Saint-Exupéry would say, the design was an elegant solution: in the end, there was nothing left to remove, although decades later, he would discover that he had perhaps removed too much.

Even with all his weight-saving measures, when Arnold added every-thing up, he had a problem common to most airplane designs—the empty weight was more than he'd planned: 438.5 pounds empty, or 28.5 pounds above his original design goal. He thought, however, that even at the higher weight, he could fly more than double Heinonen's distance, and he proposed two routes. His primary route went from Los Angeles to St. John's, Newfoundland, and his backup route went from Fairbanks, Alaska, to Miami, Florida.

In retrospect, Arnold's predictions were wildly optimistic. However, his ideas impressed Hamner and other A&M engineering professors, and they submitted his design paper to a regional student competition sponsored by a professional engineering organization, the Institute of the Aeronautical Sciences, now the American Institute of Aeronautics and Astronautics.

Held the end of April 1960 at a luxury hotel in Dallas, the competition included twelve other schools as well, including aeronautical engineering powerhouses such as Notre Dame, the Air Force Academy, and the Geor-gia Institute of Technology. Students from each school presented papers on esoteric topics such as "midcourse interplanetary guidance" and a "turbo-athodyd engine" to a panel of judges culled from four major air-craft manufacturers. Arnold's paper was the only one about the design of an actual airplane, and perhaps that persuaded the judges to award him first place. The award came with a prize of three hundred dollars, a tidy sum for someone with a family and an expensive hobby.

With an airplane design under his belt and his degree in hand, Arnold might have been satisfied that he had met most of his youthful goals. He was a pilot, half a mechanic, and now an engineer. However, having an engineering degree and being an engineer are two different things. He had designed an airplane, but would it really fly? And could it really set a record?

The only way to find out was to build and fly the airplane. His youthful exuberance shining through, my father wrote in the report to his profes-sors documenting his design that he would build and fly his new design "as soon as time and circumstances permit."

He had no idea that time and circumstances would unfold in ways that would both hinder and help his pursuit of his dream.

7

Stagnation

We here at Headquarters have noticed an increasing number of
letters from members, readers and enthusiasts that mention the
clipping of wings or installing larger engines in commercially
manufactured aircraft.

Experimenter, April 1955

WHEN I STARTED TO BUILD AN AIRPLANE IN THE MID-1990S, I
found an abundance of books, manuals, videos, classes, and magazine
articles to teach me about construction techniques and the FAA rules
involved in amateur-built aircraft. However, CAA rules in the 1950s provided little guidance to either builders or field inspectors regarding even
something as basic as the definition of an amateur-built aircraft. A few
builders, who had each spent hundreds or even thousands of hours
constructing airplanes, collided with CAA inspectors unwilling to issue
experimental certificates. Searching for consistency across the United
States, CAA officials turned to Paul Poberezny and the EAA for help with
questions such as: "What constitutes a homebuilt airplane?" and "How far
can a kit manufacturer go?" The second question took decades to resolve,
but the first question quickly divided amateur builders into two camps:
those who thought it okay to call a modified production airplane a homebuilt, and those who thought only an original airplane built by an amateur could qualify as a homebuilt.

The CAA wasn't completely against modifying production aircraft
such as J-3 Cubs. Rules existed that allowed anyone to make changes,
such as the addition of a different engine or a larger fuel tank or new
instruments. But the CAA had to determine that the changes were safe

and then approve them so the aircraft could still be certified as a standard production aircraft. Professional designers who thought they had improved the performance of a standard airplane could even apply for a "supplemental type certificate" that allowed the designer to sell modification kits or modified airplanes, and a mini-industry grew that offered improved aftermarket aircraft parts such as air filters, exhaust systems, and extended-range fuel tanks.

But the CAA drew the line at amateurs making a change to a production airplane and then recertifying that airplane in the experimental amateur-built category. From the CAA's point of view, the issue wasn't a matter of safety so much as the intent of amateur building and fairness to manufacturers of standard production aircraft. One aircraft with one modification that hadn't been through a rigorous safety analysis could hardly be deemed a major threat to public safety, but it violated the spirit of homebuilding, which was supposed to be about education and recreation, not just slapping on a bigger engine for the purpose of flying around your friends and family. And it wasn't fair to the original aircraft manufacturers or the manufacturers of modification kits, who had to pay thousands of dollars to sell their products to the public.

Unfortunately, the CAA had muddled the modification issue by allowing, even encouraging, builders to use some certified parts that enhanced safety, such as landing gear, wheels, propellers, and engines. Using some parts from salvaged airplanes was also permissible, including entire wings or control surfaces, but CAA rules also stated, "It is not intended that this provision be used to avoid obtaining approval of major alterations to aircraft previously certificated in another category." This was the reason the CAA rejected *Little Poop Deck* for an experimental certificate: Poberezny had merely altered the Taylorcraft to improve its performance. *Little Audrey*, on the other hand, was made from the fuselage of one airplane and the wings of another, and Poberezny had fabricated many new parts, making the plane eligible for a certificate as an experimental aircraft.

Despite his own experience with the clip-wing Taylorcraft, Poberezny, now more mature and a government employee himself, came around to the CAA's way of thinking on altering production aircraft, a view that enraged many EAA members, who made their feelings known during meetings and in *Experimenter* letters and articles. Poberezny and his supporters argued that, in addition to violating CAA rules, modifying production aircraft went against the true spirit of homebuilding. How could you call something homebuilt if you just modified it?

Those in favor of allowing modified production airplanes to be certified as experimental aircraft argued that there was no reason not to certify them: they used the aircraft for pleasure flying only, not for commercial operations, so the modified craft put no paying passengers at risk. And not everyone was capable of designing an airplane from scratch; in fact, many early homebuilders had gotten their start by modifying production airplanes. Some, like Duane Cole, argued that thousands of Cubs and similar light aircraft past their prime could gain new life with homebuilders after the addition of a few modernizing parts and larger engines. Since those aircraft were out of production, the original manufacturers shouldn't care, especially those who had ceased business.

Homebuilding might grow more quickly if participants could obtain experimental certificates for modified standard aircraft; but on balance, Poberezny thought, advocating the privilege was too risky. Amateur builders already had plenty of freedom to do what they wanted, so why create conflict with the CAA over a rule that wasn't needed? In the end, Poberezny elected not to lobby for a rule change, but the controversy came at a cost—at the end of 1957, EAA membership continued to grow, but only about half the original 250 members still belonged.

Despite the anger created by the controversy, the membership continued to elect Poberezny as president each year. No one else could match his organizational skills, enthusiasm, charisma, commitment, and energy.

*   *   *

While the controversy over what constituted a homebuilt raged, the CAA saw kit-built aircraft as a means to help reinvigorate dwindling interest in aviation in the United States. The number of new student pilots had dropped to under forty thousand—from three times that many after World War II—and between 1952 and 1954, one in six airport operators had gone out of business. Congress passed a resolution to encourage model building among elementary school children and the building of real airplanes from kits among high school students. Models were abundant, but it wasn't clear where the kits were supposed to come from, since designers of homebuilt airplanes still sold mainly plans and a few parts for purchase.

The CAA had yet to rule on what might be allowed in a kit anyway. Clearly, kits that contained plans, instructions, and raw materials were okay, but many homebuilders thought the prefabricated Baby Ace fuselage that Poberezny offered might violate the rules.

In addition to noting the dearth of kits, other EAA members saw that existing plans rarely offered designs that put them ahead of the tired old Heaths and Pietenpols of the 1930s; for an organization dedicated to innovation, there didn't seem to be much innovating going on. In addition, even with CAA rules now allowing passengers in homebuilts, only a handful of designs had more than one seat.

Enter the Design Competition, announced in the February 1957 *Experimenter*. The goal of the competition was to design a "good utility airplane" with folding wings so it could be stored in a garage and towed to the airport, in the same way that people towed boats to lakes. Recognizing that some spouses and families might better support homebuilding activities if they could ride in the completed airplane, the original contest rules also required an airplane with at least two seats. The passenger rule was dropped when some designers complained, but the EAA stacked the deck to favor two-seaters by assigning them more points toward the five-thousand-dollar prize, which would be awarded at the 1958 fly-in.

The 1958 date proved too ambitious, and the competition slipped to 1959 and then to 1960. By 1959, a promising-sounding twenty-four designers, including one from France, had entered their projects, and EAA leaders and members looked forward to the judging at the 1960 fly-in.

*   *   *

As the 1950s closed, homebuilt aircraft were becoming embedded in the mutating DNA of US aviation. Congress and the Federal Aviation Act of 1958 morphed the CAA into the Federal Aviation Agency, later the Federal Aviation Administration. In addition to assigning power over operations to the FAA, the act also moved rulemaking from the Civil Aeronautics Board to the FAA. In theory, this consolidation of power for both rules and operations would make it easier to make changes, both good and bad, to regulations regarding amateur-built aircraft. EAA membership totaled more than eight thousand, and FAA data showed that almost half of the roughly one thousand airplanes registered in the experimental category were built by amateurs. Homebuilt rotorcraft, the term for small helicopters, were becoming popular, and one homebuilder in California had produced a jet-powered airplane using the same type of engine used in an air force trainer. Moreover, homebuilding ceased to be a purely male domain when Californian Joan Trefethen completed her Stits Playboy. Homebuilders even received credit for introducing innovative design features that had found their way into production aircraft, such as Steve Wittman's landing gear and the flattened fuel tanks used on the wingtips of Cessna's 310 twin-engine airplanes.

The EAA renamed the *Experimenter*, now titled *Sport Aviation*, with the words "and the Experimenter" in small type to acknowledge the organization's roots and emphasis on homebuilding. Most members thought the new title was a good thing: it reflected the idea that the EAA was about all sorts of flying for pleasure, and not just about homebuilding, a concept that they felt would attract even more members.

Even with the magazine's name change, homebuilding was still the mainstay of the EAA, and was widespread enough that members began complaining about a lack of landing gear, tubing, engines, wheels, propellers, spars, and assorted gizmos and gadgets required to complete something capable of flight. *Sport Aviation* contained more than thirty pages of homebuilding topics, such as articles on how to select building materials and on construction tips ("how to get smooth cuts in wood"), as well as design debates, including: "Straight or curved lower longerons?" (Answer: It depends—curved if you're using wood because it's easy to bend, but straight if you're using steel tubing.)

The annual fly-in, now called the National Fly-In, having outgrown the Gran-Aire facilities, had moved to Rockford, Illinois. Dozens of homebuilts with names such as the *Mighty Mong*, the *Flying Flea*, and the *Termite* arrived in 1960, along with a record-setting fifteen hundred members, one coming from Bombay, India. Although members from Canada and Europe had attended past fly-ins, the expansion into Asia seemingly prompted a name change the next year, to the International Fly-In.

Dreams of speed and space flight took hold as members spent one evening of the five-day event watching movies filmed at Edwards Air Force Base about the rocket-powered X-15, a dazzling machine that screamed over the desert at more than two thousand miles per hour piloted by, among others, a test pilot named Neil Armstrong. Most homebuilders would have been thrilled to fly at one-tenth the speed of the X-15, and hopes ran high for the design competition entries. But of the twenty-four designers who had signed up, only two had flown their airplanes to Rockford, and neither had completed the fifty hours required for prize eligibility.

The disappointed judges examined the two entries, determined to learn something despite the poor showing. They soon discovered that the two designers had spent more time building than documenting—the plans and construction manuals they supplied with their planes were woefully inadequate. What was the point in entering a nice airplane in the contest if no one else could build it? The judges declared the contest null and void. Competition director Bob Whittier reported that a wide variety of problems had overcome the designers: "Some men found that after family and business responsibilities[,] . . . completion of a plane was simply out of the question. Others started out with far-out designs[,] and . . . [some] took on the task of doing two or more tough things at once, such as making a plane of unorthodox configuration out of brand new materials, and found they had bitten off more than they could chew."

Whittier was also "galled and embarrassed" that no one had managed to come up with something better than the aging Pietenpol, but on a brighter note he pointed out the high quality of workmanship in all of the homebuilts that came to the show. Designers weren't yet cranking out innovations, but at least people were building aircraft that weren't falling out of the sky.

Whittier and his fellow EAAers weren't discouraged—recognizing that new aeronautical advancements take time, they delayed the competition judging for two more years. Their optimism was rewarded when six monoplane entries showed up at the 1962 fly-in, four with low wings and two with high wings. Three of the airplanes were single-seaters, and three were two-seaters.

Judging had actually started five months before the fly-in as designers submitted plans for review to twelve volunteer EAA judges located around the country. At the fly-in, each designer gave a presentation about his airplane to the nine judges in attendance to clear up any missing or confusing information in the six-inch stack of documents each entrant submitted before the event.

Based on five main judging criteria, judges disqualified two entries for lack of documentation. Peter Bowers, a Boeing engineer from Seattle, took first place for his all-wood *Fly Baby*. Bowers's entry was a single-seat airplane instead of a two-seater (the competition rules had stated that two-seaters were preferred), but his creation fared well on other points: it was a true sport airplane that could operate from small fields, was easy to build and fly, and had folding wings to allow garage storage to save money on a hangar.

The *Fly Baby* may not have been revolutionary, but another airplane at the 1962 fly-in more than made up for that. Edgar Lesher, an aeronautical engineering professor from the University of Michigan, brought an unusual-looking airplane he had designed and built, *Nomad*. The two-seat airplane used a "pusher" configuration like many of the early airplane designs—the engine and propeller were mounted on the back of the airplane instead of the front, which improved forward visibility and reduced cockpit noise and drag when compared to a front-mount tractor engine, since there was no longer a propeller slipstream washing over the airplane.

Born in Columbus, Ohio, Lesher, by age ten, hung out at local airports and, by sixteen, had read every aviation book in the local library. After earning a bachelor's degree in math from Ohio State and a master's in aeronautical engineering from University of Michigan, Lesher worked first in the aircraft industry and as a professor at Texas A&M and then at Michigan during World War II. During a short stint at Stinson Aircraft, he worked on a four-seat pusher design that Stinson hoped to sell in the postwar civilian market. The design was never produced, but it sparked Lesher's interest in pusher aircraft.

Back on staff at Michigan, Lesher wasn't a typical professor. He was interested in actually building airplanes, not in arcane theoretical research; and throughout his career, he expended more energy writing articles for *Sport Aviation* than for academic journals. Attending the 1958 EAA fly-in and seeing all the old airplanes had inspired him to design and build *Nomad*.

Constructed of aluminum, *Nomad* featured a tail mounted below the fuselage instead of above to keep the rear-mounted propeller from hitting the ground if the pilot over-rotated the nose during takeoff or landing—the tail would scrape first and protect the more critical propeller. Lesher had plenty of help designing and building his airplane;

students in his classes churned out performance calculations, and machinists and other workers in the university shops provided factory-quality tooling and expertise during the construction.

One problem, endemic to most pusher designs, wasn't easily solved—the high vibrations caused by the long shaft connecting *Nomad*'s engine to the propeller. Front-mounted propellers usually bolt directly to the engine, but to accommodate a lighter and more aerodynamically clean fuselage that narrows at the tail, rear-mounted engines usually sit somewhat forward of the propeller, sometimes as much as several feet away. If the engine could rotate at a perfectly constant speed, the long shaft wouldn't cause a problem; but cylinders don't fire continuously. They fire one at a time in a rapid sequence that gives rise to vibrations. Relatively harmless when transmitted over a few inches to front-mounted propellers, the vibrations can become catastrophic as they migrate down a long shaft. It's like the difference between balancing a wine cork versus a long pencil in your palm—one is effortless and the other nearly impossible. The vibration levels using Lesher's original shaft were about twice as high as he expected, but he found a solution in the Dodge Flexidyne coupling, an automobile part recommended by flying car pioneer Molt Taylor.

First flown in late 1961, *Nomad* attracted huge crowds at the 1962 fly-in, and judges awarded Lesher first place for "Outstanding Design." But more interesting to Lesher than all the accolades was a conversation at lunch one day with Leeon Davis. Like Arnold, Davis had read about Heinonen's record flight and thought the distance record looked like easy prey for another homebuilt. Davis designed and built an airplane, the DA-2, for a record attempt, but a move from Indiana to Oklahoma had delayed his plans. At the Rockford lunch, he made the mistake of mentioning his interest in the record to Lesher, who seized upon Davis's idea for winning the straight-line distance record and added plans for six more record attempts to his slate: altitude, distance over a closed course, and speed over four separate closed courses of one hundred, five hundred, one thousand, and two thousand kilometers. In 1962, all seven records for the five-hundred-kilogram class of airplanes belonged to Europeans, and Lesher wanted to bring the records back to the United States.

But *Nomad* wouldn't work in an attempt for the record—the two-seater weighed nearly 1,000 pounds empty, and the pilot alone would push the total weight past the 1,102-pound limit. Using design principles from *Nomad* but now focused on weight, Lesher built a new single-seat

Fig. 7.1. Ed Lesher's *Teal*, 1960s.

pusher he named *Teal*, apparently after the duck whose silhouette graced the side of the finished airplane.

Like Arnold, Lesher calculated that a fifty-horsepower engine would be optimum for setting records, but he, too, found no suitable engine that size. He instead cannibalized *Nomad* for its hundred-horsepower Continental engine. The larger engine was a good compromise: it reduced performance at the lower speeds used for distance records, but it increased performance during the pursuit of speed and altitude records.

Years later when Arnold read about *Teal*, he wondered if Lesher had read his student paper. *Teal* contained many of my father's design features: the storage of the majority of fuel in the wing, an extra fuel tank in the fuselage, drag-reducing retractable landing gear, and simple instruments. Lesher had even come up with the same wing-surface area.

With all the extra hardware needed to drive the rear-mounted propeller, *Teal* was heavy. Even without frills such as lights and an electrical system for night flying, *Teal* weighed 680 pounds empty, compared to Heinonen's 551-pound HK-1 and Arnold's optimistic 438-pound design. However, *Teal* flew faster than Heinonen's airplane owing to the lower drag, which offset the weight penalty. As for the pilot, Lesher's first idea was to find a jockey-size aviator, but he instead decided to fly for the records himself. This gave him an incentive to lose weight; and besides, he didn't want to design and build the airplane only to have someone else fly it and earn the record. Everyone knows who Chuck Yeager is, but who remembers the engineer who designed the X-1 that Yeager used to break the sound barrier?

Teal first flew in 1965; and by 1970, Lesher had set all the records he pursued, except for straight-line distance, the record my father coveted.

8

Holding Pattern

This project has been undertaken to fulfill the author's long-
standing desire to design, build, and fly an airplane embodying
his own ideas.

Arnold Ebneter, "Preliminary Design of an FAI Class 1
Airplane and Plans for Establishing International
Distance Records," Texas A&M student project, 1960

AFTER MY FATHER GRADUATED FROM TEXAS A&M IN THE SUMMER
of 1960, we moved to England Air Force Base in central Louisiana and
settled into a rental house near the base. Young military families filled
the neighborhood, so it had many the benefits of living on base without the headache of maintaining a yard to exacting military standards.
Yard work was not high on my parents' list of priorities.

Arnold checked out in the F-100D, a newer and heavier model that
required flaps to prevent the touchdown speed on landing from being
even higher than the older airplane's already almost unmanageable
170 mph. To make room for the flaps, engineers moved the F-100 ailerons
outboard, an option Arnold wouldn't have four decades later when his
own design proved too hot to handle during landings.

One month after arriving in Louisiana, Arnold was deployed to Greece
for a NATO exercise. For this deployment, he wasn't the only Ebneter
scrambling: Colleen had still not learned how to drive a car. In Texas,
everything she needed had been within walking distance of our apart-
ments; but the house in Louisiana was across the railroad tracks and
three miles away from the base, along a busy state highway. Fortunately,
the family car had an automatic transmission. The quiet neighborhood

turned into an easy training ground, and Colleen passed her driving test just a few days before Arnold departed for his three-week trip.

Life at England soon turned into a series of hectic rotations from the United States to Europe, the Middle East, and eventually Southeast Asia, although some of Arnold's trips sounded more like cruise ship itineraries than military deployments, with stops at the South Carolina coast, Bermuda, the Azores, and Spain. Departures and arrivals, however, always seemed to occur at uncruiselike early hours of the morning, with my mother and other wives dragging sleepy-eyed, pajama-clad toddlers to Base Operations, a building where their deploying husbands and fathers assembled before departing on military jets.

In August 1961, while Arnold was deployed to Incirlik Air Base in Turkey, the Cold War flared as East Germany built the Berlin Wall. President John F. Kennedy put the US military on high alert and mobilized more than one hundred thousand reservists. At the end of September, instead of flying back to the United States as planned, Arnold climbed into the back of a C-130 cargo aircraft and flew to Spangdahlem Air Base in Germany, where he joined other F-100 crews waiting for a battle if the Cold War stare-down failed.

In late October, the crisis cooled, and Arnold's return to Louisiana must have been a joyous reunion, because by December Colleen, despite her resistance to the idea of a fourth child, was pregnant again. Arnold had just made the final payment on his car, and with a bigger family on the way, he had an excuse to buy a bigger airplane. It wasn't long before he located a used Beechcraft Bonanza nearly identical to one in an ad he had drooled over fifteen years earlier while a student at Rensselaer. In addition to being able to carry two adults and four small children, the Bonanza had retractable landing gear and was much faster than the family Cessna 170.

The new airplane alarmed my sensibilities. Unlike our old airplane, which sat with its tail firmly on the ground, this new one sported a modern nose wheel so the airplane sat up straight, looking like a miniature Boeing airliner. I convinced myself this precarious-looking setup was going to tip over at any minute. The new airplane also had low wings instead of high ones, making it harder for my sisters and me to play under the wings during rest stops. None of this seemed good to me, but my parents were enchanted with their new purchase.

The Bonanza's registration number was N5125C, and my sisters and I soon appropriated the aviation pronunciation of the letter *C*—"Charlie"—as the airplane's name. And once something has a name, it's hard to get rid of it.

Most summers, we flew Charlie back to Minnesota and Wisconsin to visit my grandparents and cousins. We usually stopped for gas, restrooms, and Cokes at the airport in Paducah, Kentucky, and my sisters and I loved to exaggerate the pronunciation of "Pah-DOO-cah" in our southern drawls.

Summers also meant air shows, often at the base's "Open House" where Americans could see their tax dollars at work. My sisters and I meandered about with our parents and looked at the fighters, bombers, tankers, cargo planes, and helicopters on display, sometimes walking through the big ones and occasionally sitting in the cockpit of a small one. But with our parents both being pilots, we weren't particularly impressed with the airplanes; we had much more fun squishing the melted tar between the cracks in the concrete ramp. If it wasn't hot enough, all we could do was kick at the rock-hard substance, but when perfect squishiness arrived at a certain temperature, we could step on the black blobs and feel it oozing about under our shoes. After we took our feet away, the tar would magically return to its original shape. If it got too hot, a little clump of tar would stick to our shoes, and then we'd spend the rest of the afternoon scuffing our feet on the ramp, trying to scrape off the gunk.

Even as an adult, I like to step on blobs of soft tar at air shows.

* * *

My sister Kelly was born in July 1962, and save for a parade of cats, dogs, mice, various other small animals, and the occasional horse, our family was complete. Two months after Kelly's arrival, my father ventured back to Incirlik for what he assumed would be another routine deployment; but the United States again went into full crisis mode on October 16, when spy planes discovered Soviet missile sites in Cuba. After an agonizing two weeks on the brink of nuclear war, Khrushchev backed down and removed the offending missiles. However, the tension between the two countries remained high, and Arnold's squadron once again remained in place for an extended deployment. As the squadron maintenance officer, Arnold knew this would mean days of boredom punctuated by maintenance-check flights, which he cherished because that meant no annoying wingmen hanging around as he flew. A check flight usually took only fifteen or twenty minutes, so after finishing all the required maneuvers to make sure the mechanics had fixed the airplane, he had plenty of time to play over the Turkish countryside. All alone, he could dive to a few hundred feet above the desert valley, where, blazing along at more than six hundred miles per hour, he lit the afterburner and pulled hard, rolling out thirty seconds later at twenty-five thousand feet for a mountain-peak view without all the hard work to get to the top. During one flight, he stumbled on the town of Urgup and its ten-mile-long valley filled with yellow, black, and brown limestone "inverted caves" that ancient people had carved into a half dozen small cities. The surreal juxtaposition of his high-tech fighter and the Martian-like valley left him with few words to describe it in a letter home to Colleen.

The Berlin Wall and Cuban missile crises were just warm-ups for the rest of the turbulent 1960s. In March 1965, President Lyndon Johnson approved Operation Rolling Thunder, bombings of North Vietnam intended to put pressure on the communist government to stop its support of Viet Cong fighters in South Vietnam. On March 17, Arnold and his squadron flew to Da Nang, South Vietnam, for a three-month deployment.

One month after he arrived in Southeast Asia, the air force selected Arnold to earn his master's degree from the Air Force Institute of Technology at Wright-Patterson Air Force Base. His bachelor's degree hadn't opened doors as he'd hoped; he used some of his new skills in his duties as a maintenance officer, but the air force considered him a pilot, not an engineer. His hopes for test pilot school at Edwards Air Force Base had been dashed shortly after he got his bachelor's degree—the maximum age for attendees was thirty-three, and he never even had a chance to apply. If he couldn't be a test pilot, maybe with a master's degree he could lead the design of a new airplane for the air force.

With all the deploying and training during his five years in Louisiana, Arnold had done nothing to further his hoped-for record-breaker other than occasional tinkering with the retractable landing gear. He had yet to find a design that worked—the ones he had envisioned were either too heavy, too complicated, or both. He began to worry that the retractable gear might not be worth the effort and expense; and he didn't own any basic power tools, let alone a sophisticated machine that could produce parts with the tight tolerances required by retractable gear. Perhaps fixed gear wouldn't produce that big of a drag penalty; but he yearned for the sleek look that retractable gear would give his record setter, and he didn't want to give up yet. He was sure the engineer in him would find a solution.

Once he'd settled into his graduate-school routine in Ohio, Arnold again had to set aside his hopes of refining his student project design—classes, studying, flying Charlie on the weekends, and flying an Air Force T-33 once a week left him with no extra time. His record-setting design languished in notebooks and in his head.

While Arnold was at school, the Vietnam War continued to escalate. Although the air force had originally planned to assign him to a research job after he finished his degree, new rules dictated that he return to Vietnam to finish the one-year rotation now required of all pilots. Before he went back to Vietnam, we moved to Phoenix, Arizona, for my father's F-100 retraining at nearby Luke Air Force Base. He put his record setter and engineering career on hold once again.

* * *

While my father was in Vietnam, my mother slept with a steak knife under her pillow. My three sisters and I shared her bed—my youngest sister every night, and the rest of us taking turns joining them on a rotating schedule. We didn't think much about the knife—it seemed a necessary defense, along with the German shepherd–collie mutt my father bought before he left. He also picked up a black-and-white kitten named Patrick.

There were only a few other military families in our Phoenix neighborhood, which lay thirty minutes by car from the base. In those days, if a military member was deployed for more than six months, his or her family couldn't live on base.

My mother told us not to tell anyone our father was in Vietnam. The war had become unpopular, and students and others all over the world protested US involvement.

Even without my mother's cautions, my father's departure from Phoenix made me realize this one was different from his previous absences. Instead of heading for Base Operations at Luke, we drove to Sky Harbor Airport in Phoenix, where he boarded a civilian jetliner; he was the only person on the plane going to Vietnam. My mother cried, the only time I ever saw her in tears when he left.

My older sister, perhaps understanding the consequences of combat better than my younger sisters and me, prayed every day when we walked home from school that there wouldn't be an official blue air force car in our driveway, come to deliver bad news.

I was ten, and my job was to interpret symbols on maps and find freeway exits for my mother as we drove to shopping malls in Phoenix. My mother, despite having never gotten lost while flying all over Minnesota using nothing more than a map and compass, could never master a Rand-McNally road atlas.

* * *

Arnold had flown Charlie as much as he could during the Christmas holiday before he left for Vietnam. After that the plane would go into storage: with four children competing for the time Colleen needed in order to learn to fly the faster and more complex Bonanza, she had let her piloting skills lapse, so Charlie would be relegated to a hangar for nine months, like a horse patiently awaiting his rider's return. His new home was a little airport named Litchfield Park, located just south of Luke. The airport owner had a crop-dusting business and didn't rent hangars for a living, but a soft spot for military pilots must have led him to allow Charlie in. He even conducted a required annual inspection on the airplane at no cost to Arnold.

Arnold arrived in the Philippines on January 26, 1968, to attend a jungle survival course; and on January 30, as he wrapped up training, the North Vietnamese launched the Tet Offensive, a major ground operation that wreaked havoc with the well-tuned air force schedule. At first, the air force halted all flights to, from, and inside Vietnam not directly related to combat operations. A few days later, Arnold finally landed in Vietnam on a flaming orange Boeing 707 airliner operated by Braniff. A large, brightly colored airplane made an attractive target, and the Braniff pilots didn't shut the engines down after they landed; Arnold and the other troops streamed off the airplane while outbound passengers fought to climb on. Even with the bedlam caused by nearly three hundred bodies toting duffle bags colliding in all directions, the orange target was airborne again in ten minutes.

The next day, Arnold landed at Tuy Hoa Air Base and checked in with his new unit, the 308th Tactical Fighter Squadron, nicknamed the

"Emerald Knights," complete with bright green scarves and patches. While Arnold had been at school, tactics and weapons had evolved in Vietnam. Surpassed by the F-4 and other new fighters, the F-100 was now largely relegated to bombing missions, called "close air support," to help US Army forces in South Vietnam. For a close air support mission, F-100 pilots took off in flights of two or three and contacted a command post, nicknamed "Surfside," who then provided a rendezvous point in the sky. After reaching that point, the flight contacted a forward air controller, who gave further instructions, depending on who needed help on the ground. The forward air controllers normally flew in small, low-powered airplanes and fired rockets that exploded with a small fireworks display over a target, leaving a smoke trail for the F-100 pilots to follow.

On February 18, Arnold's routine flight ended in a shootout when an army unit defending a Special Forces camp ran into trouble. As Arnold's flight arrived on the scene, the enemy welcomed them with heavy anti-aircraft artillery. Smoke obliterated the pilots' view of the battlefield, and the hostile troops were so close to the friendly forces that it was almost impossible for the fast-moving pilots to distinguish between them. The pilots were stuck in the "friction of war," a term introduced in Carl von Clausewitz's nineteenth-century treatise *On War*—in this case, a stray bomb might kill friendly forces; but if they did nothing, the North Vietnamese would likely overrun the Special Forces camp.

Artillery shells whizzing around him, Arnold spotted what he was sure were enemy troops and dove into the fray to drop his bombs. The cockpit of the F-100 was a cocoon separating him from the pandemonium below, and the scene was familiar—it looked and felt just like the hundreds of practice bombings he had made during training. He'd never been shot at before, but he was flying so fast, and was so focused on his target, that he paid no attention to the murderous bits of metal streaking by him. According to the citation that accompanied the Distinguished Flying Cross that the air force awarded him for this flight, he "delivered his bombs with pinpoint accuracy" and the North Vietnamese retreated. However, Arnold knew that almost everyone received this award at some point during his tour. In fact, the air force tended to pick an action for the award as soon as possible, so pilots wouldn't do something stupid later in their deployment in an effort to get the medal.

*   *   *

Tuy Hoa in 1968 was very different from the Vietnam Arnold had left nearly three years earlier. As the stalemate dragged on, the air force settled in for the long haul and, except for the lack of base housing and families, Tuy Hoa facilities rivaled any stateside base. The pilots had private rooms in air-conditioned trailers, although they were usually too busy to enjoy the nice quarters. During the Tet Offensive, Arnold and his fellow pilots flew two or three times a day; and even late at night the base sounded like Chicago-O'Hare during rush hour—a cacophony of maintenance trucks zipping up and down the flight line, F-100 engines whining as they taxied before announcing their takeoff with a roar, and the low-pitched throbbing of C-130 cargo airplane propellers during engine run-ups.

Despite the continuous flying, Arnold was determined to keep his engineering skills sharp, even if he couldn't practice on real airplanes. In a letter home, he asked Colleen to find all the model airplane engines he had stashed around the house and send them to Vietnam, where he and several other pilots attached them to two-foot-long model airplanes they had built.

Unlike the real airplanes the pilots flew, their models spent more time crashing than flying. One pilot's P-40 initially looked promising as it wobbled around in two circles, but a few seconds later the model entered a loop and then dove onto the concrete ramp, smashing itself to bits.

At least the P-40 got off the ground. After watching Tuy Hoa's soft sand ruin a dozen models as they tried to take off and land, Arnold decided to put the biggest tires he could find on his model. The gawky result looked like flying landing gear with a biplane attached, but the *Tuy Hoa Sandhopper* survived.

By early July, the Tet Offensive had petered out, US marines had abandoned Khe Sahn, and US and allied forces began chasing the North Vietnamese Army around the countryside again. Most of Arnold's flights became routine "tree-busting" missions to clear out trees and brush so that helicopters carrying ground forces could land. During his spare time, he negotiated via letter with my mother regarding our plans for a month-long driving expedition to Minnesota and Wisconsin.

In the early morning hours of July 29, 1968, as we prepared for our cross-country drive, Viet Cong attacked Tuy Hoa. At 1:37 A.M., a sapper squad detonated a satchel charge that woke up the entire base. US security forces counterattacked as rescue crews pushed airplanes to safety and battled flames that engulfed two C-130 transport aircraft. Gunships from a nearby base joined the melee, feeding flares and additional smoke into the disarray on the ramp.

While US and Korean ground forces fought the assault, Arnold and the other pilots raced out of their rooms and milled about for a few minutes, hoping to be useful. Then someone pointed out that, since their only weapons were .38-caliber pistols, maybe it would be best if they jumped into a nearby bunker and stayed out of the way. They all agreed and scurried to the shelter, where they stayed for the rest of the fight.

The next day, we watched the attack on TV. Since an official car hadn't pulled up to tell us otherwise, we assumed my father was okay, and we headed east.

Two days later, my father learned that for his next assignment he was to be an aeronautical engineer at the Air Force Armament Laboratory at Eglin Air Force Base in the Florida Panhandle. This was the sort of news that warranted a phone call home, using the Military Auxiliary Radio System to patch across the Pacific; but we were somewhere between Albuquerque and Oklahoma City. While he waited for us to get to Minnesota, he dreamed about converting his Texan and Cajun daughters into Gators and plotted the trip from Phoenix to Eglin, with stops in Victoria, Texas, and Alexandria, Virginia, to see old friends. He would miss flying the F-100, but his new assignment should have regular working hours and fewer deployments. Now he could really get some building done and find out if his design would work.

Arnold counted the days to his final flight on October 1, not knowing that this flight would also be the last time he ever climbed into an F-100. After he landed, the other pilots in his squadron toasted him with a bottle of champagne. He decided the occasion merited a glass and indulged. He had survived 224 combat flights intact, while receiving only two holes in his airplane. It was time to head back to his family, flying Charlie, building his world-record airplane, and eating my mother's everyday breakfast of fried eggs, toast, and bacon.

*   *   *

With the Air Force Armament Laboratory, an Army Ranger Camp, and two units flying F-4s and other jets, Eglin Air Force Base teemed with activity. Jets screeched overhead at all hours as they headed off to drop bombs on a range or launch missiles over the Gulf of Mexico. Arnold was no longer making the noise, but he was happy to have a job as a real engineer.

The dream job soon fell apart. He was primarily an advocate for the lab's funding in the Pentagon's budget process, a job that Arnold's bosses considered a prestigious position in the air force food chain. Arnold longed to work on the design of a weapon instead. He initially thought some flying on the side might make up for the disappointing job, but the F-100s that belonged to the test wing were reserved for the test pilots. He settled for a C-54, a lumbering cargo airplane with four engines, four propellers, and four crewmembers.

With the air force apparently determined to waste his engineering skills, my father turned to designing a new seat for Charlie. The Bonanza could carry four adults, so Maureen, Kathleen, and I would normally squeeze into the two backseats, and Kelly would sit on my mother's lap. With us growing taller, that wasn't going to work much longer. While at Tuy Hoa, he had sketched out a bench seat to install in the baggage compartment for my younger sisters, and he now filled in the design details, borrowed a welding kit to make the frame, and found a local upholsterer to make the cushions. After getting the FAA to bless his design and installation, he took us up for the seat's maiden flight. The howls from the back of the airplane soon after takeoff made him realize he had missed something. In his zeal to design the seat, he had forgotten about my sister's requirement: there was no window in Charlie's baggage compartment. A few days later, he ordered a window kit from Beechcraft, the Bonanza's manufacturer. Charlie would serve for a few more years as a family airplane, at least until my sisters and I all grew to more than one hundred pounds each.

A decade after graduating from Texas A&M, Arnold finally acquired some parts for his homebuilt airplane: a used engine and propeller he bought for one hundred dollars from a lieutenant who owned a J-3 Cub. The engine, a sixty-five-horsepower Lycoming model, was an antique even in 1970, and parts were hard to come by, but it was still a great deal. My father stored the engine in Charlie's hangar at the Crestview Airport, about thirty miles north of Eglin, and brought the wooden propeller home to protect it from the humidity. It fit nicely under the double bed in the master bedroom.

Arnold cleared off his drafting table and started laying out detailed plans for his airplane. His conceptual design had been just an idea and

Fig. 8.1. The original propeller for the E-1, second from the top, 2012.

some initial calculations about the art of the possible. Now he had to define the details that would make everything work—exactly what materials to use, how to assemble the airplane, how to build the retractable landing gear, and most important, how to keep the airplane as light as possible. Each individual detail, too, had many additional pieces—subsystems, components, preparation, tools, and so forth—and many of those pieces interacted, so that changing even one detail often led to changes in myriad other parts of the airplane. If he altered the material for the wing, he would have to modify the way it attached to the fuselage; if he used a different engine, the new shape and power level would require a change in the cowling and exhaust system, among other things.

He first focused on designing the retractable landing gear to reduce the parasite drag on the plane. Designers take advantage of the induced drag from the wing to help an airplane slow down for landing, but parasite drag is just a nuisance. And while induced drag mostly disappears at high airspeeds, parasite drag increases with the square of the airplane's speed, so an airplane flying at 160 mph has four times as much drag as it would at only 80 mph. Low-speed airplanes don't need much defense against parasite drag, because the penalty isn't very high, but designers of high-speed aircraft obsess over reducing parasite drag because the payoff is huge. Every extra bit of drag at high speed either lowers the airplane's top speed or requires additional thrust to maintain the top speed. Bigger engines don't always help; they usually weigh more and may require a bigger cowling, which in turn has more drag, setting up a relentless design battle.

The best way to reduce parasite drag is to streamline the airplane as much as possible, and most airplanes that fly faster than about 150 mph have retractable landing gear. An airplane that flies slower than about 120 mph will almost never have retractable landing gear, since the small benefit does not compensate for the extra complexity and weight. Instead, low-speed aircraft often use wheel pants and other fairings to streamline the gear.

Arnold's airplane was in a design gray area, flying between about 120 and 150 mph, where the tradeoffs aren't so clear. In his original design, Arnold had calculated he could save about fifty pounds of drag by building retractable gear, and he had been sure he could design a mechanism that weighed less than ten pounds. But like many things in engineering, the solution wasn't as easy as it at first appeared to be. In addition to bringing the gear up and down, the mechanism had to have a backup system; and the whole system required a handle or knob in the cockpit and associated plumbing, along with lights or some other indication that the gear was working right. The gear itself would also be heavier than fixed gear, due to the hinges and linkages that enabled the gear to fold into the fuselage or underneath the wing.

While Arnold grappled with the gear, he drew dozens of designs, carefully plotting the outline of each part on vellum drawing paper and making hundreds of calculations to estimate weights. To get new ideas, he spent hours researching the landing gear on other airplanes and examining the gear on airplanes he saw at air shows. Nothing worked; his designs were all too heavy, but he was sure it was just a matter of time until he hit on the right solution.

Although the landing gear seemed to have an infinite number of possible combinations of sizes, shapes, components, and materials, decisions about the wing were more pedestrian. In 1970, engineers still had a limited set of materials for building an airplane—mostly wood, aluminum, and steel tubing with fabric, although composite materials were entering homebuilt markets.

Arnold's original design called for a "wet wing," an aluminum wing that he would seal so it could serve as the fuel tank. It would be easier to build separate fuel tanks and make sure they didn't leak before he installed them in the wings, but that would add weight to the airplane and wouldn't let him use the full volume of the wing for carrying fuel. However, his wet wing posed other problems.

Ribs and spars made from aluminum are easy to build, but attaching an aluminum skin to the ribs requires hundreds, even thousands, of small fasteners called rivets. Each rivet needs a small hole in both the skin and the rib, and every hole creates the potential for a fuel leak in a wet wing.

Arnold figured he had two ways to fortify the wing against fuel leaks. He could dab sealant on every rivet and other possible openings, or he could encase the entire wing in fiberglass. The sealant would weigh less and be tedious to apply, but the fiberglass wasn't a surefire answer. He had no experience working with fiberglass, and even something as simple as covering the wing could have disastrous results if he didn't do it right. He also wasn't sure how well the fiberglass would hold up when attacked by gasoline, so he decided to use the sealant, a decision that would come back to haunt him thirty years later.

Although happy with the design changes and refinements to his record setter, Arnold found it impossible to start building the airplane. He still didn't have any tools, and with no garage and six people crammed into three bedrooms, he had no place to build. Charlie's hangar at the Crestview airport was an option, but there wasn't much room available with Charlie already in there, and Crestview was a forty-five-minute drive from Eglin. That might work for one day each weekend, but a ninety-minute round-trip in the evenings in order to work for only an hour or so didn't seem efficient.

Even if he had found tools and a place to build, Arnold was, by late 1970, delivering C-54s to various locations around the globe, trips that once again took him away from home for weeks at a time. When he wasn't ferrying airplanes, he was busy maintaining his military pilot proficiency, mostly by flying at night and on the weekends so he could work a full schedule at the lab.

It was starting to look like the propeller under the bed would stay there.

9

Young Aviation Turks

Through the homebuilder the cumulative growth of many minds,
working toward a common goal, add much to general aviation technology. New ideas, spawned by you, the homebuilder, germinate
from the faintest desire into dreams; and these dreams become
reality.

Richard Killingsworth, Chief Master Sergeant, US Air Force
(Retired), designer and builder of the DSK-1 Hawk, 1974

BY THE MID-1960S, HOMEBUILDERS HAD STILL NOT MADE THE GREAT
contributions to aircraft development that Leslie Long, Paul Poberezny,
and others had envisioned. Peter Bowers's award-winning Fly Baby was
a nice design, but its wood construction and single seat could hardly
be called a giant leap in technology, and the other 140 or so Buttercups,
Cougars, Tailwinds, Baby Aces, Pietenpols, Playboys, Midget Mustangs,
and other models at the 1962 fly-in implied that homebuilding was more
about variety than innovation. For Bob Whittier, who chronicled the fly-
in during the 1960s, the variety resulted from initiative made possible by
the freedom exercised by individuals in the United States. Amateur builders weren't just bystanders who watched others exercise their freedoms,
but were instead active participants, citizens with an "uncommon degree
of individualism, ambition and perseverance." The fulfillment of the right
to build wasn't just about the desire to make something, but was almost
demanded as a patriotic duty to those who had given their lives for that
freedom and pursuit of happiness.

As innovation limped along, a minicraze developed for new homebuilt
designs wrapped around converted automobile engines, a source that had

largely been abandoned a decade earlier for the sturdier, certified aircraft counterparts. Amateurs now sought out the newer technologies and lower acquisition and operating costs of auto engines, especially the flat, air-cooled Volkswagen and Corvair engines, which were aircraft-engine look-alikes. New VW-powered designs abounded, including the exotic-sounding Sonerai and a multitude of racers.

The number of aluminum designs, too, grew steadily during the 1960s. Despite the availability of aluminum as a building material since before World War II, and its use on almost all modern factory-built airplanes, many homebuilders were slow to accept the material. For one thing, aluminum could be expensive. For another, it required specialized tools, although the basic tools weren't expensive. Mostly, many designers didn't understand aluminum and were skeptical of the material. With wood, you could look at it and see if it was aircraft quality: guidelines and standards specified the acceptable distance between tree growth rings, the number of knots, and so forth. How were you supposed to know if your piece of aluminum was any good? Although manufacturers use strictly controlled processes to ensure aluminum quality, many homebuilders seemed to prefer nature's uncontrolled processes, and only a handful of the two major aluminum designs from the 1950s, John Thorp's T-18 and Robert Bushby's Midget Mustang, showed up at the fly-in each year during the 1960s. However, a new generation of designers graduating from college in the 1950s and 1960s had no qualms about metal or even composites. Armed with engineering degrees, textbooks, and slide rules, young designers churned out airplanes that produced eye-popping performance numbers and were easy to fly and build, to boot. Ladislao Pazmany, an immigrant from Yugoslavia by way of Argentina, introduced the amateur-built PL-2, a two-seat aluminum aerobatic aircraft with enough range for cross-country flying, a design adopted by the air forces of several Asian countries as a trainer.

In 1968, the twenty-five hundred amateur-built aircraft registered in the United States surpassed the number of transport aircraft operated by the airlines, and the annual EAA fly-in evolved as well. With nearly a half million participants, an on-airport campground the size of a small town, and night air shows, the one-week event had worn out its welcome with the Rockford Airport manager. When Rockford city officials threatened to raise rents and curb flying, Steve Wittman convinced EAA officials to come to Oshkosh, which he had long advocated as the best place for the fly-in. Poberezny had tried Oshkosh one year in the 1950s, but chaos had ensued when he invited too many other flying organizations to join the event. After a successful Oshkosh fly-in in 1970, a twelve-year lease with the city of Oshkosh sealed the deal, and the EAA began constructing permanent buildings at the airport in order to teach classes on various aircraft construction techniques: welding steel tubing, cutting and gluing wood, riveting sheet metal, and covering aircraft with fabric.

In 1972, homebuilders finally got some of the futuristic designs they had been longing for. The fly-in spread out a buffet of tasty-looking new airplanes that mixed and matched every possible engine and building technique: VW-powered designs such as Ken Rand's composite construction KR-1; Bob MacDonald's S-2 and Pazmany's PL-4A, both made from aluminum; at least four new tube-and-fabric biplanes that used certified engines; and the stars of the show, two pusher airplanes—Jim Bede's aluminum BD-5 and Burt Rutan's wooden two-seat VariViggen—and Richard VanGrunsven's thoroughly conventional but aluminum RV-3.

Jim Bede had previously designed the BD-1, which evolved into the Yankee, an FAA-certified two-seater built by American Aircraft, and the BD-2, an aircraft he hoped to fly around the world nonstop, unrefueled. He never made the around-the-world flight, but he did set a closed-course distance record in 1969 in the C-1d weight class, flying back and forth for seventy hours nonstop between Columbus, Ohio, and Kansas City. Bede turned those design experiences into the four-seat BD-4, which he offered in 1969 with a kit touted as requiring only nine hundred hours of construction time using basic hand tools most homeowners would have, such as a ¼-inch drill. Bede claimed his "bolt-together fuselage and patented Panel-Rib construction" meant a builder could turn out a wing during a long weekend. Far beyond the ordinary materials kit, the BD-4 had everything a builder would need, including prefabricated fiberglass parts, welded steel fixtures, nuts, bolts, and even the seat belts. Some thought a four-seat airplane shifted homebuilding from sport aviation to transportation, and still others thought the "erector set" kit flouted FAA rules. But Bede insisted that the builder still had to provide 80 percent of the labor; the FAA agreed and approved the kit in 1973.

With the BD-4 featured almost monthly in *Sport Aviation*, a homebuilding newcomer could easily get the impression that everyone was building a Bede plane, but Bede had moved on to an even bigger idea—a one-person pusher that would cruise faster than two hundred miles per hour using a fuel-sipping engine. He envisioned flying the BD-5 from California to Illinois nonstop on less than thirty dollars' worth of fuel. Bede brought the yet-to-fly prototype on a trailer to Oshkosh in 1971 to show off to the eight hundred customers who had already plunked down two-hundred-dollar deposits for the aircraft based solely on information packets. BD-5 fever was already spreading faster than a lethal virus.

Powered by a thirty-six-horsepower Polaris snowmobile engine, the BD-5 prototype flew on September 12, 1971. The version Bede planned to sell used a German-produced Hirth engine and first flew on July 11, 1972, theoretically far enough in advance to collect the flying time required by the FAA to demonstrate the plane at Oshkosh in 1972. But failures besieged the Hirth: pieces separated from each other in flight, fuel lines pinched off gasoline to the cylinders, and the engine somehow ingested foreign matter. Oshkosh attendees settled for white jackets emblazoned with black-and-red trim and the BD logo, along with films of the airplane flying over Kansas that left them drooling. The collection of kits and parts Bede brought with him enticed many pilots, and even some nonpilots, to fork over deposits and down payments for kits, a decision many would later regret as Bede transformed into one of the most polarizing figures in homebuilding history. Supporters considered him a visionary genius who could revolutionize not just homebuilding but all of aviation; detractors considered him an aviation snake-oil salesman. But in 1972, all things seemed possible.

Burt Rutan began working on his first design, the VariViggen, in 1963 while still an aeronautical engineering student at California State Polytechnic College. The all-wood VariViggen, named after a Swedish fighter airplane that used similar design elements, was so far from being a conventional airplane that it left reporters searching for words to describe it. Not only was the audacious airplane a pusher, but also it used canards—pitch control surfaces on the front of the airplane instead of the back. Although many early airplanes, including the Wright Flyer, used canard configurations, it didn't take designers long to realize that control surfaces in the back worked better. Yet here was an airplane that defied that logic.

After graduating from Cal Poly, Rutan worked as a performance engineer on the F-4 and F-15 fighter airplanes at the Air Force Flight Test Center at Edwards Air Force Base. In his spare time, he finished the VariViggen design and tested it using a one-fifth scale model in an improvised

Fig. 9.1. Jim Bede's BD-5, 1970s.

Fig. 9.2. Burt Rutan flying his VariViggen, 1970s.

"wind tunnel" fashioned from a rack clamped to the luggage carrier of a station wagon. The residents of Lancaster, California, where he lived, were used to odd goings-on at the base, so it's unlikely anyone looked twice at the spectacle of a station wagon barreling down a dusty road topped with a bizarre-looking airplane that seemed to commit a multitude of sins against the laws of aerodynamics.

Rutan completed the VariViggen in his garage in Lancaster in early 1972, but he had to wait a bit to fly it—he had accepted Jim Bede's offer to make him director of development testing at Bede's company in Newton, Kansas. After moving to Kansas, Rutan squeezed in enough testing on the VariViggen to fly it at Oshkosh, where it won the Most Outstanding Design award. Whenever it took to the skies, all motion on the ground ceased as the crowd glued their eyes to the airplane whose science-fiction look earned it a role in the 1975 film *Death Race 2000*, an apocalyptic satire featuring five hotrods and drivers who earned points for killing pedestrians as they raced from New York to California. Rutan fans would have to endure more than an hour of bad acting and gratuitous violence to see the VariViggen, which portrayed a French enemy aircraft that met its demise by crashing in a fireball after being outmaneuvered by a car driven by David Carradine.

Richard VanGrunsven, nicknamed "Van," arrived at Oshkosh 1972 from Oregon in his new RV-3, an all-aluminum airplane that was the most conventional-looking of the debut craft. In 1962, with the hoopla surrounding the design competition, few people had noticed the Stits Playboy that Van had flown to the Rockford fly-in from Michigan, where he was stationed at Kincheloe Air Force Base. Vision problems had kept the then twenty-three-year-old out of air force pilot training—he'd served instead as a communications officer for three years—but he had earned his civilian commercial and flight instructor certificates by the time he graduated from Portland University with an engineering degree. Van had grown up immersed in Oregon's rebellious homebuilding culture, and his father had learned to fly at Leslie Long's field, located three miles from the VanGrunsven family home, so Van knew George Bogardus and had heard many stories about Long.

Van had joined the EAA at seventeen, in 1957, but attending college and serving in the air force gave him no time or space to build his own airplane, so he purchased a Playboy from another builder not long before the 1962 fly-in. He soon sold that Playboy and bought a damaged one with no engine. In addition to repairing the second Playboy and attaching a 125-horsepower Lycoming O-290G engine, he improved the airplane's performance and handling qualities by adding new wingtips, a larger tail, and several new fiberglass parts—an engine cowling, propeller spinner, and wheel pants. He also added a bubble canopy, a type of canopy that projects beyond the sides of the cockpit. In comparison to a canopy set flush with the cockpit, it enables the pilot to move his or her head around more and see better.

After fifteen months spent modifying his Playboy, and eighteen months of flying it, Van decided to reduce the plane's weight. The nose was especially heavy, which meant he had to pull harder on the stick to rotate the plane skyward for takeoff and landing. It was a good airplane, but he thought he could do better.

By now out of the air force and employed as an engineer back in Oregon, Van designed a new wing. Two struts on each side of the wing in Ray Stits's original design might have looked like toothpicks compared to the rest of the airplane, but the skinny pieces still added weight and drag. Van discarded the struts and moved his new wing somewhat forward on the fuselage, which reduced the nose-heaviness and let him trim twelve pounds of ballast from the tail. After installing new landing gear and making a few other modifications, he had shaved eighty-five pounds from the airplane, which now cruised at 148 mph, 13 mph faster than the original, and needed only three hundred feet to stop after landing—half the original distance. Van designated his new airplane—which now bore only a passing resemblance to the original Playboy—the RV-1, the "1" indicating his optimism that future airplane designs would also use his initials.

Van put the plans for his RV-1 on the market as a Stits Playboy modification, but only one other RV-1 was ever built. Then someone sweet-talked him into selling his RV-1; Van hated to lose the airplane, but giving it up motivated him to come up with something better. Starting from scratch, he designed an airplane about the same size as the Playboy but different in every detail, particularly in the use of aluminum, which Van thought was the best material for building an airplane.

By building a nearly perfectly smooth wing and fuselage and adding fiberglass fairings everywhere possible to further reduce drag, Van squeezed so much performance out of what some denigrated as an "archaic airfoil" that the RV-3 won the 1972 Oshkosh fly-in's "Best Aerodynamic Detailing Features" trophy and went on, in 1973, to win an "efficiency contest." The RV-3 was speedy in flight, but Van had to operate out of a 670-foot-long runway at his private airport, so he also added flaps and a set of unique "drooped ailerons" that added lots of drag when needed for making short landings.

In addition to introducing new airplanes, the 1972 event also showed why the EAA had by then become the second-largest association for pilots in the United States, despite its roots as a refuge for quirky aviation addicts. Inspired by the lure of new designs and the EAA's approach to affordable flying, aviation aficionados descended on Oshkosh in droves to worship at the Poberezny church that promised better aviation. More than five thousand aircraft landed at some point during the fly-in, and most had been built in factories, not garages.

Economics seemed to drive the sudden interest in homebuilt aircraft—one manufacturer reportedly spent nine million dollars to certify a four-seat airplane to the FAA's satisfaction, which meant that the certification costs alone worked out to eighteen thousand dollars per airplane if five hundred airplanes could be sold. Adding in the manufacturing costs and profit meant that the airplane would cost well more than that, probably at least forty thousand dollars, well out of reach for most pilots, given that a decent suburban house cost about thirty thousand dollars.

For a homebuilt aircraft, each builder provided the labor and had only to satisfy the FAA that the single airplane he or she built was safe to fly. Even better, the FAA would usually let the builder perform the maintenance on the airplane, further reducing ownership and operating costs.

A cottage industry sprang up to meet the needs of homebuilders, who had once struggled to find parts. More than fifty exhibitors displayed wares at Oshkosh in 1972, selling aircraft plans, instruments, radios, engines, landing gear, fabric, paints, and even insurance.

With the FAA's blessing, in 1973, of both the BD-4 and BD-5 kits, builders could now buy a kit with confidence that the resulting airplane would qualify for certification as an experimental amateur-built plane. Other designers with plans and materials kits took note, and a new race was on.

* * *

In 1975, a new Burt Rutan airplane, the VariEze, pronounced "very easy," was the star of the Oshkosh fly-in. The VariViggen from 1972 had been just an appetizer for the main course, and hearts pounded and jaws dropped as pilots spotted the new model and deliriously proclaimed, "That's it! That's what I've been waiting for!"

Even though Rutan had intended to use the VariEze only for research on canards, pilots thought it was everything they wanted: a speedy, easy-to-build, exotic-looking airplane with two seats and better range than the VariViggen. Many pusher designs had suffered from excess vibration, but since the VariEze, like the VariViggen, did not have a conventional tail in the way, Rutan was able to bolt the propeller directly to an engine mounted in the very back of the fuselage, preventing the vibration problem in his design. Without a pilot and passenger in place, the tail-heavy airplane was prone to tipping back, so Rutan added a nose gear that retracted once the plane was on the ground, forcing it to kneel and leading some to compare the VariEze to a camel.

The VariEze was much more than an improved version of the VariViggen. The newer airplane used composite materials that slashed construction time by two-thirds or more. Composites also allowed for smooth surfaces and complicated curves not possible with fabric, tubing, wood, or aluminum, at least not with the tools most homebuilders had. Like the BD-5, the VariEze supposedly could fly nonstop from California to Illinois for only thirty dollars' worth of fuel; and when Rutan designed the airplane, he had in mind a plan to break some of Lesher's records.

Designer Ken Rand had introduced composite construction using polystyrene foam in his KR-1 airplane, on display at the 1972 EAA fly-in, but his technique used a mix of wood and composite pieces made from foam and a boat-repair cloth, called Dynel, that could stretch in any direction. Rand made composite "sandwiches" by epoxying a layer of Dynel over a piece of foam cut and sanded to the shape of the part, resulting in a very light yet strong part that wouldn't corrode like aluminum, rust like steel, or rot like fabric and wood.

Rutan took composite construction to the next level. Except for a few specialized pieces such as the landing gear and canopy, everything on the VariEze was made from composites. Rutan used a hot wire to carve his foam to the correct shape and then covered it with two layers of unidirectional cloth placed at right angles to each other. The wing was built by first laying up the spar, adding a few rib templates, and then carving the rest of the wing with the hot wire.

The new technique was inexpensive, easy, and fast; reportedly, a wing could be built in two days. Builders might have a flying airplane in a few

Fig. 9.3. Gary Hertzler with the VariEze he built, photographed in about 2010.

months instead of a year or more and didn't need expensive power tools such as band saws and rivet guns. Buyers lined up in droves, but they would have to wait a bit. The VariEze that Rutan brought to Oshkosh was only proof of a concept, and it needed some improvements before he could offer plans for a working airplane.

Even though the plane's design was immature, Dick Rutan, an air force pilot, flew his little brother's VariEze during the fly-in to beat one of Lesher's world records, the distance over a closed course. For a closed-course record, the pilot flies several circuits around a fixed set of points on the ground, landing back at the point of departure, much like running laps around a state-size racetrack. Dick required two attempts to break the record: his first try resulted in an emergency landing in Green Bay when the Volkswagen engine blew up. Resourceful helpers scrounged a second Volkswagen engine from another airplane, slapped it on the VariEze, and two days later Dick tried again, this time breaking Lesher's record by more than 83 miles. The record didn't last long, though; a year later at Oshkosh, Leeon Davis, who had put his own record-seeking dream on hold during Lesher's quest, smashed Rutan's record by more than 600 miles to set a new C-1aI closed-course distance record of 2,263 miles.

Another engine failure and excessive maintenance convinced Burt Rutan to abandon the Volkswagen engine in the VariEze along with the C-1aI straight-line distance record; he couldn't count on the cranky engine to last for the flight's projected thirty hours. Instead, he improved the VariEze's design and added a certified engine, the Continental O-200. No longer working for Jim Bede, Rutan began selling VariEze plans in July 1976 from his company, Rutan Aircraft Factory, in Mojave, California. To make sure his builders knew how to use his simple but new construction technique, Rutan spent eight months traveling around the United States and Europe giving seminars. More than six hundred people showed up for his first class, near Saint Louis.

Rutan eventually added one more airplane to his homebuilt line, the Long-EZ, a larger version of the VariEze that operated in the heavier C-1b class for aviation records. On December 15, 1979, determined to set a record that would last more than one year, Dick Rutan departed the Mojave airport in a Long-EZ and, despite fatigue-induced hallucinations during the flight, landed safely more than thirty-three hours later back at Mojave. His 4,800 miles obliterated the previous closed-course record of 2,955 miles. Eighteen months later, a more fatigue-savvy Dick clobbered the C-1b straight-line distance record by flying 4,563 miles from Anchorage, Alaska, to Grand Turk Island in the Caribbean. Almost forty years later, both records still stand.

Five completed RV-3s appeared at Oshkosh in 1975. In addition to wowing crowds with formation flights, Van's airplanes looked the same, something unheard of in the homebuilding universe. With a plans-built airplane, every builder started with the same set of plans and materials, but construction techniques and finishing touches varied widely from airplane to airplane, making each a unique craft custom-built to the owner's specifications. However, with the RV-3, Van offered parts and a design that would be difficult to improve, resulting in airplanes that varied only in their paint jobs and instrument panels.

Some EAAers thought this uniformity was a good thing since it might improve safety, because builders were less likely to make ill-informed design changes. Purists thought the sameness was terrible, because the whole point of homebuilding was to make a unique product, not just copy someone else's, and standard designs might stifle innovation.

Even Van had doubts about his RV-3 compared to the better performing VariEze and BD-5, especially with builders snapping up four thousand or more of Rutan's plans and Bede's kits. But not everyone would want a pusher design, and some might shy away from composites. Van thought there might be a bit of a market for his own kits, so he pressed on and designed the RV-4, a two-seat version of the RV-3.

Van and others had been skeptical of Jim Bede's ability to deliver BD-5 kits, but the RV-3 designer didn't know his competition was about to implode. Bede had hoped to begin delivering engines by the end of September 1973, but the two-stroke Hirth continued to have problems, as predicted by many of Bede's detractors. Instead of the intake-compression-ignition/power-exhaust sequence of four-stroke engines, two-strokers—designed for chain saws, motorcycles, and snowmobiles—alternate rapidly between compression and power as they simultaneously intake and exhaust air. It's a great way to get a lot of power out of a little engine, but all those extra power strokes and the mingling of exhaust gases with intake air makes for extra heat and highly polluting blue smoke to deal with. Installed in the BD-5, the Hirths were prone to overheating and failures. And while the engines may have been cheap to purchase and operate, they had to be overhauled every three hundred hours of flying time, making them not much better than engines from the 1920s.

By 1975, a few BD-5s had been built and flown with the Hirth engine. A few other BD-5s used a modified Honda Civic engine that proved reliable; but Honda wasn't producing engines for Bede's customers, and builders were getting impatient. Adding to the engine woes, many BD-5 builders hadn't received their kits or had been shipped only partial kits.

Thinking he might distract the groundswell of disgruntled kit builders, Bede showed up at Oshkosh in 1975 with an even hotter and more improbable version of the BD-5: the jet-powered BD-5J. The jet model used a compact French TRS 18 engine that managed to produce two hundred pounds of thrust, about three times its sixty-six pounds of weight, not bad considering that the engines used on the best military fighters at the time produced thrust only about four times their engine weight. The US Air Force was intrigued enough by the BD-5J to bring one to Edwards Air Force Base for an evaluation, but test pilots found it wanting in the performance required to fly some basic maneuvers used for fighter training.

Bede's publicity director decided that a demonstration team of jets would be just the solution to keep up enthusiasm for the BD-5 while they sorted out problems with the propeller-driven version. Given that the Thunderbirds, the US Air Force's demonstration team, had recently traded in their gas-guzzling and noisy but crowd-pleasing F-4 fighters for fuel-efficient, whispery T-38 trainers that put on a less dramatic show, there was plenty of room for other jet teams to move into the air show scene. Debbie Gary, the only female airshow pilot in North America at the time, wound up on the team, along with Bob Bishop and Corkey Fornof, and they flew air shows during the summer of 1975, including at Oshkosh. Gary especially enjoyed traveling in Bede's DC-3, a cavernous tail-dragging cargo airplane built in the 1930s and 1940s that could swallow up all three BD-5Js, along with the pilots and support equipment.

The BD-5J air show team lasted only one summer, meeting its demise along with BD Aircraft. The microjet's hype couldn't staunch the propeller version's fiscal hemorrhaging, and Bede had bet the rest of the company on the microjet. Encouraged by Curtis Pitts's ability to get his homebuilt aerobatic biplanes certified for factory production, Bede had poured everything he had into qualifying for FAA certificates for the BD-5 and BD-5J. In 1979, with only about fifty BD-5s built and an estimated four thousand kits ordered, and no BD-5J certificate in sight, Bede declared bankruptcy. Since so many builders had never received their kits, many

Fig. 9.4. Richard VanGrunsven with an RV-4, photographed in about 1985.

suspected Bede had used their money to finance the BD-5J fiasco; and the bankruptcy court seemed to agree. Part of the settlement in 1988 required that Bede refrain from selling kit aircraft for at least another ten years. Even so, it was not the last time that Jim Bede's vision would outstrip the realities of the homebuilding market.

As Jim Bede slid into bankruptcy, Van flew the first flight of his two-seat RV-4. Builders may have lusted after both versions of the BD-5, but in the end the unsexy but still aerobatic and efficient RV-4 gave thousands of builders all over the world something that worked.

With flashy new designs and better kits, homebuilding began moving from the fringes of aviation toward the center, and even the manufacturers of factory-built aircraft took notice. A few small companies, such as Bellanca and Aero Commander, had been exhibiting their aircraft at the EAA fly-in since the mid-1960s, but larger companies, such as Beech and Mooney, had viewed homebuilders and their annual county-fair-like fly-in as a sideshow, not a serious market or venue. But after Oshkosh attendance surged past the half-million mark each year, the manufacturers could no longer stay away. With that many aviation-minded people showing up, surely a few of them might be interested in buying a production airplane. By the mid-1970s, the Big Four—Beech, Mooney, Cessna, and Piper—started hauling their latest models each year to Oshkosh, where their engineers, in addition to selling airplanes, prowled the home-built displays looking for innovations they could incorporate into production aircraft. Roy LoPresti, at one time the chief engineer for Mooney, reportedly got from a homebuilder the idea for smoothing the lip inside an air intake to reduce drag.

By the late 1970s, the stars seemed to be aligning for the homebuilding community. Designers offered more than two hundred kinds of aircraft kits and plans, including those for biplanes, monoplanes, replica fighters, hang gliders, helicopters, sailplanes, amphibians, and a new airplane that revolutionized homebuilding in a way that even Ed Heath would not have predicted.

*   *   *

As Burt Rutan and Richard VanGrunsven eked out some success, others paid an even higher price than Jim Bede for chasing their dreams. With homebuilding barriers falling, many fledgling aircraft designers, including one of Arnold's coworkers, caught the bug. Richard "Dick" Killingsworth, originally from Alabama, had risen to the rank of chief master sergeant, the top enlisted rank in the air force. Killingsworth had boundless ideas and the energy and talent to put them into practice. In the spring of 1973, he was one of about two dozen men nominated for a position at the Pentagon where he would have been the top enlisted advisor to the four-star general who ran the air force.

When he didn't get the prestigious job, Killingsworth decided to retire and sell aircraft kits. He had earned his pilot's license in his own airplane, a two-seat Cessna 150 trainer, even arranging for a local flight school to let him use his GI Bill to pay for much of the cost of the airplane during the training.

Like Arnold, Killingsworth used the license as the first step toward becoming an aircraft builder and designer, although he was more interested in making money than setting records. To get started, he bought a kit for an aluminum airplane called a "Jeanie's Teenie" that had been featured in *Popular Mechanics*. Before selling the Teenie kit to Killingsworth, the previous owner had put together the wing. Looking for a way to complete the partially assembled kit as quickly as possible, the chief hit upon a novel shortcut—he made the fuselage from a two-hundred-gallon bomb-shaped external fuel tank he'd pulled from an aircraft salvage yard in nearby Pensacola. After cutting a few holes in the tank, Killingsworth mated it to the wing and called his new creation the DSK-1 Hawk.

Arnold sold the Lycoming engine he had bought for possible use in his record setter to Killingsworth and did some stress analysis on the Hawk's design. He decided the airplane would hold together, although he cautioned Killingsworth that the fuel system could lead to an engine failure. If the airplane climbed too steeply, the fuel would run to the back of the tank and away from the valve that moved the fuel into the engine.

On May 26, 1973, Killingsworth flew his first flight in the Hawk. He spent a busy summer putting in the FAA-required fifty hours on the airplane and then took it to Oshkosh to display to potential kit buyers.

In 1974, the Hawk made both national and international aviation news with an article in *Popular Mechanics* and a mention in *Jane's All the World's Aircraft. Popular Mechanics* dubbed the airplane "the homebuilt you have to see to believe." Killingsworth had already received orders for more than 250 sets of plans, at fifty dollars each, produced by his company, DSK Airmotive. In addition to selling plans, he offered kits of materials and parts to builders. Realizing that some people didn't have ready access to surplus fuel tanks, he designed the DSK-2 Hawk II, which featured a fuselage built from aluminum. His wife was learning to fly, and he intended the Hawk II to be her airplane. He also had ambitious plans for a DSK-3 Falcon, which would be a stretched, two-seat tandem version of the Hawk, and a DSK-4 Eagle, a two-seat side-by-side airplane.

On April 12, 1975, as Killingsworth took off from Coastal Airport, a small grass strip located near Pensacola, the Hawk's engine quit and the plane crashed into trees off the end of the runway, killing the forty-four-year-old. In addition to his wife, he left behind five daughters and a son. The National Transportation Safety Board report cited a complete engine failure due to fuel starvation caused by an inadequate design. They noted that Killingsworth had made a maximum performance climb at an angle of about fifty degrees, the maneuver Arnold had warned against. DSK Airmotive soon folded, and only a handful of the airplanes "you ha[d] to see to believe" were ever built.

* * *

EAA members who turned to the last page of their February 1977 issue of *Sport Aviation* noticed a full-page black-and-white advertisement with the head of a bald eagle covering most of the page and the words "The Eagles Are Coming!" at the top. The person who placed the mysterious ad wasn't a mystery, given the Christen Industries logo at the bottom of the page. A Stanford graduate and pilot since he was a teenager, Frank Christensen had originally worked during the early days in what would become Silicon Valley, but left in 1972 to pursue his aerobatics and homebuilding interests. He loved flying Pitts biplanes, which by 1973 had transitioned from strictly homebuilts to factory-built aircraft, and he thought he could improve on Pitts's design even though it had already proved nearly unbeatable in aerobatic competitions.

Christensen developed an improved inverted oil system that let the Pitts, or any airplane for that matter, fly upside down indefinitely, as long as the fuel system still worked. The engines on airplanes used for normal flight have pickups for oil only at the bottom of the oil reservoir, called a sump; when these airplanes turn upside down, the oil falls to the top of the sump (which is now at the bottom of the inverted airplane) and the oil no longer enters the engine for cooling and lubrication. This is bad; fly like this for more than a few seconds and you can wreck the engine or worse. Christensen's improved design added pickups to the top of the oil sump and extra plumbing to make sure the oil would come from the right set of pickups: bottom for normal flight and top for inverted flight. He also developed a manual fuel pump and an improved canopy that fit the two-seat Pitts airplanes.

Christensen sold thousands of his new products to Pitts owners, but he still thought the airplanes had some problems, such as small cockpits and poor forward visibility. After unsuccessfully lobbying Curtis Pitts for some changes, Christensen hatched his Eagles, which he planned to unveil at the 1977 EAA fly-in.

In August, many fly-in attendees first sought out the six Rutan VariEzes that made it to Oshkosh and parked in a circle with their nose gears retracted, which some thought resembled a homebuilder prayer meeting. But with the first Eagle sighting, fickle builders abandoned the VariEzes to feast on Christen Industries' new design as pilot Bob Herendeen swooped down the flight line showing off the airplane's pop art paint scheme and aerobatic capabilities. Elsewhere on the field, an Eagle resting on a luxurious red carpet held court among visitors, who snatched

Fig. 9.5. Parts from the Christen Industries Eagle kit, 1970s.

up hundreds of slick marketing brochures housed in professionally designed display boards.

The Eagle was actually four different airplanes, single-seat and two-seat versions that could be purchased with two different engines. The Eagles were similar in performance to the Pitts aerobatic airplanes, but what set homebuilders buzzing were the kits, each composed of twenty-six separate packages that came with everything—prefabricated parts, materials, tools, and step-by-step manuals that made an Eagle less like a homebuilding project and more like assembling a very complicated piece of Ikea furniture. At the end of the one-week fly-in, Christen Industries had taken more than one hundred orders.

Some FAA inspectors at the fly-in looked warily at the hubbub surrounding the ostentatious little airplane. Surely, some of them thought, this kit with completed ribs and other fully formed parts can't possibly meet the rule adopted in 1962 that required an amateur builder to construct a "major portion" of the airplane, as in Jim Bede's kits.

After Oshkosh, Christensen met twice with an FAA official in Los

Angeles who believed the Eagle kits violated the "major portion" rule, also called the "51 percent" rule. It was up to Christensen to prove the FAA wrong, but his computer programmer who analyzed the kit contents found that, indeed, builders would construct less than half the airplane. However, the analysis also gave Christensen his way out: the wing ribs used hundreds of small pieces of wood, and if builders cut those hundreds of small pieces themselves, they would build more than the required 51 percent. After seeing the modified pieces, the FAA agreed that the Eagle kits obeyed the rule, and soon other manufacturers included complete parts in their kits as well, attracting builders with more money than tools and time on their hands.

Homebuilding would never be the same again, and the new builder-friendly kits had arrived in time to help win the biggest battle the light-plane community would fight in the first century of powered flight.

*   *   *

In 1988, the ten-year moratorium on Jim Bede's sales of kit aircraft ended, and Bede, never one to let past reality intrude on blind optimism about his next design, announced the BD-10J, a new jet he thought would push homebuilding into the realm of supersonic aircraft. His new company, Advanced Aircraft, planned to sell six BD-10Js to a hotel chain to replace the Pitts biplanes used by their aerobatic team. In some ways, Bede seemed to have learned his lesson: instead of trying to develop an airframe like the BD-5 and then finding an engine for it, he designed the BD-10J around the General Electric CJ610 turbojet engine, essentially the same powerplant used by the US Air Force in their supersonic T-38 trainer, sans the afterburning engine. Bede envisioned the empty BD-10J as weighing about fourteen hundred pounds, about one-fifth the weight of the T-38, so he believed his little jet would be capable of supersonic flight without the afterburner assist. Even at only a fraction of the T-38's price, the BD-10J wasn't for the financially faint of heart: the basic kit cost $160,000 and a used engine would be at least another $40,000. At that price, even the ultraexuberant Bede thought he might sell only fifteen airplanes.

The BD-10J made its first flight on July 8, 1992, from the airport in Mojave, California, and then fell into oblivion.

On July 13, 1985, Burt Rutan had announced he was getting out of the homebuilt-plans business. Unlike Bede and Van, Rutan had never embraced kits, and the plans he sold for his designs eventually came back to haunt him. Since paper is cheap, plans are profitable—selling one thousand plans at fifty-dollars each yields fifty thousand dollars. Not bad, but Rutan discovered the downside when people who had bought VariEze plans a decade earlier were now getting started and calling for advice. With no new revenue stream, Rutan had a hard time keeping up with the demands of his builders. He continued to support his existing builders, but decided to move into the aviation mainstream, casting his lot with Beech Aircraft and new commercial designs.

As Bede stagnated and Rutan shifted, the often-overlooked Van soared further into the homebuilding stratosphere. After the RV-4 sold like hotcakes, he moved to fulfilling the demands of his next customer base: those who wanted an airplane where people sat side by side, like in a car. Other potential customers had never flown taildragger airplanes and wanted tricycle gear. Even though a side-by-side airplane offended Van's aerodynamic sensibilities—a fatter fuselage would be slower than his sleek RV-4 design—he caved in to customer demand. But he drew the line at the retractable landing gear some wanted. His calculations showed that, at best, retractable gear might add seven or eight miles per hour to his designs, and he felt that the extra cost, weight, and complexity wouldn't be worth it.

Van's side-by-side design, the RV-6, debuted in 1986. With a used engine and basic instruments, a builder could construct an airplane for less than fifteen thousand dollars, but Van's airplanes still couldn't get any respect in some quarters. Former fighter pilot Don Norris wrote an article in the August 1987 *Sport Aviation* saying he had chosen to build a Bushby Mustang II rather than a Van's model because "the RV-4 has a fat wing." Instead of leaving it at that, Norris challenged RV pilots to "a simulated dogfight to settle any questions you may have."

Van, having other business back east, showed up in an RV-6 at the Parkersburg, West Virginia, airport not long afterward to take on Norris. The challenger, observing Van's quiet gunslinger-like confidence as he unloaded bags from the RV-6, already knew he was in trouble.

The two pilots lined their airplanes up next to each other on the end of the runway. Norris expected them to take off together in a side-by-side formation, but as soon as they pushed the throttles forward, the RV-6 scooted ahead of the Mustang. Van zipped to twenty-five hundred feet and circled, waiting for Norris to catch up. The two then turned their airplanes head on, as though they were fighter airplanes meeting up in battle. The goal for each was to try to maneuver his airplane behind the "enemy" into what would be a simulated gun-firing position.

Norris never had a chance. Within seconds of turning back toward each other, Van jumped behind the Mustang, and no amount of turning by Norris could shake him.

Norris decided to try another tactic. He dove toward the ground and, after gaining speed, pulled into a vertical climb, with the Mustang's nose pointed straight up in the air. Van dove after him, also pulling up into the vertical position. Despite the RV-6's spectacular takeoff, Norris thought the "fat" RV-6 wouldn't have enough power to climb with the Mustang, but Van stayed right behind him until both airplanes ran out of airspeed and had to dive back toward the ground. Climbing and diving in vertical maneuvers is similar to going up and down a hill in a car without pushing harder on the accelerator while heading uphill: the car slows as you reach the top of the hill but then speeds up again going downhill.

After several more minutes of fruitless diving and climbing with Van following the Mustang closely the whole way, Norris called on the radio: "I'm convinced."

Van's confidence in his airplane matched his confidence in his aircraft business. He never had a long-range plan, but simply had a philosophy of keeping cash reserves in case he saw an opportunity, figuring that if he had to rely on a bank for financing, opportunities might pass by. He believed in hitting singles, not home runs, and in providing airplanes that worked for people, not necessarily airplanes they lusted for. After all, we might wish for the Maserati sports car displayed at the entrance of the car show, but in the end most of us buy the Ford sedan.

Builders seemed to agree with Van's philosophy, and one of them, Chuck Berthe, a respected test pilot with an aeronautical research corporation, built an RV-4 and tested it with standard air force procedures. Berthe, liking what he saw, offered Van, who had never even been an air force pilot, let alone a test pilot, a backdoor entrance to membership in the Society of Experimental Test Pilots, whose membership roster includes Chuck Yeager, John Glenn, and Neil Armstrong, to name a few.

Berthe also asked Van to help write and present a paper at the society's annual symposium. Arriving at the Beverly Hilton in Los Angeles in September 1991, where civilians were decked out in their finest suits and military officers wore dress blues, Van was initially cowed by what he considered the "gods of the industry." But once Berthe warmed up the crowd, Van relaxed and even got a few laughs at some of his ad-libbed jokes. The duo urged the professional testing community to get more involved in helping homebuilders, since, at the time, amateurs were doing most of the designing and flight-testing of lightplanes. There was little, if any, money in helping homebuilders, but test pilots could provide advice and perhaps fly first flights for nervous builders.

At the time, I was a captain stationed at Edwards Air Force Base, working on the flight-test program for the air force's newest cargo airplane, the C-17, and I watched Berthe and Van give their presentation. I knew several people who had built airplanes, and I had even taken a ride in one, an open-cockpit biplane called an Acro Sport, where I worried more about falling out of the cockpit as we did loops than about how well the airplane was constructed. However, like much of the audience, I had only a vague notion of what homebuilding was all about.

Berthe and Van discussed some of the differences between professional and amateur flight-testing; unlike professionals, amateurs don't normally have access to large teams of flight-test experts, highly accurate instruments specially developed for testing, and control rooms on the ground to monitor flight conditions and help out if there's a problem. However, the methods used to test lightplanes are still the same, and we laughed while Berthe narrated a video showing him performing aerobatics in his RV-4. Suddenly, homebuilts were cool. After attending at least two dozen symposiums held by the Society of Experimental Test Pilots, I have forgotten nearly every one of the hundreds of papers presented about professional flight-test programs for everything from the F-16 to the Boeing 787, but the homemade video of the homemade airplane always stayed with me.

Homebuilding had grown up.

10

Colleen's Cub

You have no idea what your life will be like tomorrow. You are a puff
of smoke that appears briefly and then disappears.

James 4:14, *The New American Bible*

ON JULY 2, 1975, AFTER WAITING NEARLY SEVEN YEARS, EVERY-
thing came together for Ed Lesher's assault on Heinonen's 1957 distance
record—airplane, weather across his planned route, and Ed. He planned
to fly from Saint Augustine, Florida, to Phoenix, Arizona. Although he
would likely have had a tailwind with a west-to-east flight, he chose to fly
east-to-west because he couldn't fly at night. The westerly route gave him
four more hours of daylight.

Lesher had first gone to Florida in 1971, thinking he would wait only
a few weeks to make the flight. However, even with good weather, he twice
cancelled because he wasn't able to sleep the night before the planned
trek. A doctor prescribed some mild medication, but it wasn't until 1975
that the weather cooperated again.

Lesher took off just after sunrise, equipped with a baseball cap, navigation charts, a canteen of water, and hard candy. To help fight boredom,
he kept to a rigid schedule: on the hour, he switched fuel tanks and
computed his ground speed; at fifteen minutes past, he drank some
water; at thirty minutes past, he recorded instrument readings; and at
forty-five minutes past, he ate candy. After almost twelve hours, he
crossed into Arizona and skirted a wall of thunderstorms in front of a
mountain pass.

"What am I doing here? Should I make a 180?" Lesher asked himself.

He knew an airport lay twenty-five miles north, but that was short of the record. Lesher cut south instead, and he soon saw Tucson and improving weather in the distance; a few minutes later he had broken Heinonen's record, and he decided to land forty-five miles ahead at Phoenix's Litchfield Park Airport rather than take more chances. He had flown 1,835 miles, enough for a new record.

Not to worry; my father was sure his airplane would beat that by at least a thousand miles.

*   *   *

As Arnold pondered landing gear designs and Killingsworth pumped energy into his ill-fated homebuilding business, the Vietnam War had lurched toward an uncertain conclusion. A bombing campaign over the 1972 Christmas holiday finally produced an agreement between the United States and the North Vietnamese that ended the war in January 1973.

With the end of the war came funding cuts, and the air force started pushing people into jobs they didn't want, hoping some of them would leave voluntarily in lieu of being kicked out. In April, my father received notice of an assignment to run a Reserve Officer Training Corps detachment at Parks College in Cahokia, Illinois, near Saint Louis. He thought the assignment must be a mistake—normally ROTC jobs are filled by volunteers, and he hadn't volunteered for anything—but the nameless people who make assignments assured him it wasn't an error and reminded him he had only seven days to decide to take the assignment or retire.

Arnold hadn't even considered retirement until the assignment crossed his desk. A contractor ran the bombing range at Eglin, but they would be swamped with veterans and retirees clamoring for a handful of engineering jobs. At forty-five, he was too old to fly for the airlines. With Maureen and me almost in college and no other apparent options, my father agreed to the move.

Upon his arrival, there was some good news. One Parks College perk was free classes for instructors, so that fall he enrolled in two courses and finished the powerplant part of his mechanic's license, which had eluded him for so many years. The rating might look good on his resume, and he could save a few dollars by working on Charlie's engine instead of taking it to a mechanic.

Arnold still wanted to design airplanes, and the US aerospace industry was hiring again after a slump in the early 1970s. He sent resumes to Beechcraft and Cessna in Wichita, and while he waited to hear back, an ad in the Saint Louis paper caught his eye: Boeing needed engineers in Seattle. A few days later, a Boeing interviewer in Saint Louis suggested that Arnold was a perfect fit for a product safety job they were trying to fill. Arnold didn't know much about product safety, but imperfect as the job sounded, it was better than an air force that no longer seemed to want him. In August 1974, he retired from the air force, and for the second time in a year, Arnold, Colleen, and their kids, dogs, cats, cars, and Charlie skittered around the Midwest for several weeks, followed by a journey to unfamiliar ground on the West Coast.

* * *

Arnold rented the first house he found in Bellevue, a suburb east of Seattle. In addition to being near good schools, the location was an easy commute to his job about ten miles south, at the 727 plant in Renton. It was also within walking distance of bus lines to downtown Seattle and the University of Washington, where I had been accepted as a freshman in January 1975, my entry delayed one quarter by the unexpected move.

Bellevue had an airport that would have been perfect for Charlie and building an airplane, but there were no hangars available. The weekend after he arrived in September 1974, Arnold flew Charlie around the Seattle area and found a hangar at Harvey Field in the rural town of Snohomish, about thirty miles north of Bellevue. The hangar wasn't fully enclosed, and the airport was a bit of a drive, but it would prove to be a fortuitous choice.

Noble Harvey and his son, Eldon, along with a family friend, established Harvey Field on the family homestead in 1944; but the airport's first flight actually took place on May 7, 1911, when famed barnstormer Fred Wiseman brought his biplane to Snohomish for an exhibition. The flight was much like Ed Heath's attempts in New York a few years earlier: Wiseman took off from a ball field on the Harvey property and crashed a few hundred yards away in the field that later became the airport.

Like many small airports after the war, Harvey initially boomed and then fizzled in the late 1940s, but Eldon hung on, and by 1947 he had built hangars and a flight school alongside the short, grass runway. One of the business's earliest purchases was a slightly used Aeronca Champ; and more than sixty years later, the Champ still earns money for the Harvey family. Skydiving began at the airport in 1961 with the Seattle Skydivers, the oldest skydiving club in the United States. Eldon's son Dick and Dick's wife, Kandace, took over airport management in the early 1970s, adding a paved runway and getting FAA approval for veterans to use their GI Bill at the flight school.

Harvey's tiny runway and surrounding obstacles make for challenging approaches and landings, but aviators love the airfield for being much as it was in 1944. On any given day you can sit in the airport's restaurant and watch a who's who of aircraft parade by, including colorful homebuilts, powerful twin-engine airplanes, whirling helicopters, and graceful balloons. It's not hard to imagine Charles Lindbergh and *The Spirit of St. Louis* floating across the power lines at the end of the field, touching down on the grass runway, and joining fellow pilots for a cup of coffee.

After settling into Seattle, Arnold now had the time to build his record setter. His Boeing job didn't require much travel, and he rarely worked overtime, but he once again had no place to build. The rental house had no garage, and Charlie's hangar was open to the elements in front. With two kids in college and two more right behind them, there was no money for another hangar.

Even with all the bills, Arnold had to buy a new toy, an amazing piece of equipment from Hewlett-Packard, the HP-45 calculator. With his Boeing employee discount, the calculator still cost more than two quarters' worth of my tuition at the University of Washington, but it was unbelievable what it could do. Error-prone computations that took an entire evening with a slide rule and a mountain of tables in textbooks could be done without mistakes in just a few minutes. Arnold could now fiddle endlessly with his record-setting design, and I borrowed the calculator occasionally to help with my chemistry and physics tests.

Arnold also discovered the Boeing Surplus Store, located just a few miles from his office. He wandered the aisles of the aviation flea market, peering at the old manufacturing equipment, tools, airplane parts, fasteners, and scrap metal piled everywhere like stray cats hoping for a home.

Figuring materials good enough for Boeing airliners would be more than adequate for a homebuilt airplane, Arnold spent the next several years assembling a grab bag of materials, mostly aluminum in all imaginable forms: sheets, strips, stringers, rods, angles, bars, tubes, and channels. After he and Colleen bought a house, it wasn't long before the garage looked like a mini Boeing Surplus, with tubs and cardboard boxes jam-packed with tubing and other aluminum pieces, accompanied by rolls of aluminum sheet standing nearby. On nearby workbenches and shelves, airplane parts overflowed onto other workbenches cluttered with old models, abandoned toys, telescopes, and tools.

When my father wasn't tweaking his design and collecting parts, he flew Charlie alone on weekends, which he spent sightseeing around the Seattle area. As Maureen and I developed our own social lives as teenagers, we stopped going to the airport on Sundays, and our whole family no longer fit into Charlie anyway. Once we kids stopped flying, my mother, too, mostly abandoned my father, diverting her attention to an Anglican church congregation that met just a few blocks from our house and to working part-time, first as a cook at a preschool and then as a page for the King County Library in Bellevue.

After three years of flying by himself, my father was a little bored; and in the summer of 1977, he joined Snohomish Flying Service as their chief pilot, filling his evenings and weekends by instructing pilots in the use of every airplane in the Harvey fleet. That same summer, we flew to Portage for a family reunion to mark the fiftieth wedding anniversary of my father's parents. With Charlie now too small, the six of us piled instead into a rented twin-engine Cessna 310.

After landing in Portage and unloading our bags into my grandparents' car, my father poked his head inside the airport's wooden hangar that he had helped build during high school. There sat the same Cub he had soloed in thirty-three years earlier, beckoning him like an old friend waiting to catch up on old times.

Even my mother had never seen this airplane, and with the Cub's hallowed status making it a member of our extended family, we paused to take pictures. I had just turned twenty, and I remember having, for the first time, an inkling that my father was once young too, with his own hopes and dreams.

During our return trip, we stopped for fuel and a weather check in Great Falls, Montana, and Arnold learned that the clouds would be too low to land at Harvey. He added extra fuel to the Cessna and filed a flight plan for Paine Field in Everett, which had an instrument approach.

The cloudless skies as we approached the Cascade Mountains from the east made it hard to believe that fog and rain would greet us in just a few miles, but as we neared Paine Field, voices coming from the radio didn't sound promising. Weather conditions were just barely good enough for us to land—clouds at two hundred feet above the ground and visibility one mile in fog and rain.

My father dialed in the frequency of the instrument approach, and I could hear the familiar Morse code identifier over the speaker, the quiet beeps indicating all was well with the system on the ground. But we still might not see the runway—our altimeter or the instrument landing system receiver might be a little off, or the clouds might lower briefly just as we reached the minimum altitude, or my father might not keep the needles that guided us to the runway perfectly centered.

One of those things happened to the pilot in the airplane in front of us, and he announced, "Missed approach." He circled around to try again.

Knowing he had plenty of fuel to fly back across the mountains and land in good weather, my father entered the murk. Our descent through the cloud layer should have taken only about a minute, but it seemed to last much longer, the cockpit completely still except for the humming of the engines and the reassuring beeps. We had been gone for a week, and I wanted to get home to see my boyfriend and get back to my summer job.

At exactly two hundred feet above the ground, my father tightened his hand on the throttle to initiate a climb away from the ground we still couldn't see, and I figured we were heading back east to land in Ellensburg.

A split second later, my sisters and I all cheered as we broke out of the clouds, perfectly aligned on the mix of red, green, and white lights that outlined the runway and a safe landing below.

It would be the last flight the six of us ever took together as a family.

*   *   *

In the late 1970s, Arnold bought a used A-75 Continental engine. The engine was a lighter-weight variation on his original design, which called for a Continental A-85. At 170 pounds, the A-85 was more than one-third of his planned empty weight for the airplane and a starter and generator would add another thirty pounds or so, which meant five gallons of gas not in the tanks. Arnold could live without the starter—he could hand prop the airplane to start it, something he had done many times in his early flying days—but he wouldn't compromise on the generator.

At least part of his planned eighteen-hour record-setting flight would be at night, which meant the airplane had to have red, green, and white position lights, and he also wanted a radio and some rudimentary navigation equipment. With no electrical system, he could use a handheld radio, but, at a minimum, he needed a battery to power a navigation system and the position lights. With a big enough battery, he could eliminate the generator, but a large battery might weigh more than what he saved on the generator.

The A-75 engine he bought helped a little, since it weighed about ten pounds less than the A-85. The new engine produced only 75 horsepower, which meant the airplane would lose a little performance during climbs, but it would still cruise at about the same speed and consume the same amount of fuel. At the time, it seemed perfect.

* * *

By 1980, my father had passed his fiftieth birthday, and the propeller still lay under the bed, with only a periodic cat to keep it company. Maureen and I had both graduated from college, and I'd joined the air force to become an engineer, a decision that, although made in a moment of boredom, would work out spectacularly well. With only my two younger sisters left to finish college, a financial revival appeared to be on the way for my parents.

But now, my mother wanted a Cub.

After a twenty-year hiatus from piloting, Colleen wanted to fly again. It was one thing to ride along as a passenger, but she missed being in control. After eighteen years of Charlie, Colleen had decided a Cub was more her speed; and in the middle of December, Arnold spotted an ad in the *Western Flyer*. "Here's a Cub up at Floathaven Seaplane Base that says 'basket case.' Whatcha think?"

"Sure," said Colleen, and he flew up to Bellingham a few days later to find a Cub in dozens of pieces, with no fabric, no engine, and no propeller. One wing looked like it might be salvageable, and the other was a total wreck, but the price was right.

He returned a few days later in a car with a trailer to tow the parts home, and he moved his new project into the garage to keep company with the Boeing Surplus collection. The next spring, he drove ten hours round-trip to Walla Walla to rescue a set of wings. The remnants of two Cubs would become one.

In the meantime, an engineer in Arizona was getting ready to extend the C-1aI world distance record yet again.

*   *   *

When he wasn't working at Boeing during the day or flying at Harvey during evenings and weekends, Arnold sanded rust off the Cub's welded steel tube fuselage and rebuilt wrecked or missing parts. After six years, he had finished the major components—wings, fuselage, tail—but he set the project aside to move to a new house in Woodinville, located twenty minutes from both Harvey Field and his new Boeing job in Everett, twenty-five miles north of Seattle.

During the move, someone carried the propeller into the house and leaned it against a corner in the dining room, where it fit nicely with my mother's décor: framed sketches of balloons, and cabinets that displayed, instead of china and fine silver, a jumble of old altimeters, tachometers, radios, and instruments identifiable only to Arnold. Some months after the move, Colleen started telling people, "If he ever builds that airplane, I'm going to write a book and call it 'The Propeller under the Bed.'"

The new house came with a two-car garage, perfect for airplane building and just in time for putting fabric on the Cub. Instead of using old-fashioned cotton with dope, Arnold used a newer covering system called Stits Poly-Fiber, developed by Ray Stits at Flabob Airport. The Poly-Fiber was simple to use, although the forty-page instruction manual that came with the materials must have given some homebuilders pause. After reading the directions, Arnold glued polyester fabric to the Cub parts and then used a household iron to shrink the fabric until it formed a taut surface. Colleen stitched the wing fabric to the ribs, and then Arnold sprayed on several layers of coating to protect the fabric from sunlight, followed by a few coats of Cub Yellow paint.

At dawn on a Sunday morning, he attached the tail of the fuselage to a trailer hitch on his Volkswagen and, towing the fuselage on its own wheels, crept on back roads to his new hangar at Harvey Field. He then sped back home, loaded the wings on the roof rack, and took them to join the fuselage for final assembly.

With a little luck, my parents might fly in their new Cub on the fortieth anniversary of their first flight together.

*　*　*

Not everyone read the detailed directions Ray Stits provided with his product—unfortunately, with disastrous results in the case of one home-building legend. By the early 1980s, Steve Wittman, with his prodigious designs, racing exploits, and ability to coax two hundred miles per hour out of a few horsepower, had become an elder statesman of homebuilding. In 1983, he became semiretired in Florida but maintained a summer home in Oshkosh. To make the annual trek, Wittman built the O&O, which stood for "Ocala and Oshkosh." The O&O was a slightly larger version of his popular 1950s design, the Tailwind, built primarily out of wood and fabric.

On Thursday, April 27, 1995, Wittman and his second wife, Paula, a pilot herself, departed Leeward Air Ranch near Ocala about 9:30 A.M., planning to fly nonstop to Oshkosh via their usual route. Because they had not filed a flight plan with the FAA, which triggers a search-and-rescue effort within thirty minutes after an airplane becomes overdue, no one called the FAA until Friday, after the Wittmans failed to arrive in Oshkosh.

Several people in northeastern Alabama had reported noises that sounded like explosions or sonic booms on Thursday, so search-and-rescue teams focused on the rugged terrain in that area. Close to nightfall on Saturday, searchers discovered aircraft debris near a mine. Sunday morning, Paul Poberezny and four others flew to Alabama to help find their friends, and just before noon on Sunday, searchers found the missing airplane's fuselage, erasing any hope that Steve and Paula had survived.

Any concerns about the ninety-one-year-old Wittman's age were quickly dispelled: the O&O had obviously come apart in flight. Strewn over more than a mile, the wreckage pattern looked more like the aftermath of a jet fighter or airline accident than that of a typical light aircraft, which tends to arrive at the accident scene largely in one piece.

National Transportation Safety Board investigators quickly established that both wings had separated from the airplane, but more ominously, both ailerons had also separated from the wings, and most of the fabric attached to the right wing had delaminated. The ballooning effect from the detached fabric sent the ailerons into a condition known as flutter, in which the ailerons and wings began oscillations that ripped the

O&O apart. Flutter can be catastrophic within a few seconds, and even trained test pilots sometimes cannot react in time to recover. Wittman probably had no chance to save Paula and himself.

In deference to modern materials, Wittman had used Stits Poly-Fiber on the *O&O*, and the National Transportation Safety Board found that he had not used the fabric system in the way Ray Stits intended. Instead of using an iron and Stits's special products, Wittman had attached the fabric as though it were cotton, using nitrate dope, a product that had served him well for five decades' worth of racing airplanes. But Stits's modern polyester fabric couldn't absorb the dope as cotton or linen did, and the fabric eventually detached.

At the time of the accident, I had started my own homebuilding project, and Wittman's error shocked me. If a giant could make such a mistake, what chance did the rest of us have? Homebuilders talked about the accident for years, and it remains a sober reminder that designers and builders need to stay abreast of the new processes often required by new materials. However, in a final testament to Wittman's skills, his mistake performed flawlessly for a decade before it took his life.

* * *

As the Cub neared completion in the summer of 1989, my mother misplaced her driver's license. When she went to the Department of Licensing for a replacement, she failed the eye test. Except for needing reading glasses as she aged, she thought she had no vision problems; but she scheduled a visit with an eye doctor.

After ruling out macular degeneration, her doctor asked for further tests, which found an arteriovenous malformation, a congenital cluster of arteries and veins in her brain that had grown over time. Colleen's cluster pressed on her optic nerve, explaining her vision problems. Although many such malformations are now treatable, in 1989 there was nothing to do except watch it and hope it didn't hemorrhage and cause a stroke.

Although Colleen insisted otherwise, my sisters and I found it hard not to connect this disturbing news with her childhood brain surgery. My grandmother had always claimed the surgery was the result of an accident—her five-year-old brother hit her in the head with a swing, or perhaps banged her head on the floor over a piece of gum. But those

Fig. 10.1. Colleen's Cub and Arnold, Colleen, and granddaughters Mary (*top*) and Kelly (*bottom*), 1991.

stories had never made any sense to me. Whatever happened, there was a point when, as a child, she couldn't raise her head without vomiting. Surgeons at the University of Minnesota hospital operated and removed a hematoma from the front of her skull. And although she spent a month relearning to walk, she had apparently made a complete recovery.

After taking both a daytime and a nighttime driver's test, Colleen regained her driver's license; but her piloting days were over, although she could still fly an airplane with Arnold along. He registered the Cub with the FAA in Colleen's name, and on November 12, 1990, nearly ten years after seeing the initial ad, and narrowly missing their fortieth anniversary date, Arnold test-flew Colleen's Cub for the first time.

Two weeks later, the Snohomish River, which skirts Harvey Field, threatened to spill over its banks, and Arnold flew Charlie to higher ground at Paine Field in Everett. With no radio, Colleen's Cub couldn't talk to the tower controllers at Paine, so Arnold moved it a few miles north to the non-towered Arlington Airport, where it patiently waited for a week as the floodwaters saturated Harvey.

After the water and holidays receded, Colleen finally flew her Cub in January. It must have been bittersweet, knowing she had the airplane she longed for, but realizing she would never again know the freedom of being alone in an airplane: counting antlike cars at a stoplight that holds no sway over you; feeling a crosswind as it pushes your machine sideways across a tapestry of fields knitted together by roads and rivers; playing tag with a rainbow in a wispy cloud; and wondering what the earthbound mortals might be thinking as you pass overhead. Are they jealous? Do they want a flight? Or do they just want your pesky noisemaker to go on its way? My mother would never know that feeling again.

11

Doldrums

The plain fact is that the amateur-built aircraft has become the only economically feasible way of developing new civilian airplanes for purposes other than transporting executives at company expense.

Bob Whittier, *Sport Aviation*, October 1972

ON JULY 7, 1983, A SUPER CUB, A LARGER AND MORE POWERFUL version of the Piper J-3 Cub, collided with a van while taking off in Los Lunas, New Mexico. The pilot hit his head on a camera mounted in place of the front seat and suffered extensive brain damage, and the passenger, a cameraman sitting on the fuselage floor in front of the camera, was seriously injured. The pilot of a glider towed by the Super Cub managed to release the towrope, fly over the collision, and land safely on another runway.

The Super Cub occupants had planned to film the glider for a commercial for a local bank, but the airport manager, believing the operation unsafe, had complained to the FAA and closed the airport. When he saw the Super Cub taxiing, the manager drove his van onto the runway to stop the takeoff; the pilot saw the van, but believed the driver would clear the runway once the pilot started his takeoff roll.

In the end, the National Transportation Safety Board blamed the van's driver, along with the pilot's reduced visibility while flying the Super Cub from the rear seat of the airplane. The pilot's wife sued Piper Aircraft, claiming negligence due to the reduced visibility and the lack of a shoulder harness, which would have prevented the injuries. The Super Cub had been manufactured in 1970, eight years before the FAA required aircraft to be built with shoulder harnesses—and even then, they were required only in the front seats to prevent people from hitting their heads on the instrument panel. It apparently hadn't occurred to the FAA that rear-seat occupants might need protection from ill-thought-out camera installations.

In May 1986, despite the fact that the Super Cub met all FAA requirements when manufactured, and despite clear evidence of buffoonery on the part of the pilot and the airport manager, a jury ordered Piper to pay the pilot $2.5 million. Although later reduced to a little over $1 million dollars, the judgment was just one in an ever-increasing series of lawsuits that threatened to drive light airplane manufacturers out of business.

In 1977, the combined total of all lawsuits against the light airplane industry was $24 million; by 1985, that number had increased nearly tenfold, to $210 million. Largely because of liability costs, the average price of single-engine piston airplanes doubled between 1980 and 1984. Deliveries of all general aviation airplanes plummeted, from nearly 18,000 in 1979 to 1,085 in 1987, the lowest number since record keeping had begun in the late 1920s, except for three years during World War II, when no civilian airplanes were produced. By 1985, manufacturers claimed that increased costs of engines alone added an average of $5,000 to a new airplane, and one manufacturer said liability insurance added $70,000 to his production cost per plane, easily doubling the price of a small airplane.

Sales of larger and higher-performing general aviation aircraft costing at least $300,000, such as business jets and piston-driven twin-engine airplanes, didn't suffer as much, because buyers of planes in this class were less sensitive to prices. With higher-end airplanes driving profits, Cessna Aircraft Company stopped producing single-engine piston airplanes by the mid-1980s, and the other three large manufacturers—Piper, Mooney, and Beechcraft—dropped all but a handful of models. By the time the corporate bleeding stopped in the early 1990s, the industry had shed one hundred thousand jobs, many of them in Kansas, home to much of the lightplane industry.

To be fair, not all of general aviation's downturn could be traced to product liability. When the free fall began in 1979, industry experts blamed the United States' sluggish economy and assumed deliveries would pick back up as inflation and unemployment dropped; however, as the stock market hit record highs in the mid-1980s, consumers bought boats, sports cars, and motorcycles, but not airplanes. Some in the industry thought the problem was a lack of new designs. But the increased cost of learning to fly, owing to higher fuel prices, drove away many younger students, who had no Vietnam-era GI Bill to help defray costs. At the same time, the increasingly complex airspace around urban areas and busy airports made it harder to learn to fly. Radios and precise navigation equipment, long considered optional, were becoming de rigueur, adding to rental expenses and requiring extra hours of instruction. The number of newly minted private pilots dropped from sixty-eight thousand in 1980 to thirty-six thousand in 1984. By the late 1980s, between reduced military pilot production and reduced civilian pilot production, the airlines, for the first time in their existence, had trouble hiring enough pilots.

Manufacturers complained, too, about high labor costs associated with the skilled aerospace labor force, and when they weren't blaming machinists, they blamed the tens of thousands of used airplanes still in the fleet that displaced new sales and added to the companies' liability woes. As the Super Cub case had shown, as long as an airplane was still flying, a manufacturer could be held liable for design defects, despite the airplane having been certified by the FAA at the time of manufacture. Improvements to an aircraft design could be used as evidence in court that the original design was flawed to begin with, providing a major disincentive for manufacturers to fix problems. Even new airplane designs suffered from the liability albatross. In 1991, one designer abandoned his idea for a new two-seat trainer after learning that insurance would add $21,250 to the $42,500 suggested price of his new airplane.

In 1984, homebuilders outproduced lightplane manufacturers for the first time—for the first three quarters of 1984, registrations of amateur-built aircraft increased by 1,358, compared to 1,082 factory-built single-engine piston airplanes. The total number of homebuilt aircraft now stood at just over ten thousand, a small, but ever-growing slice of the nearly three hundred thousand civil aircraft in the United States. So many homebuilts were entering the market that FAA field inspectors lobbied their employer to drop one of the required airworthiness certificates for homebuilts. Until that point, inspectors had first issued an airworthiness certificate before an aircraft's first flight that was good only during the flight-test period of around twenty-five to forty hours. After flight tests were completed, the inspector issued a second certificate with no expiration date. After three decades of experience with an increasing number of homebuilts, the FAA decided issuing two certificates was a waste of time that didn't add to safety. Since 1985, homebuilders have received only one airworthiness certificate, with no expiration date. The FAA representative still puts limits on the aircraft—for example, passengers are not allowed—during the flight test phase, called Phase I. Once the flight tests are complete, the builder makes a logbook entry and is free to fly the aircraft in normal operations, called Phase II.

Amateur builders of aircraft didn't emerge unscathed from the product liability era; prices of certified parts as mundane as wheels and fasteners climbed along with airframes and engines. By the mid-1980s, the EAA headquarters had trouble finding liability insurance for chapter fly-ins, and the cost of insurance for the 1985 Oshkosh fly-in quadrupled from the previous year, adding $150,000 that had to be passed along as increased entrance fees. Even without actually building aircraft, kit producers felt the crunch: one designer reported that 30 percent of the cost of his kits was for liability insurance.

A handful of homebuilders and designers, too, found themselves at the wrong end of lawsuits. In 1979, a pilot sold a homebuilt aircraft to another pilot, who crashed the airplane five days later, killing himself and a passenger. The widow of one of the victims sued the previous owner for $10 million, even though he was not the original builder. The lawsuit was eventually dropped, but only after costing the pilot considerable expense and stress as he defended himself. In 1992, Burt Rutan beat back a lawsuit that alleged a crash was caused by a defective VariEze fitting. After Rutan pointed out that the builder hadn't installed the fitting correctly, and that the intoxicated pilot had been performing aerobatics, which were beyond the VariEze design limits, the jury unanimously found in favor of Rutan.

Despite the collateral liability damage to the homebuilding community, amateur-built aircraft emerged as a partial antidote to the skidding lightplane deliveries in the United States. Kit manufacturers began offering higher-end homebuilt aircraft to mainstream aviation enthusiasts who could no longer buy a new production airplane that met their needs. In addition to the Christen Eagle, homebuilders could choose from a menu of two-seat airplanes, such as the Sequoia Falco and the Swearingen SX300, both of which promised cruise speeds of two to three hundred miles per hour, faster than most light twin-engine piston airplanes. Basic kits cost around $40,000, but even after adding the engine and instruments, a factory-comparable airplane could be had for under $100,000.

As the cost of parts continued to soar, some homebuilders turned to ultralight aircraft. In 1982, the FAA introduced new regulations that allowed aircraft weighing less than 254 pounds to fly without registration and without meeting standard airworthiness requirements. The machines were limited to carrying only the pilot, were not allowed to fly faster than about sixty miles per hour, and were restricted to flying outside clouds during the day and largely to rural areas. But for many pilots, it was like a return to the pre–Air Commerce Act days of the early 1920s. Kit prices for ultralight craft ranged from $5,500 to $9,000, and the industry of about fifteen producers sold twenty-one hundred kits in 1985 alone. Market surveys showed that most of these kit buyers were already pilots, and the ultralight industry salivated at the thought of four hundred thousand potential customers.

Lightplane manufacturers who had once seen homebuilding as a potential threat now grabbed the lifeline tossed to them by the amateurs and formed a coalition of alphabet-soup aviation organizations: EAA, AOPA, GAMA, HAI, NAAA, NAA, NATA, NBAA, and IAM, among others. The coalition held seminars and workshops, lobbied Congress, and urged its members to send letters to their congressional representatives asking them to support tort reform to limit the liabilities of aircraft manufacturers. No one was looking to escape lawsuits altogether, and everyone agreed people had a right to sue in cases of outright negligence or deception by a manufacturer. But with airplanes lasting for decades, a time limit on liability, called a statute of repose, was needed. Various senators introduced tort reform bills beginning in the mid-1980s, but none went anywhere as the powerful and well-funded Association of Trial Lawyers of America blocked the bills at every stage, which threatened to extinguish the lightplane industry and, along with them, homebuilts. It appeared that, in just a little more than a decade, a small number of lawyers might permanently wipe US homebuilding from aviation's DNA, something forty-eight state legislatures had failed to do five decades earlier.

*　*　*

In the midst of the crisis, sixty-eight-year-old Paul Poberezny was elected chairman of the board of the EAA in 1989, and he stepped down as EAA president after thirty-six years of service. The membership elected another Poberezny, Paul's son Tom, to fill the void. Tom Poberezny, having grown up thinking that everyone welded airplane fuselages in their garage, had blazed his own aviation path as a champion aerobatic pilot; he had even missed his graduation ceremony from Northwestern University in order to compete in his first aerobatic contest. In 1971, he formed the Red Devils aerobatic team with Charlie Hilliard and Gene Soucy, and the trio traveled the air show circuit for years in their red Pitts Specials, thrilling crowds with formation aerobatics that, in many cases, outstripped what the Air Force Thunderbirds could do with their less-versatile jets. The three reformed the team in 1979 as the Eagles Aerobatic Team after Frank Christensen invited them to try his new Eagle. As a teenager, Tom had worked for the EAA, helping with grounds and building maintenance both in Hales Corner and at the Rockford fly-in. After graduating from college in 1970, he worked several EAA jobs, including financial planning, operations, and fly-in planning, and he became fly-in chairman in 1975. In the 1970s, he had also become president of the EAA Aviation Foundation to fund and plan for the new EAA museum, which opened in Oshkosh in 1983. While Tom did not always see eye to eye with Paul, passing the baton from father to son made for a seamless transition.

Shortly after taking over as president, Tom surveyed the EAA membership and found that many were concerned about the dwindling interest in aviation among younger generations. Not long afterward, the EAA created the Young Eagles program, which called upon homebuilders and other general aviation pilots to provide free rides to kids aged eight to seventeen. Since then, more than two million Young Eagles have been flown, inspiring many to pursue aviation careers or become homebuilders.

As the Young Eagles program took off, the exhausted US lightplane industry had yet to do anything to ensure the new generation would have something to fly. In 1992, manufacturers decided to focus their tort reform efforts on just the statute of repose, instead of worrying about other components of the congressional bills previously proposed, such as how liabilities would be decided when multiple parties were found responsible. New bills introduced in the House and Senate eventually passed, and President Bill Clinton signed the General Aviation Revitalization Act into law in August 1994.

After the bill's passage, Cessna announced it would start producing new airplanes within two years, the time it would take to rehire skilled workers, convert old drawings to new computerized processes, build a new manufacturing facility, and bring online tooling not used for the past eight years.

By the end of the century, the new law seemed to be working, and more than twenty-five thousand aerospace workers were back on the job.

While legislation to revive the lightplane manufacturers wound its way through Congress, kit manufacturers who stepped in to fill the void found a demanding new set of customers more interested in flying than building. Some manufacturers, such as Lancair, who sold three-hundred-mile-per-hour homebuilts of composite construction, began offering "quick-build" kits that arrived with more and more parts fully assembled, in some cases nearly an entire wing or fuselage. Instead of the typical two- or three-thousand-hour build time, quick-build kits promised assembly times of less than one thousand hours. Some manufacturers thought the quick-build kits went too far, but as in the case of the Christen Eagle in the 1970s, the FAA ensured the new kits conformed to the "major portion" rule to allow certification as amateur-built aircraft. By the 1990s, the FAA had developed a checklist to make the major portion compliance process easier, but applying it was still something of an art form. Since an amateur using hand tools might take fifty hours to complete something that a kit manufacturer using an assembly line might knock out in two hours, time alone wasn't a good measure to define whether a builder had completed a "major portion" of the construction of their aircraft. The FAA's checklist instead focused on tasks, which made it easier to massage a wide variety of kits into compliance.

Even with the quick-build kits, a few potential aircraft owners wanted little or nothing to do with the building process, prompting some entrepreneurial aircraft mechanics to offer their services, and *Sport Aviation* created a "Builder Assistance Programs" heading in the classified ads section. Some mechanics specialized in certain models, such as Lancairs, while others offered assistance in specific manufacturing processes, such as composites or tube-and-fabric. At least one advertiser left no illusions about how much of the airplane he or she intended to build: "Assistance with your wings, fuselages, or turnkey aircraft. Professionally built by A&P [airframe and powerplant mechanic]." In other words, ship me your kit, and I'll let you know when it's ready.

But paying a mechanic to assemble a kit violated every rule in the FAA's playbook on amateur-built aircraft. First, one or more amateur (i.e., unpaid) builders were supposed to construct the "major portion" of the aircraft for it to be certified as amateur-built. Some thought that perhaps mechanics could get around the rules by building an airplane and then selling it to the person who wanted it, but that violated the second requirement for an amateur-built aircraft: it was supposed to be constructed solely for the recreation and education of the builder. While the FAA realized that some people were serial builders who built an airplane, flew it for a few years, sold it, and then built another airplane, they didn't intend for people to build airplanes and then sell them immediately. Even if selling a completed aircraft could be viewed as compliant with the rules, it also wasn't fair to the struggling aircraft manufacturers, who, with insurance and certification expenses, couldn't compete with a homebuilt. On the other hand, many kit manufacturers and would-be kit buyers complained that competition was a moot point, since the major airframe manufacturers weren't building much of anything anyway.

In 1994, the FAA sat down with EAA officials and representatives from the Small Aircraft Manufacturers Association, which had many kit manufacturers as members, to sort out what the FAA now termed "commercial assistance." Within a year, the agency published new guidelines that told builders what they could and couldn't do to preserve their ability to certify an aircraft as an experimental amateur-built. A builder could employ commercial assistance, as long as the builder still completed at least 51 percent of the aircraft. If a kit was rated as, say, 60 percent builder-assembled and 40 percent factory-made by the kit manufacturer, a builder could use commercial assistance to complete up to 9 percent of the building, since that would still let the builder complete 51 percent. Builders could also ask people for unpaid help, could pay for services not considered part of the building checklist, such as customized interiors and painting, and could pay someone for instruction. The rule developed in 1952 and further refined in 1962 stood fast, and commercial assistance programs largely faded from the pages of *Sport Aviation*.

* * *

After the General Aviation Revitalization Act passed and Cessna started building again, some new manufacturers moved into the lightplane market, most notably Cirrus Aircraft, which offered sexy and speedy four-seat airplanes that included a ballistic recovery parachute a pilot could deploy to lower the plane to the ground if things got out of control in the air.

Even with the liability reforms, the new airplanes were at least as expensive as the airplanes from the 1980s. Instead of passing along liability costs to customers, manufacturers drove higher prices with bigger engines, plush interiors, and high-end stacks of avionics. Potential owners had moaned for updated equipment for years, but when the manufacturers finally produced it, many pilots balked at the cost. Sales of single-engine airplanes picked up, but by the end of the century it was apparent that sales wouldn't be returning to the prelitigation days anytime soon. The market further stagnated after the terrorist attacks on September 11, 2001.

Taking another stab at fully reviving the lightplane industry, in 2004 the FAA introduced an entirely new category of pilot certificate, the sport pilot, with light sport aircraft and light sport mechanics to go with it. Sport pilots could fly airplanes weighing less than 1,320 pounds, about the size of a Piper Cub, with only one or two seats and fixed landing gear, along with a few other restrictions. Moreover, sport pilots could earn their licenses in only twenty hours, half that required for a private pilot certificate. But the best part for many was that, as long as a sport pilot had a valid driver's license, he or she didn't have to periodically pass an FAA flight physical and obtain a medical certificate. Anyone with a higher rating, such as a private or commercial pilot, could simply let an existing medical certificate expire and continue to fly in light sport airplanes; it wasn't even necessary to tell the FAA. The only catch was that those whom the FAA had ever denied a medical certificate weren't eligible to become sport pilots, even if they had driver's licenses. The new rules came too late for my mother to fly her beloved Cub by herself but had the potential to give many other pilots the freedom to fly again in both certified aircraft and homebuilts.

The FAA made it as easy as possible for sport pilots to get airplanes. Certificated airplanes, such as Cubs and Aeronca Champs, could be operated as light sport aircraft, as long as they met the requirements. Manufacturers of light sport aircraft seemed to have endless certification options: a traditional airworthiness certificate; certification as a primary category aircraft, a certification introduced in 1992 that had so many restrictions attached to it that few designers ever used it; a set of international airworthiness standards, which led to a flood of imported eastern European airplanes; and the light sport aircraft certification itself. Not only that, light sport aircraft could be offered fully or partly assembled, and partly assembled aircraft did not have to meet the "major portion" rule for kits. Pilots willing to take some classes could also be eligible to earn a certificate that allowed them to do the maintenance on some light sport airplanes.

The new rules harkened back to desires that the EAA membership had expressed in the 1950s; and after three years, more than fifty new airplane kits were available that cost as little as one-fourth of a factory-built. Between 2004 and 2007, the FAA also issued two thousand sport pilot certificates and registered more than four thousand light sport aircraft. Ten new models appeared at the 2007 Oshkosh fly-in, now called AirVenture, including Van's RV-12 and Cessna's entry into the market, the Cessna 162 Skycatcher.

Pilots gushed over the Skycatcher the way they had over the BD-5 three decades earlier, everyone apparently having forgotten Jim Bede's cautionary tale of overpromotion spinning into the ground. Cessna CEO Jack Pelton proclaimed that, with the Skycatcher, "we're going to teach a whole new generation of pilots how to fly."

The trainer seemed as though it would live up to its billing, with roomier insides than the old Cessna 152 aircraft, an instrument panel that resembled the cockpit of a regional airliner, and a price tag of $109,500. Just like the BD-5, it seemed too good to be true, but customers ordered more than eight hundred Skycatchers after the Oshkosh debut. And, as in the case of the BD-5, the dream slipped away almost immediately.

To keep manufacturing costs down, Cessna decided to have much of the Skycatcher fabricated in China. The fact that the final assembly would be done in Kansas didn't quell some customers' fears, which were exacerbated by two accidents early in the airplane's development—even though the accidents had everything to do with the Skycatcher's design and nothing to do with the manufacturing. Many customers cancelled orders, and when Cessna, unable to keep costs down, raised the Skycatcher's price to $150,000, many more cancelled. Finally, in late 2013, Cessna abandoned the program after selling only two hundred airplanes.

It might be easy to assume that, as an old manufacturer possibly bound by tradition, Cessna couldn't compete in a new market that required innovation, but many light sport manufacturers floundered as they found it impossible to produce airplanes under the $50,000 threshold many thought was needed to boost general aviation. Even the kit version of the RV-12 cost about $70,000. Van may have been able to keep down the cost of the basic airframe, but he had no control over the cost of engines, wheels, brakes, avionics, and dozens of other parts. If he cut the cost of his airframe in half, it would hardly put a dent in the price of the airplane.

By 2014, sport pilots and light sport aircraft had yet to bring aviation back to its glory days, had there ever been any glory days to start with, but the new rules have had a noticeable impact. About half the pilots flying Harvey Field's Aeronca Champ currently do so under the sport pilot rules, many of them former private pilots who no longer want the worry and expense of a biannual FAA medical exam.

Perhaps the FAA, homebuilders, and manufacturers will someday find a way to build and fly airplanes at one-tenth the cost of today. Aircraft are more like boats than they are like automobiles, and—unlike the maritime industry, which offers everything from canoes and rowboats to yachts and oil tankers—the aerospace industry has yet to find the right mix of low- and high-end aircraft that makes aviation accessible and still maintains the magic of flight.

*　　*　　*

The turn of the century ushered in not only light sport aircraft but also a new challenge for homebuilders and dreamers: private access to spaceflight. In 1996, entrepreneur Peter Diamandis launched the XPRIZE, a competition that promised to award ten million dollars to the first privately financed manned spaceship that proved the viability of commercial space travel. Just as Raymond Orteig had hoped to stimulate commercial aviation and air travel seven decades earlier with his twenty-five-thousand-dollar prize for crossing the Atlantic, Diamandis hoped to pry a portion of space travel away from governments and put it into the hands of the private sector.

To earn the prize, a team had to fly two manned flights within a two-week period. The winner wasn't expected to go into orbit, but merely to reach the edge of space, defined by the Fédération Aéronautique Internationale for record-setting purposes as one hundred kilometers, or about three hundred thousand feet, above the earth's surface.

Burt Rutan was first in line for the new space race, which had more than a dozen competitors by the middle of 1997. Rutan even announced that he would eventually create a space tourism company, a twenty-first-century version of post–World War I barnstorming. He envisioned a future where amateur builders would assemble spaceships out of parts bought from Aircraft Spruce and Specialty, the mail order company that catered to homebuilders.

By 2004, twenty-six teams from the United States, United Kingdom, Canada, Russia, Argentina, Israel, and Romania had entered the competition, spending more than a hundred million dollars combined as they pursued the XPRIZE. Rutan's company, Scaled Composites, reportedly spent twenty million dollars, most of it contributed by Microsoft billionaire Paul Allen.

In 2003, Rutan wrote a *Sport Aviation* article to let the world know how he planned to conquer space. Because of the thick atmosphere at lower altitudes, a rocket uses most of its fuel just trying to leave the launch pad and travel the first few miles after liftoff; so Rutan decided to carry his spaceship to fifty thousand feet above the ground before launching. NASA had used the technique for decades, dropping small research vehicles such as the X-15 from a B-52 bomber. But Rutan couldn't afford a B-52, even if he'd been able to buy one—international treaties discourage private ownership of modern strategic bombers. Instead, Rutan built his own mother ship, *White Knight*, an ungainly looking craft with long booms under the wings. The booms held the parked fuselage high enough off the ground to permit a crew to maneuver *SpaceShipOne* underneath it and attach the smaller craft to the larger one. Given its shape, *SpaceShipOne* might have resembled a bomb if not for the starry paint job that looked more worthy of Disneyland than a space program.

On September 25, 2004, I listened as several Scaled Composites pilots gave an update on *SpaceShipOne* at that year's annual symposium presented by the Society of Experimental Test Pilots. The pilots gave no hint regarding possible launch dates, but when the presentation was over, I turned to another attendee and said, "I think they'll make it."

"Maybe," my neighbor said, frowning.

Four days later, Mike Melville, who had started out as a welder and been the first employee at the Rutan Aircraft Factory in the mid-1970s, became the FAA's first civil astronaut as he rocketed to 337,000 feet above the Mojave Airport in *SpaceShipOne*. Returning from space, Melville could see San Francisco and San Diego off his wingtips as he glided to a landing, where he was congratulated by Tom Poberezny, who had traveled from Wisconsin to witness the launch.

Five days later, on October 4, Brian Binnie reached 367,000 feet, and Rutan's team, now called Mojave Aerospace Adventures, took home the XPRIZE. By then, Rutan's space tourism company was well on its way—about two weeks earlier, he and Richard Branson had reached an agreement to create a new company, Virgin Galactic, with the goal of giving well-heeled astronaut wannabes the ride of their lives.

12

Seeping in Seattle

Well now the propeller has graduated to the dining room and I don't
dare look under the bed—there is a new speed-distance plane being
built in the garage to replace the J-3 that finally matriculated to the
airport, where it has resided for the last 5 years!
Found in 2012 on a scrap of paper in Colleen's handwriting

IN THE EARLY 1980S, GARY HERTZLER, AN ENGINEER WITH ALLIED
Signal in Arizona, built a Rutan VariEze and then tinkered with the
exhaust system and air inlet, added a special propeller that optimized his
cruise performance while sacrificing a bit of climb capability, and coated
the airplane with exceptionally smooth paint. Beginning in 1982, he won
an award for fuel efficiency three years in a row. Realizing the potential
of his airplane after taking part in the efficiency competitions, he flew
to California in July 1984 to take on the C-1aI distance records. On Friday
evening, July 14, Jeana Yeager departed Bakersfield in Hertzler's VariEze
to set a new C-1aI closed-course record. While Dick Rutan and Hertzler
flew alongside in Rutan's Long-EZ, she cruised between Bakersfield and
Merced, landing at noon the next day.

Hertzler then ferried his airplane to the Rutans' base at Mojave and
tried to get some sleep before taking off at midnight carrying two quarts
of water and two granola bars. His airplane was a bit more sophisticated
than Lesher's—in addition to lights and an electrical system, Hertzler
had a VHF Omni-Directional Range, a piece of electronic equipment that
simplified navigation.

Hertzler followed Interstate 40 to the east and climbed to 11,500 feet
to clear the high terrain in Arizona. He flew all night with no problems;

but the next afternoon, clouds in Indiana forced him to fly low to the ground. Sixteen hours into the flight, his two sleepless nights and tangling with the weather had taken their toll. He still didn't feel drowsy, but from his slow reaction times as he flew the airplane, he could tell he was tired, and he decided to land in Martinsburg, West Virginia. He knew it had been a good choice when he later saw the barely legible handwriting in the logbook entry he made right after landing. Hertzler's new record was 2,214 miles, 450 miles farther than Heinonen's original record, but it could have been worse for Arnold: when Hertzler landed, the VariEze still had enough fuel to fly another three hundred miles.

In 1986, Dick Rutan, along with copilot Jeana Yeager, set the biggest homebuilt aircraft record ever, when they became the first to fly any aircraft nonstop around the world, unrefueled, in yet another of Burt's designs, *Voyager*. *Voyager* now resides at the National Air and Space Museum.

*   *   *

Not long before my father finished the new Cub, my parents took a trip to Wisconsin, and a high school friend invited them to drive to Oshkosh for the 1990 fly-in. The overabundance of airplanes, equipment, people, demonstrations, and overall euphoria that permeate the air at Oshkosh was like catnip to Arnold. All things seemed possible, and he returned home motivated to start building.

But not the record setter. He wanted a BD-5, and he soon found a used kit for nine hundred dollars.

A few months later, Arnold realized why most BD-5 kits were never finished: even after two decades, there still was no suitable engine. But the kit wasn't a complete waste. Arnold salvaged one part—a U-shaped piece of metal that supported the BD-5's reclining seat. The part was perfect for the tilted seat he wanted in his record breaker, and it solved another problem. Since the wing was the critical element in his design, he had never thought much about the fuselage, which was just along for the ride, something to carry him, the instruments, and the engine. In the 1970s, he had changed his fuselage material from steel tubing to aluminum once he discovered the cornucopia of metal available from Boeing Surplus, and now the salvaged Bede piece locked in the details of his fuselage design: every decision after that had to fit around the BD-5 part.

Arnold retired from Boeing in 1991. As a safety expert, he still wasn't designing airplanes, and he wanted to spend more time flying; but given his age, Boeing wasn't interested in hiring him as a pilot. After thirty-one years, it was time to find out if his record-setter design would work.

*   *   *

Building an aluminum airplane might seem like a daunting task, but thousands of EAA members, including myself, have learned the basics in a single weekend workshop. Aluminum sheets and strips not much thicker than a piece of construction paper are very wobbly, but if you bend a strip at a ninety-degree angle, it becomes very stiff and strong. Bending a bunch of aluminum strips transforms them into parts called stiffeners. Attach several stiffeners to a piece of an aluminum sheet, and you get a strong structure. Sheets can also be made stronger without stiffeners by bending the edges over about one-half inch; you can use this technique to make ribs and formers that give shape to wings and fuse-lages. Stiffeners, ribs, formers, and sheets, along with a thick, strong piece of metal for the wing spar, make up most of the load-carrying structure on an aluminum airplane. Builders can use screws, bolts, or rivets to get the aluminum parts together, but screws and bolts are heavy, so designers and builders use them only when high strength is needed or when a part needs to be removed frequently. Most aluminum aircraft parts are riveted.

Rivets look like very small bolts or screws—most are less than a half inch long and perhaps an eighth inch in diameter—with no threads on the shank and no slots on the round head. To use a rivet, first take two or more parts that need to be connected, clamp them together, drill a hole through all the parts, and place a rivet through the hole. The rivet shank should poke out by about an eighth inch or so. The shank is then smashed to make it bigger than the hole so the parts stay together; the smashed rivet end essentially performs the same function as the nut on a bolt.

For an aluminum airplane, do this about five thousand times.

The smashing part is what gets hard. Rivets can be squashed using a hammer-size hand tool known as a squeezer, but doing that thousands of times is tedious, and the tool can't reach all places on an airplane. Many homebuilders use rivet guns, the same equipment as commercial manufacturers. *Gun* is a bit of a misnomer, since the gun doesn't shoot

Fig. 12.1. E-1 ribs and spar under construction, with plywood rib template at the wingtip, 1990s.

rivets. It resembles a drill, but instead of a drill bit, it has a face that you press against the head of the rivet. You put a heavy piece of metal called a bucking bar over the shank of the rivet and pull the gun's trigger. The gun responds by hammering the rivet/metal/bucking bar combination very rapidly, about forty or fifty blows in one second. If everything goes right, the bucking bar deforms the rivet shank to the right size and you're done. Otherwise, it's time to use your drill to remove the rivet and try again. It looks like the drawing in fig. 12.2.

Although, like many builders, my father mostly worked alone, my mother sometimes helped with riveting. With her small hands, she could easily get the bucking bar into places Arnold found impossible. Slowly, the parts started coming together.

In 1996, Arnold applied for an FAA registration number. The FAA application had a box for the model name of the airplane, and for lack of anything better, he wrote down E-1, perhaps thinking there might be an E-2 or even E-3 someday.

Many homebuilders ask for a registration number that combines a

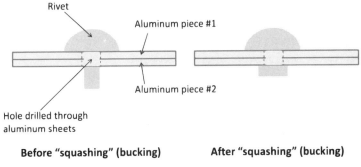

Rivet

Aluminum piece #1

Aluminum piece #2

Hole drilled through
aluminum sheets

Before "squashing" (bucking)   **After "squashing" (bucking)**

Fig. 12.2. Riveting basics.

significant number with their initials, such as N123BY, but Arnold wanted something connected to an airplane he had flown. His first two choices were already in use by other airplanes, and the balloon from his twelve-hour flight in 1951 didn't have a registration number since it belonged to the navy. Instead, he struck gold with the number from the balloon he used for his check ride, N7927A. General Mills had turned in the registration when they stopped using the balloon, and the number sat unclaimed for forty-five years.

*   *   *

In 1998, Arnold started building his tapered wings. Each wing rib had to be progressively smaller as the ribs marched from the fuselage toward the wingtip. In a rectangular wing, every wing rib is identical and interchangeable, but Arnold would build only two ribs of each size, one for the left wing and one for the right. He thought the gain in aerodynamic efficiency outweighed the production inefficiency, especially after he hit on an ingenious method for making each rib.

By 1998, software prices were falling dramatically, and many home computer users snapped up programs that previously only professionals could afford. Arnold found an inexpensive computer-aided design program, and he used it to lay out his airfoil and then instantly resize it. During one of my trips home, he showed me how he could print a rib pattern on his Boeing Surplus fanfold dot-matrix printer, glue the pattern to a half-inch sheet of plywood, cut out the plywood pattern with his band saw, and then use the pattern to form two ribs from aluminum. If he made a mistake, it was no big deal—just toss the ribs in the scrap heap, run back to the computer, print another pattern, and do it again. Before the evening was over, I had made one of the ribs for the E-1, my total contribution to the construction.

By the end of 1998, the E-1 was starting to look like an airplane.

* * *

My mother's arteriovenous malformation continued to grow, sapping her vision and her life. One day, she ran her car into a ditch. She wasn't sure what had happened; but not long after, she gave up driving and my sister Kelly ferried her everywhere. Colleen stopped flying her beloved Cub, and with hangar rent, insurance, and maintenance, Arnold could no longer justify the expense of keeping it. In June 1998, he sold the Cub to Richard Bach, author of *Jonathan Livingston Seagull*. Bach was delighted to have the meticulously restored Cub, and he used it as the basis for a book, *Out of My Mind*.

In the spring of 1999, in what would be sort of a farewell tour, my parents drove around the United States to visit old friends and family. They stopped in California, Arizona, and Louisiana before picking me up at Eglin Air Force Base for a short trip to Lakeland, Florida, and a smaller, southern version of Oshkosh called Sun 'n Fun that provided adult beverages at ten in the morning. After dropping me back at Eglin, they continued north to see relatives in Wisconsin and Minnesota before returning to Seattle.

A few weeks after we returned from an Alaska cruise that summer, my mother developed a headache and couldn't raise her head without feeling nauseous, the same symptoms she had had before her brain surgery as a six-year-old. After various misdiagnoses as the flu and allergies, her eye doctor prescribed a heavy-duty steroid that controlled her symptoms, even if it didn't cure anything. Whenever the doctor tried to reduce the dose, her right eyebrow and eyelid drooped, so he increased the dose again.

My sisters and I consulted each other about this ominous turn and decided it was the beginning of the end. My father acted as though nothing was wrong; no matter how lousy my mother felt, she fixed his breakfast every morning.

One day at the end of August, my mother couldn't get up, and my father took her to the emergency room. The steroids had given her diabetes, and the doctors decided she should try to control the disease with diet. My brother-in-law installed grab bars in the bathroom in case she got woozy. My father still thought everything would be okay.

With this latest news, I started making plans to go home for the Columbus Day weekend. But right before I bought my ticket, Kelly said my mother was doing better, so I decided to stay in the DC area, where I had moved in August.

Saturday morning, the phone rang.

"This is your father."

It was 6 A.M. in Seattle, and I could count on one hand the number of times my father had ever called me. I knew it was going to be bad.

"Yes?"

"Your mother just died."

* * *

The rain stopped as my mother's funeral ended, but the gloom lingered. The funeral procession got stuck in traffic on the way to the cemetery, and my sisters and I joked uneasily about our mother being late for her own funeral.

Forty-nine years earlier on this day, October 12, my father had taken my mother for their first airplane ride together. Normally they would be celebrating this day by flying somewhere for lunch, but instead he was burying her.

Approaching the cemetery, we passed Harvey Field, and I noticed a yellow J-3 Cub perched on the tarmac. I wondered aloud if it might be my mother's airplane, but everyone thought I was crazy. Richard Bach now owned her Cub, so what would it be doing here?

As the priest finished his blessings, we heard the drone of an approaching airplane. We looked up and watched it fly toward us, skimming just below the low-hanging clouds. Directly overhead, the pilot rocked his airplane's wings in tribute to my mother and then flew away. A minute later, another airplane flew over and did the same thing. Then another, and another, until we were dizzy from craning our necks to watch them. Some rocked their wings and some dipped their noses to pay their last respects. A helicopter hovered briefly and someone on board tossed out carnations. My sisters and I ran to pick them up as they hit the ground. I still have my carnation, pressed inside a book about airplanes.

When it seemed there could be no airplanes left at the airport, we spotted a little yellow Cub in the distance. Richard Bach circled my mother's final resting place repeatedly, climbing higher and higher on each pass, before finally heading west and disappearing. "Gone west," the words pilots use to honor a fellow aviator who has passed away.

Before I returned to DC, I taught my father how to cook the breakfast of eggs, bacon, and toast that my mother had made him for forty-five years. I opted for microwaving the bacon. He avoided the airport for two weeks, the longest period he had ever voluntarily abstained from flying in his adult life. He pored over old photos and scrapbooks. The partially built E-1 sat in the garage, cold and lonesome.

As Christmas approached, packages addressed to my mother arrived at my father's house. Things she had preordered for Christmas—Yule logs, nuts, cheeses, and sausages—made for a haunting holiday as we ate them, knowing we had all planned at least one more Christmas with her. I felt guilty because I hadn't come home for Christmas in 1998.

Months passed, and my father began to rebuild his life. He got a new cat and spent most of his time at the airport. Meanwhile, his unfinished dream sat in the garage alone, forgotten, another casualty of my mother's sudden death.

*   *   *

Arnold settled into a new lifestyle with no Colleen to make breakfast and dinner, no Colleen to feed the cats, no Colleen to pay the bills. He was shocked when he realized how much he now had to do for himself every day. Plus, no Colleen to help work on the airplane.

In addition to there being no Colleen, the garage was cold, further sapping his motivation.

His design also had a problem common to many airplane designs. Just as no battle plan survives first contact with the enemy, no aircraft design survives first contact with the building process. His record setter had gained weight, weight that would make a record impossible.

No Colleen, a freezing workplace, a fat airplane—it was too much to deal with at once, so the airplane waited.

In July 2000, nine months after my mother's funeral, my father attended the annual fly-in in Arlington, Washington, about ten miles north of Harvey Field. The Arlington fly-in is a mini-Oshkosh, with tens of thousands of attendees instead of hundreds of thousands, dozens of vendors instead of hundreds, and a few local air show pilots instead of internationally recognized performers.

As Arnold wandered the grounds at Arlington, he noticed a tiny engine made by an Australian company, Jabiru. The interest in ultralights during the 1980s' general aviation skid had produced several compact but powerful and reliable engines. The smallest engines were still best suited to ultralights, whose builders usually hung the engine on the back of the airframe; but larger engines by Rotax and Jabiru could be covered with a front-end cowling or buried in a fuselage. Arnold had looked at a Jabiru engine at Oshkosh a few years earlier, but the cooling fins on the cylinders had a weird design that offended his engineering sensibilities. However, the engine had now been flying on homebuilts for several years and had a good reputation. It was certified in Australia, but not in the United States; however, that wasn't a problem for a homebuilt.

At Arlington, Arnold took a closer look at the engine and had an epiphany. Jabiru had redesigned the engine, and he liked what he saw—the engine now looked like a miniature version of the Continentals and Lycomings he was used to. And best of all, the eighty-horsepower version was thirty pounds lighter than the bulky Continental engine he had been planning to use for the past forty years. The Jabiru also included everything he needed—a starter, generator, magnetos, and exhaust pipes, which would have added even more weight to the Continental installation. And, at twenty-four inches wide, the narrower Jabiru meant he could eliminate the chubby cheeks from his original cowling design that resembled a squirrel with a mouthful of acorns. Although the cheeks would have made for a distinctive midget-racer look, they would have been harder to build and caused additional drag.

Energized, Arnold collected Jabiru brochures and drove home to see if he could make it work on the half-built airplane in his garage. It sounded like a Jim Bede too-good-to-be-true promise, but it wasn't—engineering and materials advances in the past forty years had made possible a holy grail of an engine that would delight homebuilders around the world.

However, with a lighter engine, he had a new problem—the airplane was out of balance. The lighter engine acted like the too-far-back paperclip on the model airplane from his childhood—the nose would want to come up too much, and the wings would lose lift, causing the airplane to dive to the ground. Adding weight to the engine to rebalance things would defeat the purpose of getting the lighter engine, so the only option was to move the engine forward, just like moving the paperclip forward. That meant a longer nose, which added a little weight, but only a few pounds.

Arnold got back to work.

*　*　*

Even with the engine problem solved, the E-1 had a long way to go before it could fly. The airplane still needed instruments, radios, control cables, brakes, and dozens of other small parts, such as fuel caps, lights, and antennae. Homebuilders don't have to use FAA approved parts, but they still have to install equipment required by the FAA, although the list is surprisingly small and based on a commonsense approach not often found in large bureaucracies.

First, to know how fast they are going, pilots need an airspeed indicator, which many pilots would agree is the most important instrument in the cockpit. If the speedometer in a car fails, a driver can match the speed of the surrounding vehicles and be reasonably safe. However, pilots don't normally fly around other airplanes, and there are serious consequences for flying too slow or too fast. Fly too slow and you can lose lift and stall the airplane. Fly too fast and you can rip a wing off the airplane. Without an airspeed indicator, pilots do have cues to help them recognize if they are slow or fast—get too slow and the nose rises high above the horizon and the airplane starts to sound like it is gasping for air; get too fast and the airplane dives at the ground and the cockpit gets noisy. But looking at the airspeed indicator is the best way to know what's going on—it conveys a lot of information at just one glance. It tells you if your speed is just right; and, if you're too fast or too slow, an airspeed changing rapidly in the wrong direction will remind you that you'd better do something in a hurry to fix the problem.

Pilots also need to know how high they are above the ground and where they are going, so an altimeter and magnetic compass are next on the equipment list. Many airplanes have sophisticated navigation systems on board, such as GPS, but all the FAA requires is the lowly magnetic compass.

Fig. 12.3. Original instruments in the E-1, a typical basic homebuilt panel, 2005.

Since pilots can't just pull over to the side of the road if the engine quits, aviators keep an eye on the health of the engine via a tachometer and instruments that display oil pressure and temperature. A fuel gauge also lets the pilot make sure there is enough gas to keep the motor running.

If the airplane has retractable landing gear, there has to be some sort of indicator that tells the pilot if the landing gear is up or down.

A few other things are required for safety—seat belts, shoulder harnesses, external strobe lights to increase visibility to other pilots, and an emergency locator transmitter. If the airplane crashes, the transmitter sets off a signal that helps search-and-rescue crews find the airplane. It isn't required for single-seat aircraft, so Arnold left it out to save weight.

For an airplane that will fly around only during the day and not be used for commercial operations, that's all that's required. To fly at night, the airplane needs a few other pieces of equipment—some lights and a source of electricity.

The list gets a lot longer if the airplane is going to fly in all weather conditions, and some homebuilders put together instrument panels that rival the panel of a 747. But Arnold didn't want or need any of that, and besides, there was barely room for the equipment he needed.

Not long after he started building again, Arnold confronted his landing gear demons for the last time. The laws of physics continued to conspire against his quest to find a retraction mechanism that weighed much less than the fifty pounds of drag it would save. He knew that in the battle of form versus function, function usually loses if the designer is too insistent on maintaining the form. That had happened to the BD-5; Bede's insistence on a pusher configuration at all costs doomed him to design an airplane with a fuselage too small for a suitable engine. But Arnold didn't want an airplane with spiffy-looking retractable gear if it wouldn't set a record. Plus, his time at Boeing had made him more safety conscious, and he shuddered at the image of the ensuing fireball likely to occur if the gear didn't extend and he landed belly up and skidded along the ground, spewing fifty gallons of fuel as pavement, rocks, or tree stumps shredded the E-1's wings. Like Richard VanGrunsven opting out of retractable gear a decade earlier, Arnold conceded the battle to function and attached fixed gear to the E-1.

In 2003, he began the long process of installing the engine and finishing the small details needed to fly, including the propeller, but not the one in the dining room. An inspiration for four decades, the original propeller wouldn't work with the Jabiru engine, and it became a nice bit of artwork hanging in his hangar instead.

By the end of 2003, I began to realize why the E-1 was taking so long: four military moves and flying distractions had thwarted my own home-built, an aerobatic aircraft called the One Design. After nearly a decade of tool purchases, classes, practice parts, and on-and-off construction, I had managed to produce two ailerons and a fiberglass part. It was starting to look like there would be a second fifty-year project in the family, but I later abandoned the aircraft after deciding I no longer needed an airplane that could pull nine Gs.

In early 2005, with the help of a friend and my sister Kelly, my father loaded the E-1 fuselage, with the engine attached, and then the wings, resting in a cradle, into a rented twenty-four-foot U-Haul truck, and drove to Harvey Field. Rather than rent a second hangar, Arnold had doubled his hangar space by installing a hydraulic lift for the E-1 in Charlie's hangar a few days earlier. The process of using the lift required several steps. Pull Charlie out of the hangar. Lower the hydraulic lift. Push the E-1 onto three plates that held the tail wheel and main landing gear tires. Raise the hydraulic lift now containing the E-1. Push Charlie back into the hangar.

After arriving at the airport and readying the lift, the moving team pushed the E-1 fuselage onto the plates and raised the lift back up about a foot. They then pushed the still-cradled wings underneath the fuselage. Arnold used a motorcycle jack to hold the wings in place and then lowered the fuselage onto the wings. After some jiggling and jostling, the pieces slid together, and Arnold attached the wings to the fuselage with four bolts.

After a little more work, the E-1 was ready to fly.

*   *   *

The first flight of any airplane is a major event, especially for homebuilts operated by amateurs with no flight-test experience. According to the National Transportation Safety Board, from 2001 to 2010 only 12 production airplanes crashed during their first five hours of flying, compared to 102 amateur-built aircraft. Homebuilt accident numbers get better with aircraft age and taper off as the aircraft reaches one thousand flying hours, about the time that factory-built aircraft start seeing increases in accidents. Given the early-life issues, the FAA allows no passengers for at least the first twenty-five hours of flight for an amateur-built aircraft, although recent rule changes allow a second pilot in some circumstances for added safety.

Aware of the numbers, Arnold did everything he could to prepare for his first flight. He laid out a flight profile—take off, climb to three thousand feet while circling to stay above the airport, try a few turns, slow the airplane down to landing speed to see what it felt like, and then descend for a landing. He flew the profile numerous times on a simulator installed on his home computer, and mentally rehearsed the cards he would carry on his kneeboard in the E-1 to remind him what maneuvers to perform and what data to collect. He also performed "what-if" drills for emergencies: what if the engine quits on takeoff, what if the airplane won't slow down enough to land on Harvey's short runway, what if the engine quits at some other point in the flight?

Using my now twenty-plus-years' experience as a flight-test engineer, I lobbied for trucking the E-1 to nearby Paine Field in Everett to fly the first flight. Paine had a control tower, fire and rescue equipment standing by if something went wrong, and a longer runway in case the E-1 proved hard to land. However, the logistics of taking the airplane apart to move it and then reassembling it at Paine with no hangar proved too daunting, and Arnold decided to use Harvey. He'd been flying there for thirty years and knew every inch of the airspace and terrain, plus he could always declare an emergency and fly to Paine if he needed a longer runway. Harvey also had something that Paine didn't: a grass runway, which would make the first landing much easier.

The FAA assigned Steve Knopp as their designated airworthiness representative to inspect the E-1, and he was nervous. Knopp had never approved a unique design before, but his nervousness had less to do with what the FAA might think and more to do with Arnold having been one of his flight instructors. To be on the safe side, Knopp consulted an FAA employee for advice and found that the employee wanted to tag along during the inspection, not because he was concerned about the airplane, but because he too had never seen an original design before. In the end, Knopp gave the E-1 a Phase I flight-test period of forty hours and added only two restrictions for the first five hours of flying. First, all takeoffs had to be made to the south due to trees and houses located off the north end of the runway—if the E-1 fell out of the sky, Knopp didn't want it raining down on the citizens of Snohomish. Second, the size of the test area was somewhat smaller than the normal one hundred miles, which was intended to keep the E-1 closer to Harvey in case something went wrong, a reasonable precaution for an original design instead of a kit or plans-built airplane.

The E-1 passed on its first inspection, and Knopp handed Arnold his airworthiness certificate on June 30, 2005. I flew to Seattle right after the Fourth of July for the planned first flight on July 9.

The weather gods can still be cranky in Seattle in July, but we were rewarded with a good day—a few scattered clouds and light winds blowing from the south, the direction Arnold needed, given the E-1's takeoff restriction.

We arrived at the airport with an entourage that would have made my mother proud—all three of my sisters, three of my four nieces, one brother-in-law, and a host of friends and curious onlookers. I played test director and Kelly was the videographer.

My father filled the fuselage fuel tank to the brim for the first time—

he'd done his taxi tests with just a bit of fuel. About ten minutes after fueling, I noticed gas pouring onto the floor of the cockpit; the top of the tank hadn't sealed right. To stop the leak, we drained three gallons of fuel from the ten-gallon tank, and then mopped up the mess on the floor.

Fuel problem solved, another arrived. Before starting the engine, the little box on the instrument panel that displayed engine information wouldn't come on. I stuck my head in the cockpit and spotted two popped circuit breakers. After some trial and error, Arnold fixed the electrical problem by rewiring a short circuit from the handheld radio connected to the airplane. Then, after he started the engine, the radio wouldn't turn on. My sisters scrounged a spare from his hangar; it was scratchy but would do for the first flight.

As Arnold taxied, the crowd inched closer to the runway, but then he abruptly pulled off the taxiway into the grass and shut the engine down. He opened the canopy, and I ran a quarter mile up the taxiway to the E-1.

"Now what?"

"I heard a weird-sounding vibration coming from the engine area. I think we need to pull the cowling off and take a look."

I felt in my pockets for a screwdriver and came up empty. Arnold didn't have one either.

I looked back at the crowd. It would take me at least five minutes to run to my father's hangar and back, and people were getting restless, milling about and, in the case of my ten-year-old niece, Ruby, dancing. As I turned back to the E-1, I spotted an open hangar just across the taxiway and started toward it. The hangar dweller saw me coming and stepped out to check on the fuss.

I yelled, "Do you have a screwdriver?"

He ducked back into his hangar and emerged a few seconds later with the tool I desperately needed.

After our new friend helped take the twenty or so screws off the cowling, we all peered inside and saw nothing. We put the cowling back on, Arnold did a quick run-up, and everything seemed fine. Preflight jitters? A screw perhaps not tight? Who knows?

It was time to fly.

The E-1 needed only about six hundred feet of the twenty-nine-hundred-foot-long runway to get airborne, and the crowd let out a quiet cheer as the E-1 passed by. Ruby followed up with a jubilant "Go, Grandpa!" that always gets a laugh whenever we replay the video.

Arnold circled the airport, climbing higher and higher until we could barely see him, although he was too busy flying to pay attention to us on the ground. With its light controls and formfitting cockpit, the E-1 felt more like the F-100 than any other airplane he had flown. But on the first flight, there wasn't much time to become one with the E-1 yet as he had with the F-100. After checking out the engine oil and exhaust temperatures, making some turns, and doing a practice approach at altitude, he was ready to come back and do the hardest part, the landing.

He aimed for the grass runway, but the E-1 didn't want to stop flying. Halfway down the grass strip, still flying too fast to land, he added power and climbed back up for another try. The second approach was better: he touched down about one-third of the way down the runway, and then we all gasped as he bounced several feet back into the air. I held my breath until he touched down again and rolled to a stop at the end of the grass.

Arnold taxied back to his hangar and shut down the engine, but the mob that descended on the E-1 kept him from getting out. It seemed that everyone at Harvey wanted to congratulate him on the first flight, although few knew what he planned to do with the airplane. My father worried that if he told people about his dream, they would constantly bug him about when he expected to try for the world record. He had spent forty-five years working on the airplane, and at times he was no longer sure he even wanted to set a record. He was nearly eighty years old, and the idea of sitting in an airplane for eighteen hours no longer had the appeal it did at thirty.

Regardless of my father's aspirations, the E-1 wouldn't set any world records soon. First, he had to fix the airplane so it wouldn't make heart-stopping landings, and a household carbon monoxide detector riding in the cockpit had measured the lethal gas at 110 parts per million, more than twice the FAA-allowed 50 parts per million.

Those problems were easy to fix, but the fuel leak in the cockpit was a harbinger of a mistake that threatened to derail the dream.

* * *

Arnold spent several days examining the E-1 for every possible path the carbon monoxide could follow into the cockpit, slathering sealant on every hole or opening he could find, no matter how microscopic. Carbon monoxide molecules apparently don't like to be outside, because after leaving an engine exhaust, they cling to the bottom of a fuselage, searching for a way to wiggle back into the airplane and cause mischief. Arnold did his best to cover every opening on the bottom of the plane, but the control cables for the tail had to come out of the airplane somewhere, leaving behind impossible-to-seal points for the sneaky molecules to enter like bugs slipping into a house. After lengthening the exhaust stacks to divert carbon monoxide away from the airplane, he managed to get the level down to about twenty-five parts per million but never completely eradicated the molecular roaches.

The long landing was a bigger problem: the E-1 just didn't want to stop flying. After several more flights, Arnold found he could reduce the float by flying at a slower speed, but the nose of the airplane was so high on the final approach path that he had trouble seeing the runway.

The E-1 had too much lift and not enough drag for landing, so he decided to try adding flaps to the airplane, even though that meant also adding some fuel-robbing weight. Even with the light Jabiru engine and a wooden propeller, the E-1 was obese: it had gained 121 pounds in the thirty-four years between original design and first flight, and his hoped-for 3,075-mile range had dropped to 2,400 miles. Still plenty for a record, but the weight demons shaved 7.5 miles off the E-1's range for every extra pound—still, it wouldn't do him any good to have an airplane that could set a record if he couldn't land it safely. Long gone were the days when aviators crashed their airplanes and crawled, bruised and bleeding, from the wreckage to claim a prize or new world record.

My father had taken a risk when he designed the E-1 without flaps, as in the original F-100 design. But now he had no choice but to add them, and his F-100-like inboard aileron location limited the real estate available for a flap design. An army of engineers had been able to move the F-100 ailerons on newer models by redesigning the wing, but Arnold wasn't about to build a whole new wing for the E-1.

Since he already had plenty of lift, he needed a flap only to create drag, and he chose an elegant solution called a split flap, a small piece of sheet metal attached by a hinge to the bottom of each wing. Combined with an equally simple flap lever, he kept the added weight gain down to two pounds, or a distance loss of only about fifteen miles. Even with the flaps, the E-1 was hard to land; but since the airplane was supposed to set a distance record, not make great landings, he decided it was good enough.

Fig. 12.4. E-1 during a landing using split flaps below the wing, 2005.

After doing some additional tests to be sure the E-1 was safe to fly, Arnold started to collect data about the most important number on his airplane: fuel flow. To break the record, he needed to average at least 37 nautical miles per gallon (nmpg) of fuel while flying at about 110 knots, or 125 mph.

All airplanes have a speed called best range, which is the speed at which the airplane will fly the farthest on a full tank of fuel. Fly faster than this speed and you get to your destination sooner, but you burn fuel faster and can't fly as far. Fly slower than this speed and you burn less fuel, but the decreased speed also keeps you from flying as far. Cars do this too, but most people don't worry about it: they just drive the speed limit or a little bit higher and take what they get. When the fuel gets low, they look for a gas station. Try that in an airplane, and you're likely to find yourself low on fuel at the worst possible moment, such as over the top of the Rockies in the middle of the night with the nearest airport fifty miles away.

Pilots instead plan flights around the expected fuel burn rate. They select an engine setting for the altitude they plan to fly at, and that tells them what true airspeed and fuel burn rate to expect. From that, they subtract thirty minutes' worth of fuel for a reserve (or forty-five minutes' worth, if they're flying at night or in instrument conditions), and that tells them how much fuel they have left for the trip. Knowing the fuel burn rate, they calculate how long the airplane can fly. The next step is to figure out how fast the airplane will actually be flying over the ground, since there's almost always a tailwind or headwind whose speed has to be added to or subtracted from the true airspeed to get the groundspeed, which tells the pilot how far he or she can fly. Additional flight planning makes allowances for climb, descent, approaches, and the vagaries of air traffic control.

When Arnold plotted the points from the fuel flow data he collected, the diagram looked nothing like the well-behaved lines displayed in his engineering textbooks. Lines crossed that shouldn't cross, and stray points didn't line up where they belonged, like miscreant soldiers refusing to march into battle. However, even with the shotgun-scattered test points, one thing was apparent: the E-1 was getting only about thirty-one nautical miles per gallon.

How could this be? He had checked the numbers dozens of times, using spreadsheets on the computer and flying a model of the airplane in a simulator. But those numbers were just guesstimates based on theory. The flight test numbers told the truth.

Arnold had few options left for reducing the weight of the airplane, so he had to make it faster. Although the E-1 didn't have enough drag at the low speeds he needed for landing, it had too much drag at the higher speeds he used for cruising; and he suspected that the fixed landing gear, hanging out in the wind, was the primary culprit. However, he also had doubts about the propeller he was using. He thought the blades needed to be set at a higher angle, called pitch, so they would bite more air with each revolution and pull the airplane more efficiently.

His first propeller swap improved the fuel burn somewhat. But, still well short of his goal, he moved on to streamlining the landing gear. Many homebuilts have landing gear similar to the E-1's, so Arnold studied dozens of wheel pants in aircraft supply catalogs, but concluded none would work. He would have to make his own.

Wheel pants are conceptually very simple, resembling blunt footballs that cover the wheels and tires. But in practice, the curved shapes of wheel pants are hard to manufacture. A mechanic can learn to hammer aluminum into just about any shape, and there is a tool called the English wheel that can turn scraps of aluminum into works of art, but both techniques require considerable practice. As a result, most homebuilders either purchase preformed wheel pants or make their own using fiberglass.

But fiberglass isn't without its problems. It too requires practice to make, it's messy, and you have to build a form for laying up the fabric. If you're going to make only one or two parts, fiberglass is not very practical.

Arnold decided to cheat. Reasoning that most of the drag came from the turbulent flow behind each wheel and tire, he decided to cover just the backs of those parts. He first bought a set of gooseneck lamps from Target, hoping to modify the round bases, but he gave up on that and passed the lamps to Kelly for more conventional use. He then broke into his Boeing Surplus stock and fashioned two wheel pants that resembled flat footballs. When he was finished, the simple solution looked a bit odd, but it worked—he gained ten knots in airspeed, at a cost of only two pounds of metal.

In the summer of 2006, with the wheel pants in place and the new propeller, Arnold ran another series of tests and added the data points to his plot. This time, at 110 knots, he hit 39 nmpg.

The empty airplane now weighed 582 pounds, 143 pounds more than his initial design in 1960, but his estimated range with no wind was about twenty-four hundred miles, enough to break the record.

Except there was another aeronautical gremlin waiting in the wings.

Arnold had done all his flight tests using fuel only in the fuselage tank. In the fall of 2006, he put fuel in his wing tanks for taxi tests and to check for leaks. During construction, he had applied sealant over every rivet, every seam, and every other place he thought might provide an opening for fuel to escape.

He expected a few small leaks, so he planned to fill each tank with a few gallons of fuel and then step back to watch for dripping. If he didn't see any drips, he would duck under the wing to check for seeping fuel, small leaks that didn't push fuel out fast enough to drip but which still had to be fixed.

He poured fuel into the wing tanks, and then watched as fuel dribbled onto the hangar floor from dozens of tiny holes in the bottom of the wing, like an old shack that needed a new tarpaper roof in a downpour. Arnold stared in horror for a few seconds, and then ducked under the wings to draw a circle around each leak with a Sharpie pen. Then he drained out the rest of the fuel.

Thus began the war of the seeps.

Add fuel.

"Dammit! They're still there."

Circle leaks.

Drain fuel.

Let tanks dry out for a day.

Put sealant on leaks and let dry for a day.

Repeat process for two years.

It didn't help that every time Arnold went to his hangar to work on the E-1, other pilots, mechanics, and flight instructors besieged him. Sometimes a whole crowd showed up. A typical session might start with a question such as: "I have a student who needs one more cross-country flight before I sign them off for their check ride. Is it okay if I go ahead and schedule the check ride with you for two weeks from now?"

Instead of just a simple yes or no, the discussion quickly devolved into the weather at that time of year, or the instructor's dinner plans for the evening, or an upcoming air show, or whatever. Even if there were no distracting crowds, work was interrupted by constant trips to the hardware store, located five minutes away in downtown Snohomish. It seemed there was always a need to purchase tape, because Arnold had lost the roll he'd purchased the previous week, or to purchase a tape measure, because he'd misplaced the one he'd brought from home the previous week, or to purchase a wrench, because he couldn't remember whom he'd lent that wrench to the previous week.

Two milestones occurred in 2008. First, my father celebrated his eightieth birthday at a surprise party at Harvey Field in February. A few days after his birthday, the FAA presented him with two national-level awards, the Wright Brothers Master Pilot Award and the Charles Taylor Master Mechanic Award, to recognize his sixty-five years of piloting and maintaining airplanes. But more important to Arnold than the awards was the second milestone: late that spring, he celebrated having fixed the E-1's last fuel leak.

Finally seepless in Seattle, Arnold turned his attention back to the propeller. Although he thought the E-1 could now set a record, he still believed he could do better with another propeller. Thus began a game of musical propellers that continued for another year as he rotated propellers of various shapes and sizes on and off the E-1.

In May 2009, he was ready to take on the world record, but one last E-1 improvement would come along before he finally took off.

* * *

By the early 1990s, a handful of electronics companies were catering to the homebuilt market, selling kit radios and other types of equipment that were less expensive compared to certified parts. Even so, a basic set of avionics could easily cost five thousand dollars for not much capability. The demand for higher performing aircraft kits in the 1990s also drove demand for higher performing avionics, with some pilots spending tens of thousands of dollars for lavish panels that included dual radios, multiple navigation aids, autopilots, and thunderstorm detection equipment.

Even as vendors tried to introduce cheaper airframes and engines for homebuilt aircraft, avionics remained a costly problem for those who just wanted the basics. Yes, it was still possible to fly around in an airplane with nothing but a handful of instruments and no radio, but pilots who wanted to fly in and out of all but the smallest airports needed more. Radios, navigation equipment, transponders that reported position and altitude to air traffic control radars, and noise-cancelling headsets became standard equipment as the volume of airplanes and airspace complexity continued to rise in the United States.

In 2003, just as the sport aviation market was poised to take off, Dynon Avionics, a small company located a five-minute drive from Arnold's home in Woodinville, answered homebuilders' dreams with the first electronic flight information system, the EFIS D-10, produced just for homebuilt aircraft. At about one-tenth the cost of the Garmin G-1000, a comparable unit that came out that year for certificated aircraft, the EFIS D-10 packed six instruments—airspeed indicator, altimeter, heading indicator, attitude indicator, vertical velocity (climb rate) indicator, and turn coordinator—into one four-inch electronic display that fit into the three-and-one-eighth-inch hole that previously held just one of the instruments it replaced.

Dynon's founder, John Torode, an entrepreneur who formed and shed electronic equipment companies as often as most people change the oil

Fig. 12.5. Updated E-1 panel using advanced avionics available to homebuilders, 2010.

in their cars, owned at least four airplanes, two of which were seaplanes parked in the yard of his home on Lake Washington. His first idea for Dynon was to build a small, unmanned aircraft for detecting magnetic anomalies that indicated the presence of diamonds in the remnants of a volcano shaft in Africa, but he quickly moved on to making more affordable avionics for homebuilders. Torode found ways to hold down costs. First, sell only to the homebuilt market, to eliminate costly FAA certifications. Second, use commercial-grade gyroscopes instead of expensive aviation-qualified components. To produce a gyroscope output equivalent to that of a high-quality unit, Torode figured out how to calibrate each individual gyroscope to compensate for changes in temperature. He first built a chamber that looked remarkably like a kitchen oven to calibrate six gyroscopes at a time; newer-model chambers could do forty at a time.

Arnold saw an EFIS D-10 at the Arlington fly-in in 2003, but he was skeptical at first. He'd had a bad experience with a unit that ran on a personal digital assistant, and he didn't want to shell out a thousand dollars for what might be someone else's science project.

Others snatched up the D-10, and two years later Dynon added a digital engine monitor with a seven-inch display to their repertoire. Then, in 2007, Dynon combined everything into one box, the Flight Deck E180, and Arnold could no longer resist buying one. In addition to being a snazzy unit that replaced several instruments on his limited panel, the E180 could record his engine data, something that helped him as he tried out different propellers and further streamlined the E-1.

A year later, Dynon added a simple autopilot to keep the wings level and hold altitude, and Arnold bought that as well, bringing the E-1 to its final configuration forty-nine years after the original design.

In 2010, Dynon upped the ante even more, bringing out ten-inch displays that included synthetic vision, where the pilot sees a display of what is ahead of the airplane, even when flying in clouds or fog, and a moving map display, which keeps track of the airplane, terrain, and airspace, all in one easy-to-read display. For about ten thousand dollars, a homebuilder could now have a box nearly equivalent to one in a commercial airliner; and in April 2016, the FAA even began to approve D-10 installations in some certified aircraft, such as Cessna 172s.

Dynon units have been installed in twenty thousand homebuilt and light sport aircraft worldwide, including Burt Rutan's *SpaceShipOne*.

13

Where's Dad?

Put out my hand and touched the face of God.
John Gillespie Magee Jr., *High Flight*

THE FÉDÉRATION AÉRONAUTIQUE INTERNATIONALE (FAI) HAS A definition for everything involving an aviation record. A course is defined as "the shortest distance on the earth's surface between the two points concerned, measured in accordance with the WGS84 ellipsoid," in other words, the great circle route between two points. My father might fly around a thunderstorm and add twenty miles to his flight, but the distance for the record would still be the official distance between the takeoff airport and the landing airport. Furthermore, he couldn't just take off, fly until he ran out of fuel, and land; before departing, he had to "declare" the course he would follow. At least three weeks before a record flight, he had to describe his attempt on a "Sanction Application" submitted to the National Aeronautic Association (NAA), accompanied by a fee of several hundred dollars. The sanction fee is figured on a sliding scale based on aircraft weight—the heavier the airplane, the higher the fee.

The pilot must also carry at least one certified recorder on the airplane to show that he or she has met the requirements for the record. Older recorders called barographs simply recorded altitude and were used to ensure that the aircraft hadn't landed during a distance attempt; Arnold had carried such an instrument during his New Mexico balloon flights in the early 1950s. Modern record attempts use devices about the size of a deck of cards that contain a satellite navigation system, such as GPS, in addition to an altimeter. Pilots can rent the recorders from the NAA, but many prefer to buy their own. In 2008 the recorders cost about a thousand dollars each, but Arnold, like many other record attempters, decided to buy two—he didn't want to spend eighteen hours flying across the country only to find his recorder had failed.

Since weight is one of the major characteristics the FAI uses to classify airplanes for the purpose of record-setting, weight becomes the most important thing to document before any record attempt. FAI rules require that the airplane be weighed before takeoff in exactly the same configuration it will have during the record flight—fuel, cargo, any extra equipment carried, the crew, and personal items. An FAI official must weigh the airplane using certified scales and then seal the fuel caps with bright pink tape to ensure no one sneaks in a few more gallons before takeoff.

An FAI official must also meet the airplane at the landing airport to ensure that the airplane and pilot are the same ones that started the flight, make sure the pink tape is still in place, and collect the recorder to review the evidence that the record has been broken.

In addition, the FAI considers a flight incomplete if an accident during the flight causes the pilot or another crewmember to die within forty-eight hours after the accident, or if any person or part leaves the aircraft during the flight. Preparing for his 1927 Atlantic crossing, Lindbergh considered jettisoning his landing gear after takeoff to save weight and drag, and making a belly landing in Paris, until the FAI nixed the idea.

Unlike records such as those in track and field, where any certified performance better than the present record constitutes a new record, a new aviation record must exceed the old one by a certain amount. A new altitude record must be higher than the old by at least 3 percent or three hundred meters, whichever is less. A new distance record must beat the old by at least 1 percent or one hundred kilometers, whichever is less.

Hertzler's record was 2,214 miles, which meant Arnold had to fly at least 2,236 miles. Living on the West Coast meant he could just take off from an airport near his home instead of transporting his airplane to a good starting point, as Heinonen, Lesher, and Hertzler had done, but Arnold still had to pick a good place to land. In 2007, he scanned a map of the eastern United States for airports that would meet the requirement, and his eye fell on Hampton Roads Executive Airport, where I kept my airplane, near my new duty station in Suffolk, Virginia. Situated about 2,400 miles from Paine Field, Hampton Roads easily met the distance requirement, and landing there precluded any East Coast logistics problems. All I had to do was drive ten miles to retrieve my father when he landed.

Arnold decided to depart from Paine Field, instead of Harvey, for the record attempt, primarily because of its longer runway. He wasn't planning to try taking off in the E-1 with a full load of fuel until he actually made the record attempt. He had built the landing gear to withstand only 850 pounds of weight, meaning he had to burn down 252 pounds of fuel, which would take fourteen hours, before he could land. He had no desire to practice a fourteen-hour flight; and while he was confident the E-1 could take off from Harvey's tiny runway with a full fuel tank, prudence suggested he use Paine's longer runway. Paine's control tower also could help if he had a problem on takeoff, and it would provide a record of his actual takeoff time in case the FAI had any questions about the flight.

Arnold also had to consider weather, the time of day, and what equipment and personal gear to take. He scrutinized every piece of equipment, opting, as had Lindbergh, Lesher, and Hertzler, to take along only minimal food, water, and survival equipment. Like Lesher and Hertzler, Arnold also lost weight.

Weather was his biggest concern. With no equipment for flying in the clouds, he needed a day with nearly clear skies across the expanse of the United States, a tall order, especially in the summertime. Like Lesher and Hertzler, he wanted to make the flight in the summer to take advantage of the long days, but thunderstorms were likely to occur somewhere across the Midwest on any given day.

However, as Hertzler had done with his VariEze, Arnold had sacrificed by adding a few pounds to the E-1 in order to install lights for flying at night. Thunderstorms in the Midwest usually die down in the evening, so he decided to take off from Paine in mid-afternoon, fly across the Midwest at night, and then land the next morning in Virginia. Like Lindbergh, he would fly on a night with a full moon. Then all he had to do was hope he didn't fall asleep somewhere along the way.

Planning complete, he finished the hunt for the elusive fuel seeps and then sat back to wait for good weather.

The air force decided to move me back to the Pentagon in the summer of 2008, so Arnold recalculated the distance to my new airport in Fredericksburg, Virginia. It was a little shorter, but it would do.

On September 13, 2009, the weather looked like it would finally be good, and Arnold asked family members and the NAA official to meet him at Paine Field the next afternoon. The forecast across the country was good, except for a broken layer of clouds across the Seattle area and North Cascades that was supposed to clear up by noon.

At lunchtime the next day, Arnold flew the E-1 to Paine and waited for the weather to improve. The cloud layer was at three thousand feet, high enough for a flight in the valley next to Paine, but not enough for him to climb to the ninety-five hundred feet he needed to cross the Cascades. By the middle of the afternoon, despite flawless weather seventy miles to the east, the clouds at Paine had refused to part.

It would be another year before he could try again.

*   *   *

About two in the afternoon on July 25, 2010, my father and the E-1 lifted off from Paine Field.

Kelly reached me at my apartment a few minutes later.

"Well, Dad took off," she said when I answered the phone.

"What?" He'd mentioned earlier in the week that he thought the weather might be good enough to try for the record in the next few weeks, but no one had updated me since. It hadn't occurred to me that he might actually take off. Years of planning and discussing hadn't prepared me for the moment when he finally did it.

Part of me was happy he at last had a chance to demonstrate everything he had worked his whole life to acquire: his ability to design an airplane, to build the airplane, and to pilot that airplane across the country to show that it worked as designed. It was an opportunity to check off the "pilot," "mechanic," and "design engineer" boxes on the list he had envisioned in his teenage fantasies.

At the same time, I worried. I knew he had installed a crude autopilot on the E-1 just a few months earlier, but would it really keep the airplane from spinning out of control and diving to the ground if he fell asleep? And what if the electrical system failed? He'd be up there in the dark with no GPS to guide him to a nearby airport, and no way to talk to an air traffic controller for help. What if he'd calculated his fuel wrong, and he ran out of gas and had to land in some farmer's field? The full moon was supposed to help with that kind of problem, but still it would take place during the night, and night magnifies all problems in flight.

"So, when is he supposed to be here tomorrow?" I asked.

"Ummm . . . I don't know. I thought he said it would take, like, eighteen hours or something like that."

"So I guess he'll call me when he lands at Fredericksburg?"

"I guess so. He's got his cell phone."

Kelly wasn't concerned about the flight. After all, Arnold had survived eighteen thousand hours of flying some of the most dangerous aircraft in the world, so she assumed that no airplane would ever dare crash with him on board.

*   *   *

I plugged "N7927A" into an Internet flight-tracking program and got nothing at first. But when he showed up two hours later, his projected 8:30 A.M. arrival time in Fredericksburg confused more than it reassured me. I puzzled over the discrepancy; if the flight took eighteen hours, he should be landing about 11:15, not 8:30.

I decided not to worry. Whether he landed at 8:30 or 11:15, I'd be at work and would leave when he called.

I checked his progress throughout the evening and then went to bed at my normal time, waking about three in the morning to see where he was.

In my just-awakened stupor, it took me a few seconds to comprehend that his track had disappeared off my computer screen. I woke as if I had just gulped a Starbucks grande Americano. Had he landed early?

I looked closer at the screen and saw he had descended below about three thousand feet above the ground when the track ended. Ah, I thought, he must have simply descended below radar coverage. But why had he descended? Was it intentional, or because he fell asleep, or because he lost control of the airplane, or because the engine quit, or, or, or? My brain had gone from barely awake to imagination hyperdrive.

Go back to sleep, I thought. Everything is probably okay. If it's not, there's nothing you can do about it and you'll find out soon anyway. I spent two more hours not really sleeping and then got up for work.

He had not reappeared on the tracker, but a dotted line to Fredericksburg still showed a projected arrival time of 8:30 A.M. How could that be?

I left for work.

*   *   *

"Where's Dad?" my sister Kate demanded in the subject line of her email.

By then, it was about eleven o'clock and I sat in my office in Arlington.

I don't know. I don't know any more than you do right now, I thought, unsure how to reply.

Now I was sure our father was missing. Maybe. Sort of.

At nine o'clock, I had called the Fredericksburg airport, and they confirmed he wasn't there. They said they would tell him to call me when he landed.

I knew the groundspeed displayed on the tracker was just an estimate, and he could have slowed down if he had encountered a headwind. I still believed he had simply descended below the radar. Nevertheless, so many things could have gone wrong, and I was merely guessing.

Trying to collect my thoughts, I started to type an answer to Kate: "I don't know, but I'm not worried yet. Kelly said he was planning to fly for eighteen hours."

No, I was getting worried.

Backspace, delete, try again.

My cell phone rang and it was Kate, impatient I was taking so long to reply.

"Where's Dad?"

"I don't know," I said, hoping I sounded calm. No need to have two people panicking. "If I don't hear from him in another thirty minutes or so I'm going to try calling the FAA."

"Why don't you call them now?"

"I'm not sure he's overdue yet. Kelly thinks he filed for eighteen hours, which would make him not yet overdue."

"But what about him disappearing off the flight tracker?"

"I don't know. He probably just descended to get some better winds," I said, trying to convince myself as much as her.

After assuring Kate I would call the FAA if he didn't show up soon, I hung up, buried my head in my hands and wondered why I couldn't have a normal retired father who puttered around the garden or played golf all day.

*   *   *

At about eight o'clock that same morning, near Columbus, Ohio, after battling headwinds for five hours, Arnold calculated that the four gallons left in his fuselage tank wouldn't get him anywhere near Fredericksburg.

He pressed onward while he considered his options.

He could land and refuel at a small airport and then head to Madison, Wisconsin, where his youngest sister, Tere, lived. No point in flying all the way to Fredericksburg if he wouldn't set the record.

But he was so close to finally finishing his dream. He wasn't willing to give up yet.

Although the headwinds had hurt his progress, his calculations showed he should have more than four gallons of fuel left. But where was it?

The fuel might have oozed out of the wing, but he was positive nothing was leaking when he departed Paine Field fifteen hours earlier.

But who knew what might have happened during the long flight.

Fuel might also be trapped somewhere. Perhaps it had settled into a low spot in the wing, or was trapped behind an air bubble in a fuel line.

Or maybe he had simply missed some fuel.

He had divided his wet wing into six separate fuel tanks, and during the flight, he had gradually emptied each tank into the fuselage tank, watching the fuel transfer through a transparent tube. Maybe, just maybe, he had not fully emptied each tank.

He decided to try all the wing tanks one more time.

He switched to the first tank, and could see a bit of fuel moving through the tube, but only a few tablespoons at best. He kicked the airplane from side to side with the rudder, hoping to dislodge any fuel that might have settled in a small imperfection, but it didn't help.

The second tank produced the same result.

When he switched to the third tank, fuel surged into the fuselage tank and his hopes soared.

But how long would it last?

His fuel pump could transfer only about one gallon each minute, and he watched, almost disbelieving his good fortune, as the fuel gauge began to inch toward five gallons, and then slowly past.

Arnold expected the wing to run dry again at any second, but for another agonizing four minutes, fuel dribbled into the fuselage tank, until it finally stopped at nine gallons.

He had somehow missed five gallons during his previous transfers.

But his joy over the newly found fuel was short lived: even with nine gallons, he would land with only one gallon of fuel. Too risky, but he had one last trick to try.

The cloud deck above him was breaking up ahead. and according to the previous day's forecasts, there might be a tailwind up higher. He was too low to the ground to radio a flight service station for a better weather check, but it wouldn't hurt to climb up and take a peek.

Arnold pushed in the throttle, climbed to seventy-five hundred feet, and leveled off to accelerate the E-1 back to cruise flight.

He didn't take his eyes off the groundspeed on the GPS as it passed 100 knots. Then 101 . . . 105 . . . 108 . . . 110. A ten-knot tailwind now pushed him along, and the skies ahead looked clear.

He exhaled and recomputed his fuel reserve. Two and one-half gallons. He would have forty-five minutes' worth of fuel remaining after flying for eighteen and one-half hours. Not much, but enough to be both legal and safe.

Arnold had lost twelve pounds before the flight, which translated to two gallons of fuel. Without the weight loss, he would now be heading to Wisconsin. Instead, the Appalachian Mountains rose toward him, looking tiny and green compared to the crags he had crossed sixteen hours earlier.

About ten miles from Fredericksburg, he spotted the airport and called a flight service station to close his flight plan.

He tensed as he entered the traffic pattern for his landing. He had landed at this airport only once before, when I had taken him for a flight the previous December during his visit at the time of my air force retirement. The last thing he wanted was to crash on landing after coming this far; adrenalin overcame exhaustion long enough for a perfect landing at about 11:30 A.M. Eastern time.

He taxied to the ramp, shut the engine down, opened the canopy, and sat for a few minutes, still somewhat disbelieving that he had finally achieved his fifty-year dream.

Art Greenfield, an NAA official based in Washington, DC, walked up to the E-1 a few minutes later as Arnold started to climb out of the cockpit.

Once on the ground, he wobbled a bit, looked at Greenfield, and said, "I'm never doing that again."

* * *

At 11:45 A.M., I still hadn't heard from my father. Kelly had said eighteen hours. I called Arnold's cell phone and I tried calling the airport again. No

Fig. 13.1. Arnold Ebneter in Virginia after setting his world record, 2010.

answer from either. Arnold's phone went straight to voice mail, and I left a message.

By my estimate, he was thirty minutes overdue. After thirty minutes, the FAA assumes a plane is missing and starts to search.

I called the flight service station.

"Um, I'm looking for an airplane that might be overdue. I'm not sure exactly when it was supposed to arrive, but I was wondering if you could check on it for me." I hoped I sounded nonchalant.

"Sure, no problem. What's the tail number?" I could hear the tick-tick-tick of the briefer's fingers on the keyboard as he looked up N7927A.

"I'm showing he closed his flight plan about twenty minutes ago."

"Oh!" But where was he? "Does it say where he landed?"

"No, that isn't on here."

"Okay, thank you." I started to hang up, but the briefer stopped me.

"Wait, this flight plan says he took off yesterday in Washington State?"

"Yes. Um." How do I explain this? "He's trying to set a distance record."

"Wow!"

I laughed as I hung up and called Kelly. "Dad's on the ground somewhere. He closed his flight plan. I just don't know where he is."

I called Arnold's cell phone again; and this time it rang, but there was no answer. Now what? I didn't bother leaving another message.

My cell phone rang. It was Kelly.

"Dad just called me. He's on the ground at Fredericksburg."

"Good grief. Why didn't he call me?"

"He said he couldn't find your phone number."

I grabbed my purse and ran out of my office thinking, "He can fly all the way across the country, but he can't find my phone number?"

It took me an hour to get to Fredericksburg, and to my disappointment, the NAA official had left before I arrived. Arnold didn't look as tired as I expected, but the back of his flight suit was caked with perspiration stains.

I had moved my airplane to another airport that month, but I still had my hangar at Fredericksburg until the end of July, and we put the E-1 away. I took my father to a Bob Evans restaurant so he could eat anything he wanted for the first time in months. Then we drove back to my apartment, and he slept for three days.

Epilogue

We actually live, today, in our dreams of yesterday; and, living
in those dreams, we dream again.

Charles Lindbergh, *The Spirit of St. Louis*

AS MY FATHER CROSSED THE APPALACHIAN MOUNTAINS DURING
his record flight, the EAA's AirVenture was kicking off. I mentioned that
perhaps he could fly the E-1 to Oshkosh and show it off, but he was too
tired to even consider the idea. Then a couple of days later, Florence, the
wife of his cousin Carl, passed away. Arnold had planned to stop in Wisconsin on his return trip, but now the task took on a new urgency. He
departed Virginia the next morning, attended the funeral the day after
that, and then flew back to Washington State, taking two days and making several stops along the way.

Within a few weeks, the *Everett Daily Herald* ran an article about the
record, and the story began popping up in newspapers and online features
all over the world. As my sisters and I found each article, we would e-mail
each other the link. "Here's another one! This one's from Australia!"

At first my father was taken aback by how the articles focused on his
age and the lengthy design and building process, but by the evening of
August 28, when Harvey Field hosted a party in his honor, he had
embraced the fifty-year journey. He concluded his presentation by noting
that he had always wanted to work as a design engineer, but life and other
opportunities had always thwarted those plans. On the other hand,
though his path had been crooked, it had ultimately been more satisfying.
By being open to opportunities as they came along, he experienced many

more things than he would have on a straight path, and he had more than fulfilled his engineering dreams.

"If I had worked at Boeing or Cessna or Beechcraft as an engineer," he told his audience, "I would have designed one small part of an airplane. No one at those companies really designs the whole airplane anymore. But I can say that I designed every single bit of the E-1, and that I know where every single part is, what it does, and why it's there. No one at Boeing can say that about the airplanes they work on."

That fall, the National Aeronautic Association certified Arnold's distance as a US record, and then the Fédération Aéronautique Internationale certified it as a world record.

In January 2011, the National Aeronautic Association selected Arnold's record for addition to the category "Ten Most Notable Aviation Records of 2010." Richard Truly, a retired navy admiral and astronaut and former head of NASA, was also feted at the awards banquet in March, and when the event was over, he strode over to our table, introduced himself, and said, "Wow, that was quite a feat you did." Later, Arnold told me he couldn't believe someone of Truly's stature would be impressed by something that seemed to pale in comparison to the astronaut's own accomplishments.

But the biggest award was yet to come. In 2011, as they did for Heinonen, Lesher, and Hertzler before him, the Fédération Aéronautique Internationale bestowed the Blériot Medal on my father.

* * *

In a return to his roots, Arnold was selected as one of five aviators inducted into the Wisconsin Aviation Hall of Fame in 2013. Before the ceremony on October 26 at the EAA Museum, several of us toured the displays of dozens of aircraft that made history in the world of homebuilts and general aviation. As I wandered, I discovered an F-100 cockpit trainer with a set of steps that beckoned me to climb inside, and I called my father over. He climbed in and spent fifteen minutes pointing out various instruments and features to the rest of us as he imagined himself pushing the throttle forward, feeling the kick of the afterburner as he thundered down the runway once more in his favorite mount.

My father could have stayed for hours, reminiscing, but we had to leave to get ready for the ceremony, and a Boy Scout troop had arrived for their turn.

*   *   *

The land encircling Donald Rock is now a county park, and a tangle of shrubs and pines has overgrown the rock, making it difficult to see from the ground. In 2013, Arnold and his sister Tere donated a bench to the park to honor their parents, who had always encouraged their children to walk their own paths.

In 2016, Arnold donated the E-1 to the EAA AirVenture Museum in Oshkosh, but he continues to fly both Charlie and Colleen's Cub—he repurchased the latter in 2009. He still gives flight instruction, mostly in Harvey Field's Aeronca Champ.

Currently on display at the Finnish Aviation Museum near Helsinki, Juhani Heinonen's HK-1 is still the only Finnish aircraft to ever set a world record. Ed Lesher's *Teal* is part of the EAA AirVenture Museum's collection, but Gary Hertzler still flies his VariEze; in 1993, he took back the C-1aI closed-course distance record from Jeana Yeager, but he doesn't plan to challenge Arnold's record.

Someday, another dreamer will break Arnold's record. It might be another octogenarian, or it might be a college student who knows no limits, but someone will do it. That pilot may do it on his or her own or may do it as part of a large team flush with donations and sponsorships. Already at least one team of college students is working on the challenge.

Jim Bede died on July 9, 2015, without ever bringing another successful homebuilt aircraft to market.

Richard VanGrunsven continues to crank out new designs that may not give people everything they want, but which provide everything they need. More than nine thousand of Van's airplanes have flown worldwide since 1973, and thousands more are being built.

Burt Rutan retired from Scaled Composites in 2011, but Virgin Galactic continues to pursue space tourism, although no specific launch dates have been set. We may yet see the day when aspiring astronauts can launch their homebuilt spaceships off a rented mother ship for a weightless ride through suborbital space, just as young men in the 1920s and 1930s launched their gliders from cars and trucks.

Paul Poberezny retired in 2009, and son Tom retired in 2012, leaving the EAA without a Poberezny as leader for the first time in nearly sixty years. Paul died on August 22, 2013, and pilots filled the skies at the 2014 AirVenture with flyover tributes to his legacy.

EPILOGUE

Ed Heath and his contemporaries would be amazed at the options available to homebuilders today, all blessed by the FAA: original designs; plans created by Heath, Poberezny, Rutan, and others; antique aircraft replicas; and kits that arrive on the amateur's doorstep requiring a little or a lot of assembly. While purists may bemoan the demise of homebuilts made from original designs or plans, the success of kit aircraft in enticing novices to try their hand at homebuilding paradoxically helps keep alive the freedom to build from scratch. If homebuilts were available to only a few thousand people with the ability, time, and obsession necessary to create something new or from a few pieces of paper, the FAA might long ago have abandoned amateur-built aircraft as not worth their time and effort. Freedoms are fragile, and there is strength in numbers. With 180,000 members and more than eight hundred chapters, the EAA sails on, inspiring a new generation of homebuilders to achieve their dreams.

AFTERWORD

IT IS IMPOSSIBLE TO CAPTURE EVERY MOMENT OF THE HISTORY OF homebuilt aircraft in a text of this length. I tried to find events and designs that were representative and which told a compelling narrative, but I had to leave out many important aspects of amateur-built aircraft. Some areas not covered, or only touched on briefly, include amateur building in the international community, ultralights, rotorcraft/helicopters, midget racing, aerobatics, warbirds, antique restorations, flying cars, and dozens of individual designs and designers that contributed to the rich DNA of homebuilts. All of these topics are worthy of books or lengthy articles in their own right, and I hope other writers will join me in bringing this additional history to life.

SOURCES

My primary source for most of Arnold's experiences was Arnold. Our conversations were augmented by interviews with my sisters and other relatives, letters written by both of my parents, scrapbooks, personal and official photos, military records, pilot logbooks, yearbooks, magazines, newspapers, aircraft plans and drawings, and technical reports.

OTHER INTERVIEWS

Tom Adamson (professor emeritus, University of Michigan)
Robert Hamilton (president, Dynon)
Kandace Harvey (owner, Harvey Field)
Gary Hertzler
Steve Knopp
Richard VanGrunsven

I used more than one hundred articles from the following magazines, newspapers, and websites; a full list of articles is available at www.thepropellerunderthebed.com.

Air & Space/Smithsonian
Air Progress
Air Trails
AOPA Pilot
Aviation
Flight
Flying
Flying Manual
Jane's All the World's Aircraft
Mechanix Illustrated
Milwaukee Journal
New York Times
Oregonian

Popular Aviation
Popular Mechanics
Sport Aviation
Today's Pilot
Waukesha Daily Freeman

Aircraft Spruce & Specialty Company website, www.aircraftspruce.com
General Aviation Manufacturers Association website, www.gama.aero

BOOKS

Abel, Alan, Drina Welch Abel, and Paul Matt. *Aeronca's Golden Age*. Brawley, CA: Wind Canyon Books, 2001.

Anderson, John D., Jr. *The Airplane: A History of Its Technology*. Reston, VA: American Institute of Aeronautics and Astronautics, 2002.

Cole, Duane. *This Is EAA*. Milwaukee, WI: Ken Cook Transnational, 1972.

Crouch, Tom D. *Blériot XI: The Story of a Classic Aircraft*. Washington, DC: Smithsonian Institution Press, 1982.

Francis, Devon. *Mr. Piper and His Cubs*. Ames: Iowa State University Press, 1973.

Lindbergh, Charles A. *The Spirit of St. Louis*. New York: Scribner, 1953.

Parnall, Chuck, and Bonnie Poberezny. *Poberezny: The Story Begins . . .* Oshkosh, WI: Red One Publishing, 1996.

Raymer, Daniel P. *Aircraft Design: A Conceptual Approach*. 5th ed. Reston, VA: American Institute of Aeronautics and Astronautics, 2012.

Saint-Exupéry, Antoine de. *Wind, Sand and Stars*. Translated by Lewis Galantiére. New York: Harcourt, 1939.

Smith, Herschel. *A History of Aircraft Piston Engines*. Manhattan, KS: Sunflower University Press, 1986.

Wolko, Howard S., ed. *The Wright Flyer: An Engineering Perspective*. Washington, DC: Smithsonian Institution Press, 1987.

INDEX

Paine Field, 3, 144, 151, 177–78, 191, 192
Parks College, 141
Pazmany, Ladislao, 119, 120
Pelton, Jack, 161
Peters, Ross, 36–37
pilot arrests, 36–37
pilot licensing. *See* certification of pilots
Piper Aircraft, 39, 152–53
Piper, William, 39
Pitts, Curtis, 130, 134
plans-built aircraft, 72–73
Poberezny, Audrey, 62, 65, 67, 69
Poberezny, Paul, 62–69, 70, 71, 73–75, 95, 96–97, 156, 201
Poberezny, Tom, 65, 156–57, 163, 201
Popular Aviation magazine, 18, 23, 29, 34, 36, 37, 38, 66, 73
Popular Mechanics magazine, 15, 18, 20, 132, 133
Portage, Wisconsin, 40, 41, 42, 144
Portland University, 123
propellers, 12–13, 35–36, 114
pusher aircraft, 101–4, 121

Rand, Ken, 120, 126
Rankin, Tex, 37
Red Devils aerobatic team, 157
registered aircraft, 34
regulations, 30, 32; federal, 33–35, 36, 37, 38, 49–50, 51–52; state, 35, 36, 37, 38; amateur-built aircraft (homebuilts), 35, 50, 51–52, 66; experimental aircraft, 35, 37, 38, 66; equipment requirements, 174–75. *See also* experimental category of aircraft
Rensselaer Polytechnic Institute, 48–49, 53–54
Riverside Airport. *See* Flabob Airport
Rowan, Stanley, 28
rudder, 12, 43, 47, 195
Rutan, Burt, 120, 121, 122*fig.*, 123–29,

125, *126fig.*, 128–29, 134 136–37, 155, 162–64, 165–66, 188, 201
Rutan, Dick, 128–29, 165–66

Safety Regulation Release No. 194, 50
Safety Regulation Release No. 236, 51
Saint-Exupéry, Antoine de, 10, 59, 93
Scherer, John, 70–71, 72, 73
Scaled Composites, 163, 201
Small Aircraft Manufacturers Association, 159
Society of Experimental Test Pilots, 138–39, 163
Sommers, Forrest, 49
SpaceShipOne, 163–64, 188
spars, 21, 26, 126, 167, 168*fig.*
Spirit of St. Louis, 5–7, 89
Sport Aviation, 99, 101, 120, 134, 137, 152, 158, 159, 163
stabilator, 93
Stits Poly-Fiber, 70, 147, 149
sport pilot, 160
Stits, Ray, 70, 73, 124, 148, 149
supplemental type certificate, 96

Tactical Air Command, 78
Taylor Aircraft, 38–39
Taylor, Charles, 12, 185
Taylor, Molt, 102
testing, 15–16, 139
Texas A&M, 86, 94
Theena, Joe, 49
Thorp, John, 119
Three-A-Flyer, 50
Torode, John, 186–87
traffic pattern, 45
Triple-A Flyer, 50
Truly, Richard, 200
type certificates. *See* certification of aircraft, supplemental type certificates

ultralight aircraft, 156
University of Minnesota, 54